Rational Association

RATIONAL ASSOCIATION

Fred M. Frohock

SYRACUSE UNIVERSITY PRESS   1987

The paper used in this publication meets the minimum requirements of American
National Standard for Information Sciences—Permanence of Paper for Printed Library
Materials, ANSI Z39.48-1984. ∞™

Library of Congress Cataloging-in-Publication Data

Frohock, Fred M.
  Rational association.

  Bibliography: p.
  Includes index.
  1. Social choice. 2. Prisoner's dilemma game.
I. Title.
HB846.8.F76 1987   302′.13   86-23026
ISBN 0-8156-2390-9 (alk. paper)

Manufactured in the United States of America

Contents

FRED M. FROHOCK received his Ph.D. from the University of North Carolina. He is the author of *Special Care: Medical Decisions at the Beginning of Life* and a number of other books and articles on politics and morality. He is currently Professor and Chairman of the Political Science Department at Syracuse University.

Foreword

Professor Frohock's book is about democratic decision making—the relation between the decisions reached by social collectives and the contributions made to those decisions by the collectives' individual members. It could be said to be about the sense of the word "by" in the phrase "decisions reached by social collectives." Supposing that each individual member of such a collective seeks the collective decision that is the best possible resolution of the conflict of individual preferences, what arrangements will ensure such an outcome?

Contemporary collective decision theory has articulated various difficulties in the way of specifying such a set of arrangements: in discussions of the so-called Prisoners' Dilemma, or intractable-seeming obstacles to the efficacy of an individual's participation in the decision-making of large groups, of Arrow's Theorem, and so on. Professor Frohock believes that these difficulties are symptomatic of fundamental misconceptions about the nature of the relation between social groups and their individual members. He shows that such difficulties are generated by background theoretical assumptions which are at odds with the criteria governing the arrangements for collective decision which are explicit in the foreground of the discussion.

According to these criteria every individual participant is an autonomous rational agent. Each person's thought processes and preferences are to be attributable to that person *qua* pure individual, without the use of concepts which depend (in a holistic way) on the social formation or formations in which he or she is a participant. These social formations themselves are to be thought of, on the contrary, simply as resultants of the interactions of their individual members.

These are the conditions under which the theories criticized in this book suppose collective decisions to be reached. In this view the machinery for arriving at collective decisions does not concern itself with weighing the merits of the various preferences expressed, for such a judgment would have to be made from a perspective other than that of any one of the individual participants, a perspective that could only be constructed out of some prior aggregation of the preferences of those individuals. So the decision procedure must be designed simply as an aggregation machine for transforming all the individual preferences, whatever they may be, into a single collective preference. But Arrow's Theorem and the Prisoners' Dilemma show that a successful aggregation of this sort is impossible, according to the criteria of "success" commonly accepted.

Mr. Frohock's diagnosis of this situation is that these criteria belong to a tradition of political thought different from, and antagonistic to, the tradition within which the aggregative conception of social decision making is elaborated. For example, the likelihood of free riders who benefit from cooperative efforts without contributing to them, or of "dictatorship" by one group over others in the community, is objectionable only if the community in question is characterized in holistic moral terms in a way which methodological individualism disallows. This ailment, he argues, cannot be cured by any technical readjustments: it requires "substituting one tradition of political thought for another." He traces back to Aristotle the tradition which he sees as needed to put things right. Within it, people's preferences are not arithmetically *aggregated;* they are *adjudicated* qualitatively according to reasoned considerations. This involves considering not just people's bare preferences, but taking their reasons for these preferences into account. But these reasons can be understood only if these individuals are seen in the context of the social groups and institutions in which they participate. To put the matter more strongly, people capable of having reasons for their preferences are people whose nature is in part constituted by their participation in social and cultural formations. And this is a frankly holistic conception.

What is distinctive and interesting about Professor Frohock's presentation of these ideas is his technically skillful attempt to show how the aggregation conception of collective decision making collapses, as it were, under its own weight and is based on ideas that are inconsistent in a quite fundamental way.

Peter Winch

University of Illinois at Urbana/Champaign
Spring 1986

Introduction

Collective choice theory represents a number of traditions in political theory. One is liberalism, especially where this tradition of thought celebrates the individual as the locus of value and meaning in social life. Another is populist democracy, which sanctions the aggregation of individual preferences in reaching collective decisions. And still a third is a more recent tradition that introduces the formal vocabularies of modern economics to political issues and problems.

Each of these three traditions of discourse brings a family of concepts to collective choice. The primacy of individual rational choice follows the liberal emphasis on individual values, as do understandings of individual autonomy and negative liberty. Populist democracy is closely aligned with methodological individualism, a philosophy that sees wholes as nothing more than summations of parts. Economic vocabularies bring to political theory the ordering and means-oriented rationalities that seem to dominate collective choice.

There is much of value in each of these traditions and clusters of concepts. But it is the distinctive contribution of collective choice theory to demonstrate that the arrangement produced by these ideas is self-contradictory. A number of formal games and theorems tell us that some of the conceptual package must be abandoned if that consistency so important to formal theory is to be maintained. I have concentrated in this work on one of the inconsistencies in this body of theory: that between individual rationality and collective outcomes. My method is to identify the model of a political society common to this type of rational breakdown. I then try to recognize those social conditions that avoid rational discontinuity between *one* and *all* (or, as amended, *everyone*) without ushering in indefensible forms of holism.

I argue in the course of the book that the conditions ensuring rational continuity can maintain individuals as origins of social life only by amending, through the introduction of a richer (reason-giving) version of rationality, what we mean by the term "individual"—in particular, by abandoning the discrete and countable unit of methodological individualism and, as a consequence, the arithmetical composition rules generally employed to reach collective outcomes. In a sense, we must see individuals as intentional or purposive creatures, justifying and explaining their lives, and fashion instruments of rationality to accommodate such creatures.

Collective choice theory has provided us with a set of criteria to apply to institutions. State informally, we expect institutions to (1) transform preferences (or individual values) into collective outcomes, (2) meet tests of consistency (especially transitivity), (3) fulfill equity criteria (Pareto, nondictatorship, universal domain), and (4) provide individuals with incentives to participate when participation is beneficial to all (realize, among other needs, efficacy). It may be that our expectations are immodest, or just plain wrong. But such tests disclose contradictions between background concepts and the explicit features of political systems, markets, and any number of alternative and intermediate institutional forms. My conclusion in this work is that a distribution of authority in rules or procedures (somewhat in the tradition of Aristotle) is a way to meet such simultaneous tests of rationality and equity. But this proposal (which violates universal domain in Arrow's theorem) requires different senses of autonomy and authority than those found in collective choice, and in general ways amends the democratic values found in collective choice theory.

This book, in spite of its occasional use of formal vocabularies, is not a technical work. It is an exercise in theory that attempts to disclose the background languages of collective choice theory and, in this regard, is more like a moral argument than a technical treatise. A technician may want to repair or redefine individual-whole discontinuities with the formal apparatus of collective choice theory. But I do not believe that these problems admit of technical resolutions. I think that the contradictions exposed by collective choice, especially those demonstrated in Arrow's theorem, lead us to a deeper or more primary level of concepts where the problems recur in more general form. In a way I am saying that the formal machinery of positive theory does not cut deeply enough, and that the contradictions traced to this deeper level are signals that some basic concepts in political theory commonly thought to be compatible are radically opposed to one another. I offer these remarks to remind the reader that, while much of what I say will provoke students of positive theory, the work is founded on an acceptance, not a rejection, of the problems identified in collective choice theory. It would save us all time if responses to these explorations concentrate on the theoretical claims rather than on the technical languages sometimes used to illustrate and elaborate these claims.

Most of chapter 3 appeared in the *Syracuse Scholar* (Spring 1985) as "Arithmetic vs Morality: Liberalism in Collective Choice," and parts of chapter 5 appeared (in slightly different form) in the *American Political Science Review* (June 1980), as "Rationality, Morality, and Impossibility Theorems." I am grateful to the editors of these journals for permission to recycle this material in the work here.

I would also like to thank a number of individuals who helped me to understand what it is I am trying to do in this work. Jerry Kelly taught me a great deal about the formal notational systems of collective choice. Manfred Stanley, Richard Schwartz, and Tom Green made especially helpful comments on part of the work when I presented it at one of our bimonthly meetings of the Center for the Study of Citizenship group. Stuart Thorson, James Bennett, and David Sylvan were a helpful audience for some of these ideas at a meeting of the discussion group Sylvan organized during the 1985–86 academic year. I am also pleased to record my thanks to the graduate students in my seminars at Syracuse University who heard and discussed these thoughts as they have evolved over the years. But mainly I want to record my substantial debt in this work to the late James Reynolds, colleague and friend, whose understandings of the limits and possibilities of rational choice inform this discussion. Finally, I want to commend the patience and good will of my wife, Val, who in recent years has had to put up with a husband addressing problems in a language so arcane that those who speak it should be allowed in human company only for very brief periods of time.

Fred M. Frohock

Syracuse, New York
Summer 1986

Rational Association

1

Rational Problems

1

Anyone who has glanced at the reading material of small children is familiar with riddles like these: "What is white when it's dirty and black when it's clean?" "What gets wetter and wetter the more it dries?" "What is the surest way to keep fish from smelling?" Most children's riddles intrigue adults as well as children, but usually only for a short time. Once the answer is provided, the puzzle is solved by exposing the anomaly or odd use of words or general trick on which the riddle is formed.

Riddles for some are veridical paradoxes for others. What is puzzling in a riddle may be an apparent paradox resolved by introducing a hidden or more general truth. For example, the true description of a man as being twenty-one years old yet having had only five birthdays is explained by the fact that he was born in a leap year on February 29. A more pernicious puzzlement is found in falsidical paradoxes. Here the puzzlement is genuine, but the paradox is not. It is exposed by exhibiting the error on which it is based. For example, logicians now agree that Zeno's paradox of the tortoise and the hare, though a source of puzzlement (and pleasure to hairsplitters) for centuries, is based on the fallacy of supposing that an infinite succession of intervals must add up to an infinite interval.

The tougher, and thus more interesting, sources of puzzlement are the genuine paradoxes. The famous paradox of Epimenides, "All Cretans are liars" uttered by a Cretan (or, more generally, "I am lying

now"), and Gödel's theorem are two examples of self-referential paradoxes. They seem to circle back on themselves, creating a contradiction
by the maintenance of rules and arguments that, taken singly, are impeccable. Newcomb's problem, though not self-referential, is a paradox
created by the "pull" of two decision rules.[1] A genuine paradox seems to
force us in two directions at once when we cannot go in both directions
or even in one direction so long as the rules and conditions of the
paradox are maintained. In simplest terms, a genuine paradox is a self-
contradiction from valid rules and acceptable premises.

Genuine paradoxes still can be managed. They cannot be "solved"
like veridical paradoxes or "exposed" like falsidical paradoxes, but
strategies of accommodation are available. Look again at the paradox
of Epimenides. One familiar approach to the liar paradox is to avoid it
by introducing a hierarchy of truth locutions. True and false can be indicated with numerical subscripts denoting the location of statements
in a matrix of true-false types; this is Quine's solution.[2] We might say,
for example, it is $true_1$ that I am telling the truth when I say "I am now
not telling the $truth_0$". The paradox is avoided with the recognition of a
type of truth function (subscript l) that can address the truth of other
statements (subscript O). This is an arrangement of language familiar
to students of the sociology-of-knowledge, where claims within social
practices are judged by truth criteria from outside those practices. The
familiar dichotomy in the social sciences between "participant" and
"observer" is basically the acceptance of terms for subscripts representing hierarchies of truth locutions.

Scientific anomalies present more complex strategies of resolution
for puzzling events. A recent experiment in physics fires subatomic
particles through a slit on a screen. The resulting distribution of particles is influenced by whether another slit on the screen, causally independent of the particles, is open or shut.[3] This seeming violation of
causality raises questions (as such tests always do) about the retentive
power of basic concepts and the validity of critical tests. Some propose
replacing classical logic with some new logic accommodating quantum
physics (Putnam 1969). Others maintain that logic is necessary to
criticize a theory and subject it to falsification tests (Popper 1972). In all
cases of scientific anomaly, pressures are strong to explain the events
empirically. Test conditions may be discredited. Auxiliary hypotheses
are offered to save important theoretical principles (an offering some
see as preventing falsification) (Lakatos 1970). Failure to accommodate
the anomaly inevitably creates additional pressures to change some

parts of the theory while maintaining basic principles. Perhaps the basic principles must give way to a new paradigm (Kuhn 1962).

Game theory and collective choice, though no threats to understandings of physical reality, introduce anomalies to recent comprehensions of a political society. A number of formal games and theorems have demonstrated that collective or joint outcomes of rational choices can fail measures of rationality employed by individuals. Prisoners' Dilemma, Arrow's theorem, and a failure of efficacy in large groups all represent this anomaly: individuals are rational, society is not.[4] A rational discontinuity between individual and whole is obviously no dilemma comparable to those found today in physics. It is not certain that such discontinuities are even genuine paradoxes. Nor is a conflict between individual and collective a dilemma for types of holism.[5] But rational discontinuity is an anomaly for methodological individualism, the philosophy guiding game theory and collective choice. In Arrow's theorem, for example, the collective violates one or more conditions successfully met by individuals—transitivity, for example—demonstrating that the whole can be unlike any of its individual parts.[6]

An enormous and expanding body of work has explored resolutions and implications of these rational conflicts between one and all.[7] But it is still not clear exactly what concepts can be maintained and what must be jettisoned in avoiding these conflicts. My objective here is to explore a number of these anomalies and elaborate the types of changes that avoid such problems as well as what these changes mean for some assumptions and expectations in social theory.

2

Four representations are particularly graceful devices to elaborate rational conflicts between *one* and *all:* Prisoners' Dilemma, Arrow's theorem, efficacy failure, and Wollheim's paradox (the latter as an expansion on solutions to Arrow's problem). Each representation stands for variations on a single generic problem: that rational individuals in a collective state fail the measures of rationality that are successful among the separate individuals.[8] The generic form of the problem materializes (as we will see) on the hostility between arithmetical and holistic models.

Prisoners' Dilemma is a famous game in which individuals choose rationally and then find that the joint outcome of their choices is only third best in terms of a preferential ordering of four possible outcomes. The starting conditions of the game are straightforward enough. The players are rational egoists choosing autonomously in isolation from each other and in a state of uncertainty about how the other player(s) will choose. The game is usually described in terms of two prisoners, label them a and b, facing confession or no-confession alternatives, where confession is represented by subscript 1 and no confession by subscript 0. The confession story is, of course, embellishment. The dilemma occurs on any alternative within the Prisoners' Dilemma matrix and conditions (Luce and Raiffa 1958). As long as the entries in the matrix below are in a descending order of preferability ($4 > 3 > 2 > 1$), a Prisoners' Dilemma game occurs.

	b_0	b_1
a_0	3,3	1,4
a_1	4,1	2,2

Each player, a and b, prefers (as egoists) a payoff of 4. The best equitable payoff is 3,3. Since $4 > 3$ and $2 > 1$, the dominant strategy is $a_1 > a_0$ and $b_1 > b_0$. The outcome of the game is $a_1 b_1$, with a payoff to each player of 2 (on the numbers used above). Each individual prefers outcomes in an ordering of $4,1 > 3,3 > 2,2 > 1,4$. Thus the dilemma: rational strategy for the individual leads to a joint outcome only third best on the preference orderings of each player.

The problem represented by the original Prisoners' Dilemma is that separate individuals, acting rationally, find that the combination of their rational choices is not a rationally best outcome. If, however, the individuals can find a way to cooperate, an outcome that is rationally best for both individuals (3,3) can be secured. Notice that the problem is not created by uncertainty. If either player is certain that the other will cooperate, it is still rational (on a calculation of dominant strategies) to choose the exploitive alternative. Solutions to the game that recognize the problem as one of failed coordination advance a variety of devices—coercion, communication, side payments—that make it rational for both individuals to cooperate, not simply for each to be assured of the other's cooperation.

Arrow's theorem represents a more elegant failure of combination rules to produce rational outcomes when individuals are acting rationally. The intriguing hold the theorem has on us begins with a curious demonstration. We first ponder orderings like these: voter 1 ranks three alternatives $a > b > c$; voter 2 ranks the same alternatives $b > c > a$; and a third voter orders the alternatives $c > a > b$. If these three rankings are combined, an intransitive ordering is the result: $a > b$, $b > c$, and $c > a$. The trap is thus set by the famous cyclical majority. We are drawn further into it by Arrow's general theorem. The basic theorem is a proof that when there are more than three individuals and alternatives, there does not exist any social choice function (or aggregator) that satisfies Pareto, nondictatorship, universal domain, complete and transitive rationality, and the independence of irrelevant alternatives.[9]

The proofs of the theorem demonstrate how these conditions are incompatible. The most common proof is to suppose that there is a set of individuals decisive over two alternatives, $x > y$, and that everyone else prefers $y > x$. By universal domain, then, both $x > y > z$ and $y > z > x$ must be admissible orderings. Now $x > y$ on decisiveness, $y > z$ on Pareto, and, on transitivity, $x > z$ follows. The members of the decisive set prefer $x > z$, and, by also maintaining the independence of irrelevant alternatives, the decisiveness over $x > y$ spreads to $x > z$ with the application of Pareto and transitivity. This contagion effect of decisiveness can be extended to all pairs of alternatives, demonstrating that local decisiveness (over any pair of alternatives) becomes global decisiveness (over all pairs of alternatives) when Arrow's conditions are maintained. Further, there must always be a decisive set if there is anything short of unanimity in society and society selects (on whatever rule) some ordering over others. For example, if set 1 prefers $x > y > z$, set 2 prefers $y > z > x$, and set 3 prefers $z > x > y$ (the cyclical-majority orderings), majority rule selects $y > z$. Sets 1 and 2 then constitute a set decisive over set 3 and the contagion effect reoccurs. The upshot of the proof is that a society may not be able to make any collective decisions without either dismissing Arrow's conditions or violating them.

Recent work has rendered the problem more rather than less difficult with the development of theorems that use no more than two of Arrow's conditions and, with the use of other conditions, prove the impossibility outcome (Kelly 1978). Various stages in several of the proofs will be admitted later to uncover the radical individualism assumed in the theorem (hence the importance of introducing the language early). But the point here is that the conditions of rational choice can all be maintained without a contradiction at the individual level. The contradictions occur as individual orderings are combined to yield a collective ordering.

Arrow's theorem may appear to be a crisis for democracy. This view misses the complexities of democratic rule (which is sufficiently broad to include both Madison and Rousseau). The theorem does, however, point to a conflict between liberalism (as the doctrine that certain choices are to be shielded from collective regulation) and majority rule. Nowhere is this conflict better expressed than in the variations on Arrow's theorem developed by Sen, the paradox of the Paretian liberal. Sen demonstrates that no aggregation device satisfies universality of domain, the Pareto condition, and minimal liberalism (two individuals each with a protected pair, i.e., where each individual is globally decisive for two alternatives, x against y and y against x). Sen asks us to imagine two individuals and three alternatives. The alternatives are that (x) individual 1 does m, (y) individual 2 does m, and (z) neither individual does m. Then, 1: zxy and 2: xyz. Now between (x,z), minimal liberalism requires $z > x$ for society, and between (yz), $y > z$. (Roughly, individuals should be decisive for alternatives affecting themselves—better that no one do m than l (for l), and that 2 does m rather than 1 (for 2)). So yz and zx are collective choices. But xy is selected on Pareto. Again the aggregator fails, this time because (mainly) individuals are to be given protected pairs, i.e., more generally, a control over alternatives irrespective of the preferences of others (Sen 1971).

The third representation, efficacy failure, is often developed as a rational dilemma in voting. Stated informally, it amounts to this: in large electorates, the effect any single individual has on the outcome of an election is so negligible that there is little or no incentive to vote. On a strict consequentialist thesis (where the value of an action is assigned to outcomes rather than internal or intrinsic rewards), the rationality of voting is a function of the effects of an individual's vote on the outcome of the election. Efficacy, however, is, ceteris paribus, one over the number of voters (Tullock 1968). Thus, with an increase in the size of the electorate, efficacy declines; and with a decline in efficacy, the rational incentive to vote also declines.

A sequence of elections can provide an equilibrium point where efficacy and the number of voters are in balance (larger electorates declining to this point on reduced efficacy, smaller electorates increasing in magnitude to this point on the satisfaction of efficacy). But this point may not be optimal for either individual or social interests. Certainly any such point of equilibrium will be low in the traditional requirements of participatory democracy. A single election, where votes are cast simultaneously and on a secret ballot, produces a clearer dilemma. Any rational individual deciding whether to vote or not when the electorate is large will decide not to vote.[10] More generally, the rationality of cooperating in a joint effort is inversely related to an increase in group size. On a rational equivalence of individual voters, no one would vote even on the acceptance of voting as a desirable decision rule.[11]

Efficacy and coordination failures are combined in some representations. Olson's "free rider" is one such combination. Olson's arguments do not replicate Prisoners' Dilemma logic. The initial free rider problem, unlike Prisoners' Dilemma, requires concepts of a public good and efficacy. Also, the conditions of uncertainty found in Prisoners' Dilemma are replaced with an assumption of perfect information.[12] A free rider occurs in groups unable to exclude nonparticipants from benefits, which then reduces the incentives for each and every individual to assume the costs of producing group benefits. If, in addition, the contribution of any one individual to the production of a public good is negligible (efficacy is low), then it pays for the individual to take the free ride instead of participating, if he can do so without external costs.[13]

More recent work has attempted to collapse Prisoners' Dilemma and the free rider to a single representation. Hardin (1971) introduces a Prisoners' Dilemma game between individual and collective that demonstrates important similarities between N-person Prisoners' Dilemma and the free rider problem. The basic exercise requires that "collective" be defined as a series of individuals, each playing against all others in an expanded matrix. Failures of efficacy are avoided by maintaining binary-type interaction. The original free rider representation, however, stresses the effects of numerical magnitudes on the rationality of cooperation. Large groups reduce the importance of any single individual's contribution to the joint effort. One less taxpayer, for example, will make no noticeable difference in the budget of the United States (though the withdrawal of even one member's support might jeopardize the efforts of a small committee to achieve some goal). Several other products of large numbers, e.g., detection problems, increased organizational costs, etc., contribute to the rationality of free riding in large groups.[14] But mainly, and on an egoistic calculus, the nonexcludable nature of public goods and the inverse relationship of efficacy and group size favor the rationality of nonparticipation.

Some public goods resist production when group size declines beyond some numerical figure, a point seen easily when one tries to imagine a handful of people trying to construct an interstate highway system. But, generally, the free rider is developed along increasing marginal costs with a reduction in group size, with remaining participants able to produce some of the good if willing to incur the increasing costs. The likelihood of defection, however, increases as the number of players increases, with at least a hypothetical threshold between the rationality of cooperating versus defecting.

Wollheim's paradox, the fourth representation to be discussed here, may seem an unlikely candidate to introduce to the more formal problems of collective choice. Wollheim asks us to imagine an individual morally committed both to a substantive alternative, p, and to majority rule, m, as a method for resolving disputes. An election is held on p and a rival alternative, q. Alternative q wins with majority support. The individual is then faced with two possibilities: abandom p by supporting q as the outcome of the decision rule, or support p and abandon m. The problem Wollheim sets forth is one facing any individual with contrary moral commitments who is forced to act on one commitment to the exclusion of the other (Wollheim 1962). Wollheim's paradox is not developed in formal terms. Nevertheless, it serves as an extension of the rational choice model that avoids the breakdowns represented by Arrow's theorem, and it also helps elaborate the normative implications of the general resolutions to be developed here.

3

Rational breakdowns between individuals and wholes are not hard logical contradictions. They are mapping failures. Rules and premises used by individuals cannot be successfully mapped into the space defined by wholes even when the wholes are constituted by the same individuals. One consequence of this failure is that two well-known and generally accepted assumptions in recent traditions of thought are thereby denied: first, that single individuals, acting rationally, will promote the rational interests of all; and second, that collective rationality is no more and no less than the sum of individual rational actions.[15]

The variations on the failure of rational continuity thread unevenly through the representations. Prisoners' Dilemma represents a coordination failure that is caused by the isolation of individuals, an absence of assurance, and—especially—the matrix of payoffs. There is also in iterated Prisoners' Dilemma games a problem in the concept of time. Arrow's theorem represents a breakdown in combination rules.

Efficacy failure is a failure of causality in which the spatial mapping of individual and collective outcome is faulty. Wollheim's paradox represents a conflict between individual autonomy and authority. In each representation, rational continuity between individual and whole fails because some set of items (criteria, rules, principles, concepts) cannot be maintained without a conflict between one or more of the items.

These variations factor the generic failure of rational continuity into component parts—efficacy, coordination, assurance, and combination rule failures. A more complete understanding of rational breakdown between one and all is the helpful result. But a solution to the generic failure must also simultaneously solve all of the component problems, if a generic failure has been correctly identified. No less will be attempted here, though in each component case one or more of the defining conditions will have been changed in the solution. For example, efficacy is a special form of power. But the meaning of power varies in types of social practices, merging finally with a type of indispensability in certain social forms. Being indispensable, however, solves the problem of efficacy only by abandoning the causal relations on which the problem of efficacy failure occurs.

A theoretical literature has utilized the component problems in interesting, though limited, ways. Especially productive is the recognition that the disequilibrium of majority rule (the likelihood of cyclical majorities) provides disproportionate power for the agenda setter in political societies.[16] Equally interesting is the use of Prisoners' Dilemma (and the attendant dilemma represented by the "free rider") to justify coercive societies (Olson 1971) and/or a reduction in the size of the political society (Taylor 1976). Since the first of these resolving measures (coercion) is the Hobbesian approach and the second (size reduction) is the Aristotelian approach, it is an easy matter to see that the discussion of these discontinuities is a continuation of traditional themes with new techniques and languages. Enormous promise is also found in experimental work setting out the ways in which information, communication, decision rules, exchanges, coalitions, etc., affect the outcomes of formal games.[17]

None of these efforts, however, considers that each of the representations or component problems might be part of a more basic failure in the concepts employed in collective choice. The objective of the present work is to address two more general features of rational breakdowns between individual and collective. These general features suggest a resolution of individual-whole discontinuities that (a) can be generalized to all of the component problems surveyed here, and (b) establishes a different type of collective choice than that found in the tradition within which the problems are found.

The first feature is the connection of the rational problems to methodological individualism. Social choice theory in general assumes that individuals are numerically discrete units. Wholes, in turn, are aggregations, typically the product of arithmetical composition rules. But ordinary language suggests that wholes are not always equal to the sum of their parts. Wholes can, for example, be described with practice terms like "war" that do not break down into "countable" individuals. Or wholes may be represented by mass terms like "public good" that do not individuate in the absence of extraordinary measures. This recognition of a form of holism is one way to avoid rational breakdowns between individuals and wholes. We will see, for example, that the introduction of conditional orderings $(x \rightarrow a > b > c; y \rightarrow b > c > a;$ etc.) to Arrow's theorem, where conditions are reasons, avoids the impossibility results by defining individuals as members of rational classes rather than sets. Wholes formed on a fusion of reasons are organic (in the benign sense of being nonadditive).

A second feature is the moral content of the problems. All of the rational problems to be surveyed here rest on (largely unexamined) moral assumptions. These assumptions are not the standard brand of everyday moral premise that we all carry around. They are vital components in the formal demonstrations of rational failure. For example, Arrow's "dictator" outcome that satisfies transitivity is rejected because no individual can impose his preferences on all other individuals. Yet the rejection of decisive individuals makes sense only on the assumption that no individuals have overriding claims on all possible joint outcomes. This assumption, however, requires a vocabulary (of claims and the methods for justifying them) not found in the explicit language of Arrow's theorem. In general, the literature on collective choice is ambivalent between mathematical and moral equality. Individuals are arithmetically comparable units in the starting conditions of the problems (though these units may combine and even be counted more than once in the aggregate outcome). But little or no concern is given to the claims that moral equals might make on collective goods, claims that may justify decisive individuals (those, for example, with greater needs). The moral assumptions are thus both required for the rational discontinuities, and largely unexplored as possible resolutions of the discontinuities. Indeed, recent expansions of the primitive term "individual" to satisfy moral criteria, e.g., "extended sympathy" (Arrow

1977), transform and, on occasion, avoid some of these rational problems (although not with unqualified success, as we will see). A clearer understanding of moral terms promises a restoration of rationality.

Generally, the rational problems originate in an inadequate understanding of the primitive term "individual." Individuals in collective choice theory are typically seen as countable units. This conception of individuals, however, will not accommodate the moral vocabulary needed to develop the proofs and axioms. The narrative theme for the study is stated in this proposition: that the working logic of the representations requires that individuals be discrete (non-overlapping) and countable items, but the moral language needed to produce the rational breakdowns (exploitation, dictatorship) requires a different sense of the individual. Once the term "individual" is reinterpreted to accommodate moral needs, however, a different form of collective choice replaces the aggregation methods found in the representations. A corporate, rather than a numerical, society is the result.

The problems of rational discontinuity are, in general, conflicts among background concepts that, when examined, suggest the structural or institutional forms that provide a type of continuity meeting moral and rational tests. We will discover, first, that all of the rational problems fail to express the liberal community of moral agents that is fixed at the background level of collective choice and, second, that only a form of juridical democracy can represent such a community. There may be other starting points for a theory of collective choice than a liberal community. But the rational breakdowns to be surveyed here are all developed on liberal principles; and no understanding of the rational failures is complete without the recognition that liberalism is the origin of, and remedy for, the rational discontinuities between individual and collective.

The exercise is carried out in several steps.

1. Prisoners' Dilemma is addressed at both structural (the matrix of payoffs) and individual (principles of choice, evaluative calculi) levels. A typology of wholes is introduced to show the restriction of Prisoners' Dilemma representations to numerical wholes and the power of corporate wholes to resolve such dilemmas (chapter two).

2. The background assumptions of the representations are identified in an examination of Arrow's theorem. The strong reliance on two competing senses of equality and the ambivalent status of the term "individual" are described. Two concepts of community in Arrow's theorem are traced to conflicts between arithmetical and moral languages (chapter three).

3. Different senses of an "individual" are elaborated through a discussion of efficacy in a variety of social forms. The two competing models of society—numerical and corporate—are developed as different conditions for efficacy, and those social forms in which efficacy is not an issue are suggested (chapter four).

4. Means-ends rationality is contrasted with reason-giving rationality, and the reliance of aggregation machines on unconditional orderings is demonstrated. Conditional orderings are developed and the needs of such orderings for fused (nonaggregated) outcomes documented (chapter five).

5. The implications for accepting individuals as reason-giving are discussed. Two social forms—anarchy and deliberative bodies—are developed as institutions that accommodate reason-giving rationality. The failures of both populist and Madisonian democracy to solve aggregation problems are elaborated, and the success of organizational rationality in solving the rational problems is discussed (in giving up universal domain by restricting alternatives) (chapter six).

6. The solutions to the problems are developed in terms of some general theories of change and maintenance in social theory and contrasted with some recent theories of justice (chapter seven).

Note: Answers to the puzzles in the opening paragraph are a blackboard; a towel; cut off their noses.

NOTES

1. This paradox was constructed by a physicist, Dr. William Newcomb, of the Livermore Radiation Laboratories in California. It was famously examined by Robert Nozick in his "Newcomb's Problem and Two Principles of Choice," in Nicholas Rescher, eds., *Essays in Honor of Carl G. Hempel* (Dordrecht Holland: D. Reidel Publishing, 1969). See also the Martin Gardner report, "Mathematical Games," *Scientific American* (1974).

2. W. V. O. Quine, *The Ways of Paradox* (Cambridge, Mass.: Harvard University Press, 1976), where the distinction between "veridical" and "falsidical" paradoxes is also found. One can also change the reference to avoid self-referential paradoxes, as when a non-Cretan says "All Cretans are liars." But two different people uttering the same sentence may be expressing different propositions. For a discussion of semantic paradoxes, see James Cargile, *Paradoxes: A Study in Form and Predication* (Cambridge: Cambridge University Press, 1979).

3. The speculative discussion of this experiment has even challenged, on the basis of quantum physics, the doctrine of a real world independent of human consciousness. For

a nontechnical overview, see Hernard d'Espagnat, "The Quantum Theory and Reality," *Scientific American* 241 (November 1979): 158–60.

4. A collection of readings and text on these representations is Brian Barry and Russell Hardin, eds., *Rational Man and Irrational Society?* (Beverly Hills, Calif.: Sage Publications, 1982). See also the overview by Dennis Mueller, *Public Choice* (Cambridge: Cambridge University Press, 1979).

5. Individuals in corporate wholes who oppose collective outcomes are simply irrational—a pattern of judgment found in certain idealistic political philosophies. Collectivist theories in general do not suppose that societies are to be rational in the same way that individuals are rational.

6. Arrow's problem can be generated on a conflict between any two of the starting conditions: transitivity, the independence condition, universal domain, nondictatorship, and Pareto. But the conflict always occurs as separate orderings are combined into a collective ordering. In Kenneth Arrow, *Social Choice and Individual Values* (New York: John Wiley & Sons, 1963). See, for the best survey of versions of the theorem up to that year, Jerry Kelly, *Arrow Impossibility Theorems* (New York: Academic Press, 1978).

7. The bibliography in Barry and Hardin (1982) suggests the crowded state of the field.

8. The thought that the enterprise here is doomed at the start because "collective rationality" is oxymoronic can be gracefully set to rest. The assignment of rationality measures, like transitivity, to collective orderings is found within collective choice theory, not imposed from outside. It is precisely because collectives are thought to be subject to the same rationality tests as individuals that such rational problems as those discussed here have occurred. In any case, there is nothing mystifying in expecting combinations of orderings to be transitive, once transitivity is accepted as a rational test for individual orderings. The fault leading to rational breakdowns is not one of reifying societies, but of using flawed concepts of "individual" and "rationality." Once the flaws are sealed or avoided, rationality can be assigned to political societies in acceptable ways.

9. Kenneth Arrow, *Individual Choice and Social Values* (New York: John Wiley & Sons, 951). I am here using Jerry Kelly's language, drawn from private conversations and the excellent survey in his *Arrow Impossibility Theorems*. With that thought firmly in mind, let the following definitions be accepted as Arrow's meanings:

Decisiveness: A set of individuals is decisive for x against y ($x, y \in X$, where $X =$ a set of mutually exclusive alternatives) if, for every profile, u, in which (1) $x \geqslant_i y$ for all $i \in s$ (2) $x \geqslant_i y$ for at least one $i \in s$; we have $x \in v$ (where $v =$ a nonempty subset of $X \Rightarrow y \notin C_u(v)$ (or, y is excluded from the choice function, C_u, over the agendas).

Put in looser language, if x is in the agenda, y will not be chosen. Decisiveness is thus an exclusionary power.

Pareto: For all distinct $x, y \in X$, the set of all n (where $n =$ the number of individuals) is decisive for x against y.

Nondictatorship: There is no one individual who alone is decisive for x against y for all distinct $x, y \in X$.

Universal domain: (1) The domain of f consists of all logically possible profiles u. (2) At every u, the domain of $C_u = f(u)$ includes all finite nonempty subsets of X. If $u = a$ logically possible profile and $v \in X$, v is finite and $v \neq \phi$, $C_u(v) \neq \phi$.

Or, the domain is unrestricted, in the sense that every logically possible combination of individual orderings of alternatives in X must be the domain of the social choice function.

Independence of irrelevant alternatives: Let u and u' be two distinct profiles whose restriction to v are the same. If f assigns choice function C_u to profile u and $C_{u'}$ to u', then $C_u(v) = C_{u'}(v)$.

Completeness: $x R_u y$ or $y R_u x$ for all x, y.

Transitivity: $x R_u y$ and $y R_u z \Rightarrow x R_u z$.

Rationality: For every profile u, C_u has a binary relation R_u such that C_u can be explained by R_u as $C_u (v) = [x \in v (X R_u \text{ for all } y \in_v)]$.

10. Even the costs of acquiring information or using available information on the electoral system are usually assigned a level below the benefits derived from being informed in large electorates. Thus, it is rational to remain ignorant about how others vote even when this knowledge can be gained. See Anthony Downs, *An Economic Theory of Democracy* (New York: Harper & Row Pubs., 1957).

11. James Fishkin maintains that, since an obligation to participate in a collective effort fails in large groups, all attempts to appeal to general utility (e.g., Lyons' equivalence thesis) fail to restore the obligation of individuals to act to bring about the highest general utility. See *Size and Obligation* (New Haven, Conn.: Yale University Press, 1982) pp. 111–30. Thus, simple and general utility remain separated where efficacy fails.

12. Olson, *The Logic of Collective Action* (Cambridge: Harvard University Press, 1971). The "free rider" actually predates Plato. Antiphon is said to have addressed the problems that Thrasymachus and Glaucon (in the *Republic*) and then (much later) Olson discuss.

13. The standard references are: Paul Samuelson, "The Pure Theory of Public Expenditure," *Review of Economics and Statistics* 36 (1954): 387–89, and "A Diagrammatic Exposition of a Theory of Public Expenditure," *Review of Economics and Statistics* 37 (1955): 350–56; also Samuelson's "Aspects of Public Expenditure Theories," *Review of...* 40 (1958): 332–38, and Julius Margolis' "A Comment on the Pure Theory of Public Expenditure," in *Review of...* 37 (1955): 347–49. Distribution is impossible if goods are "nonexcludable" whenever available. See, for more recent statements, William Riker and Peter Ordeshook, *Introduction to Positive Political Theory* (Englewood Cliffs, N.J.: Prentice-Hall, 1973), pp. 240–71, and the helpful treatment in Duncan Snidal, "Public Goods, Property Rights, and Political Organizations," *International Studies Quarterly* 23 (December 1979): 532–66.

14. Elaborated in Riker and Ordeshook, *Positive Political Theory*, pp. 69–77. Numerous secondary studies have followed Olson's work with qualifications and amendments. Typical of these is John Chamberlin's "Provision of Collective Goods as a Function of Group Size," *American Political Science Review* 68 (June 1979): 707–16. Chamberlin argues that the supply of a public good may actually increase with an increase in group size since a reduction in individual contributions may be more than offset by the greater number of individuals in large groups. But Chamberlin also concedes Olson's main points: that nonexcludable public goods without the added virtue of supply irreducibility will diminish as the size increases. I do not propose to survey this technical literature. My concern here is with rational problems, not with the validity of particular representations except as they bear on an understanding of the problems.

15. And so the famous thoughts expressed by Adam Smith in *An Inquiry into the nature and Causes of the Wealth of Nations* (New York: Random House, 1937), p. 423, must be reexamined: "[When the individual] intends only his own gain . . . he is . . . led by an invisible hand to promote an end which was not part of his intention . . . . By pursuing his own interest he frequently promotes that of the society more effectually than when he really intends to promote it."

16. Reviewed by William H. Riker, "Implications from the Disequilibrium of Majority Rule for the Study of Institutions," *American Political Science Review* 74 (June 1980): 432–46, 447–456. See also the comments by Peter C. Ordeshook and Douglas W. Rae, and the reply by Riker, same issue.

17. See, in particular, the summaries (up to that year) in Mueller, *Public Choice,* and the collection of pieces in Peter C. Ordeshook and Kenneth A. Shepsle, eds., *Political Equilibrium* (London: Kluwer-Nijhoff Publishing, 1982).

2

Individuals and Structures
Types of Resolutions in Prisoners' Dilemma

1

Any study of Prisoners' Dilemma will reveal that solutions must be formed at two levels: structural (roughly, the social context in which individuals act) and individual (principle of choice, evaluative calculus). The first level is obvious in a trivial way when we observe that the matrix of payoffs is decisive in forming the Prisoners' Dilemma— change the matrix and one dissolves the dilemma. But it is more important, although perhaps less obvious, that solutions to a representation like the Prisoners' Dilemma aim at changing both the incentives that make different principles of choice rational and the principles of choice themselves. In reverse order, individuals must choose differently to avoid problems of rationality, but it must be rational for them to make these changes in their principles of choice.

The thought that both structures and individuals must change if rational continuity is to be achieved is on the order of an opening statement, not a conclusion. But its truth can be explored more effectively by inspecting the types of solutions the literature offers for Prisoners' Dilemma problems. There are three distinct solution sets: (1) introduce exogenous costs and benefits to modify the incentives of the players; (2) develop social practices (in effect, replace conditions of uncertainty with risk) that ensure cooperation without exogenous factors; and (3) modify the structural context.[1] The first two types of solutions render cooperation rational for individuals, while the third specifies what is required contextually for this rendering.

17

Look, for example, at the application of solution types one and two to each of the prominent problems represented by the Prisoners' Dilemma format: coordination and assurance failure. Failure of coordination, represented by the original Prisoners' Dilemma game, is drawn up on a payoff matrix that allows defection to dominate cooperation.

		b_0	b_1
A:	a_0	3,3	1,4
	a_1	4,1	2,2

Assurance failure is represented by a matrix that assigns both players a cooperative payoff that is greater than either can achieve through defection:

		b_0	b_1
B:	a_0	5,5	1,4
	a_1	4,1	2,2

The effect of the payoff matrix is undeniable. Obviously (1) less exogenous costs and benefits are required in B than in A to secure cooperation, and (2) less effort need be expended to establish cooperative social practices in B than in A. (Both observations follow from the stronger internal incentives toward cooperation created by matrix B). Even the decision rule used in the game differs from one matrix to another. Dominance is used in coordination failure (since 4 > 3 and 2 > 1, alternative 1 dominates 0), but cannot be used in assurance failure (since neither 1 nor 0 dominates the other on the payoffs). Maximin and maximax can be used in assurance failure (decision rules that converge whenever dominance occurs). Even the use of these two decision rules, however, is dependent on whether the other player will cooperate; for a reasonable guarantee of cooperation will mandate 0 > 1 (and make maximin an unreasonable choice). The strong effects of types one and two solutions can be more dramatically illustrated by

		b_0	b_1
C:	a_0	0,0	1,4
	a_1	4,1	0,0

Here the two equity cells are 0,0 and there is no Pareto cell. As a noniterated game, there is no solution for the problem represented by C; for no outcome is both stable and equitable. Neither dominance nor maximin work as decision rules. A maximax decision rule suggests 1 > 0, which leads to the worst outcome for both players. A cooperative effort on either alternative is non-Pareto. It is better in this dismal game to be exploited rather than to remain in an equity cell. One can only hope that the other player will choose to be exploited first.[2]

Structures affect individuals in yet another way. The size of the social unit bears on the rationality of defection. Taylor (1976) suggests that N-player iterated Prisoners' Dilemma games (where N-number of players play a series of ordinary Prisoners' Dilemma games) can produce mutual cooperation throughout the sequence of games if the number of players is small. Cooperation is possible through (a) conditional strategies, and (b) a modest discount rate, one that does not reduce future returns too far below the value assigned to present benefits. Both conditions are more likely to be realized by all players in a small social unit, less likely in a large social unit. The first condition requires a knowledge of how many other players cooperated in previous games, which is more easily secured in small groups. The second condition requires that the future is rated roughly equal to the present, which is proportionately less likely of all individuals as the number of players increases.

A numerically large group diminishes proportionately the arithmetical importance of any single unit and increases the simple probability that a single unit will defect. But a reduction in numbers is not sufficient. A small number of individuals, constituting a social unit, also produces the relational practices (reinforcement, stability, cohesion, personal contacts, etc.) that void the conditions of many participation dilemmas. Taylor affirms the importance of conditional cooperative strategies (only if others cooperate will I cooperate, etc.) for the resolution of the Prisoners' Dilemma, and the dependence of such strategies on knowing that, and how many, others are cooperating. Or, not just a reduction in numbers will do. The tighter sense of community commonly associated with fewer people is also needed. The cohesive society resulting from a reduction in numbers resolves the Prisoners' Dilemma by transforming uncertainty to risk, and even trust. Coordination is provided through a cohesive social unit, where defection is socially difficult if not impossible because individuals are no longer isolated from each other.[3]

2

A stronger relationship between individuals and structures is disclosed if evaluative principles are allowed to form social partitions. Sen (1974) attempts to resolve the Prisoners' Dilemma by introducing two new versions of it formed on different preference orderings. Egoists, who constitute the original Prisoners' Dilemma games, order outcomes as $a_1b_0 > a_0b_0 > a_1b_1 > a_0b_1$. The best equitable outcome is a_0b_0. The actual outcome is a_1b_1. Sen asks us to suppose two different types of players. One prefers the ordering of outcomes as $a_0b_0 > a_1b_0 > a_1b_1 > a_0b_1$. The other's preference ordering is $a_0b_0 > a_0b_1 > a_1b_0 > a_1b_1$. The first player prefers the best equitable outcome, but wants the highest personal payoff next (the exploitive cell of a_1b_0). The second player also prefers as first the best equitable outcome, and then is sufficiently other-regarding to rank as second the exploitive cell favoring the other player. It is an easy matter to see that games played by two of the first type of new player are assurance games (AG), requiring only that each be certain that the other player has a like preference ordering and will choose in accordance with it, in order for the game to produce the optimal payoff. The second type of new player generates an other-regarding (OR) game, where (again) all can gain their first-order outcome so long as the players are of the requisite type and choose accordingly. Unlike the original Prisoners' Dilemma game, the equilibrium point of each new game is Pareto optimal.

It is also clear that moral principles have been introduced to Prisoners' Dilemma, replacing the egoist principles generally used to elaborate the original game.[4] There are first the principles (equity, other-regarding) used by the players, each of which marks the players as moral individuals in different ways. There are also the intriguing possibilities of "ranking the rankings," or morally ordering the types of games generated by the introduction of new players. Sen's different versions of Prisoners' Dilemma games lead to such second-order preferences, which are concerned with whose first-order preferences are to be satisfied. Let x = set of all possible orderings and Π = set of all orderings of elements of x. Then the moral point of view is some ordering of all possible sets in x. For example, a moral principle might rank E (the egoist, or original Prisoners' Dilemma game) $> OR > AG$ as the ranking of rankings in Π.

Baier (1977) shows that several types of preferences are needed to elaborate rational choice: intrinsic (binary choice between two alternatives, or $x > y$ when only x and y are compared); derived (binary choice between two alternatives on a set of conditions, expressible as $z \rightarrow x > y$); and overall (global comparisons of x and y, or $x > y$ with perfect knowledge of x, y, all other alternatives, conditions, consequences, etc.). From these types of preferences we can derive the first-order preferences (egoist, other-regarding, which involve no references to preferences) and higher-order preferences (which rank the rankings) that yield the different types of Prisoners' Dilemma games. Among the important implications of this typology of preferences two stand out: first, individuals may have overall, intrinsic, and derived preferences that are contrary to one another (and so an individual can consistently hold opposed preference orderings); and second, second-order preferences can rank low those orderings established by first-order principles (as an egoist by first-order preferences may yet rank other-regarding orderings higher than egoist orderings when making overall choices—and indeed aspire to be an other-regarding individual on first-order preferences).

It is important to remember, however, that Prisoners' Dilemma is a game played in conditions of uncertainty, and that this uncertainty can extend to knowledge of what principles the opposing player is using. If compatible principles are found in Prisoners' Dilemma, then a Pareto outcome is the saddle-point. But like principles may not be compatible, and different principles (compatible and opposed) are possible conditions of Prisoners' Dilemma games. Even in the original game the importance of pairings is clear: egoists play to a suboptimal outcome, altruists play to an optimal equity outcome. If structures are formed from compatible pairings, no conflict between individual and collective rationality occurs. Introduce, for example, the following types of players to the Prisoners' Dilemma format: egoist, E, and the original Prisoners' Dilemma player, ranks outcomes on condition that they satisfy self-interest; benevolence, B, optimizes returns to the other player; masochism, Ma, wants the worst possible outcome for the self; morality, Mo, prefers outcomes on a "piggy-back" criterion—equal (and highest) returns if possible and a higher return to the other if not; utilitarianism, U, prefers the highest total payoff; sadism, Sa, prefers to minimize the other's payoff (regardless of returns to the self); and envy, En, always wants the greatest negative difference between his and his opponent's payoff. Introducing additional players to the original Prisoners' Dilemma format allows us to ask whether different principles of choice can be successful on their own criterion of success, and what structures are required for each of the principles to succeed.

The exercise is simple. Each principle (or type of individual) ranks outcomes as defined by the principle. Then the success of each principle can be settled by determining its effectiveness in achieving desirable outcomes in uniform and mixed principle games. Let game 1 be the original Prisoners' Dilemma, representing coordination failures (A), and game 2 be the matrix of payoffs representing assurance failures (B). Then, in games 1 and 2, the preferred outcomes for each player are:

1

2

$E = a_1b_0 > a_0b_0 > a_1b_1 > a_0b_1$ $E = a_0b_0 > a_1b_0 > a_1b_1 > a_0b_1$

$B = a_0b_1 > a_0b_0 > a_1b_1 > a_1b_0$ $B = a_0b_0 > a_0b_1 > a_1b_1 > a_1b_0$

$Ma = a_0b_1 > a_1b_1 > a_0b_0 > a_1b_0$ $Ma = a_0b_1 > a_1b_1 > a_1b_0 > a_0b_0$

$Mo = a_0b_0 > a_1b_1 > a_0b_1 > a_1b_0$ $Mo = a_0b_0 > a_1b_1 > a_0b_1 > a_1b_0$

$U = a_0b_0 > a_1b_0 \simeq a_0b_1 > a_1b_1$ $U = a_0b_0 > a_1b_0 \simeq a_0b_1 > a_1b_1$

$Sa = a_1b_0 > a_1b_1 > a_0b_0 > a_0b_1$ $Sa = a_1b_0 > a_1b_1 > a_0b_1 > a_0b_0$

$En = a_1b_0 > a_1b_1 \simeq a_0b_0 > a_0b_1$ $En = a_1b_0 > a_0b_0 \simeq a_1b_1 > a_0b_1$

Explanatory notes: The utilitarian is indifferent to the distributions of burdens/benefits when the totals are equal; the envious player doesn't care about totals so long as he gets a return equal to others. The other orderings are fairly straightforward. They are all (with the exception of the egoist and masochist) orderings that consider the preferences of others. And, in the form of binary relationships, each type of player generates a different type of game. Assume again that players choose on dominance strategies (when available). Then, between subscripts 1 versus 0 as alternatives, the choice of either subscript will be a function of both the evaluative criterion and the payoff matrix. The following are some reasonable (though only illustrative) calculations on choice strategies for each player in games 1 and 2.

1   2

$E - E = a_1b_1$ $E - E = a_0b_0$

$B - B = a_0b_0$ $B - B = a_0b_0$

$Ma - Ma = a_0b_0$ $Ma - Ma = a_0b_0$

$$\text{Mo} - \text{Mo} = a_0 b_0 \qquad \text{Mo} - \text{Mo} = a_0 b_0$$
$$\text{U} - \text{U} = a_0 b_0 \qquad \text{U} - \text{U} = a_0 b_0$$
$$\text{Sa} - \text{Sa} = a_1 b_1 \qquad \text{Sa} - \text{Sa} = a_1 b_1$$
$$\text{En} - \text{En} = a_1 b_1 \qquad \text{En} - \text{En} = a_1 b_1$$

Using the preference orderings of outcomes for each player in game 1, for E (as before) the outcome is third-best; for B, second-best; for Ma, third-best; for Mo, most preferred; for U, most preferred; for Sa, second-best; for En, second\third-best (equivalence). But in game 2, four of the players get their most preferred outcomes while Sa gets second-best, Ma a worst outcome, and En gets a second\third-best outcome. Two conclusions can be drawn: (1) the famous conflict between individual and joint rationality occurs in the original Prisoners' Dilemma matrix only with certain types of preferences, for the dominance principle can mandate a choice by some players (Mo and U in both games) that leads to a stable outcome most preferred by each player; and (2) a change in the payoff matrix can eliminate many of the conflicts (including the original egoist problem).

Now, second, let the games be mixed, consisting of different players. The outcomes, more numerous, are listed below:

	1	2		1	2
E − B =	$a_1 b_0$	$a_0 b_0$	Ma − Mo =	$a_0 b_0$	$a_0 b_0$
E − Ma =	$a_1 b_0$	$a_0 b_0$	Ma − U =	$a_0 b_0$	$a_0 b_0$
E − Mo =	$a_1 b_0$	$a_0 b_0$	Ma − Sa =	$a_0 b_1$	$a_0 b_1$
E − U =	$a_1 b_0$	$a_0 b_0$	Ma − En =	$a_0 b_1$	$a_0 b_1$
E − Sa =	$a_1 b_1$	$a_0 b_1$	Mo − U =	$a_0 b_0$	$a_0 b_0$
E − En =	$a_1 b_1$	$a_0 b_1$	Mo − Sa =	$a_0 b_1$	$a_0 b_1$
B − Ma =	$a_0 b_0$	$a_0 b_0$	Mo − En =	$a_0 b_1$	$a_0 b_1$
B − Mo =	$a_0 b_0$	$a_0 b_0$	U − Sa =	$a_0 b_1$	$a_0 b_1$
B − U =	$a_0 b_0$	$a_0 b_0$	U − En =	$a_0 b_1$	$a_0 b_1$
B − Sa =	$a_0 b_1$	$a_0 b_1$	Sa − En =	$a_1 b_1$	$a_1 b_1$
B − En =	$a_0 b_1$	$a_0 b_1$			

Again, on the ranking of preferences, and now counting the number of rank places and assigning a 4-3-2-1 order to them (4 for first place, etc.), in game 1 the egoist gets a preference-satisfaction score = 20, B = 21, Ma = 18, Mo = 18, U = 19.5 (the fraction here and with the next U is caused by the equivalence relation—I divided the total integers for each rank), Sa = 22, En = 21. In game 2, the scores are

$E = 18$, $B = 22$, $Ma = 12$, $Mo = 20$, $U = 21$, $Sa = 23$, and $En = 22.5$. The respective success of each player in securing desirable outcomes in mixed games is, in game 1: $Sa > B = En > E > U > Ma = Mo$; in game 2: $Sa > En > B > U > Mo > E > Ma$. Stable games in this exercise have two possible meanings: (a) equal payoffs to each player, and (b) players receiving a most-preferred outcome. It would seem that (b) is the more secure specification of stability in games formed on higher-order preferences, for equality of outcomes still permits different preference-satisfaction—surely a more important indicator of instability than equality of outcome. Note also that stable games in the sense of (b) are also games of rational continuity between individual choice and joint outcome.

This may be as good a place as any to remind the reader that these are non-iterated binary games, and thus the conclusions drawn from them are limited. But, also, the conditions of uncertainty in Prisoners' Dilemma, if maintained through a sequence of games and if (this is the bigger if) extended to knowledge of how many others are playing the game, will shield the binary relationships from changes. So perhaps the limits are not too severe in terms of the original Prisoners' Dilemma conditions. There are other, more severe, limits that are drawn from the nature of formal games like Prisoners' Dilemma. The payoff matrix is the main defining feature of the game, not only in the sense that (as demonstrated here) the matrix controls the rationality of evaluative criteria, but in the larger sense that dilemmas of rational coordination are set up artificially by the matrix. Since any of a number of matrices can represent real-world conditions, conclusions drawn from particular matrices are limited. Certainly the empirical success of various evaluative criteria must be advanced cautiously, given the artificial nature of formal games.

The artificiality of Prisoners' Dilemma game also qualifies the amendments that might be made on this exercise. One can, for example, assign utility functions to the different types of players. Taylor (1976) has generated types of games from various utility functions rather than evaluative criteria. In two-person ordinary (original) Prisoners' Dilemma games, altruists (for example) maximize the utility function $U_i = U_i (P_1, P_2)$, representing a weighted sum of P_1 and P_2. Where $P_2 = 0$, individual i is a pure egoist. The function can similarly be transformed into pure altruism with $P_1 = 0$. Introducing utilities for each player in the original Prisoners' Dilemma game transforms the game by connecting dominance to utility weights. The traditional suboptimal outcome of a_1b_1 occurs only if the utility functions of both players are weighted toward egoism. Utility functions express more exactly the strategies (defection, cooperation) of players. But even the interesting games produced from different functions—e.g., games of difference, games of anti-difference—are still products of the payoff matrix.

Iterating the game may be more useful, since (as many have observed) the static Prisoners' Dilemma game has almost no relevance for real-world social conditions. Among the many important revelations produced by iterated Prisoners' Dilemma games is that the dilemma of the original Prisoners' Dilemma may not be duplicated in the supergame (an indefinite number of iterations of a single ordinary game), for conditional cooperation may be rational in a variety of conditions (Taylor 1976). But it is more important here to note that the structural change that iteration brings is increased information about the other players' choices and strategies, thus closing the initial distance between players set up in the original Prisoners' Dilemma (where uncertainty, not risk, defines the conditions of choice). (If the game were iterated with knowledge of past plays canceled on each round, like those games of blackjack when the deck is reshuffled for each hand, then iteration would be formally identical to the static game.) The fact that at least one extended analysis of Prisoners' Dilemma suggests that conditions of social cohesion are vital to the rationality of cooperative strategies (Taylor 1976), supports the main point on the need to coalesce individuals to avoid this type of dilemma.

The outcomes of uniform (same player) and mixed (different player) games suggest that (1) the evaluative principles identifying different players are not as important in establishing rational continuity between individual and collective as the differences in matrices of payoffs; and (2) in both the coordination-failure and assurance-failure matrices, pairings among some types of players can still lead to rational joint outcomes. It follows that one solution to both coordination and assurance representations is a recognition of rational pairings in the form of social partitioning, or the establishment of structural segments that cluster players in rational groups.

Let a rational society be minimally defined as one in which Pareto is not violated when all individuals are acting rationally. Then in each of the two matrices, (A) coordination and (B) assurance, rational partitions must be generated if this minimum condition is to be realized.

Form M is a society of limited association, with social relations and movements restricted by certain principles. The individuals cannot form uniform games—they cannot have same-principle associations,

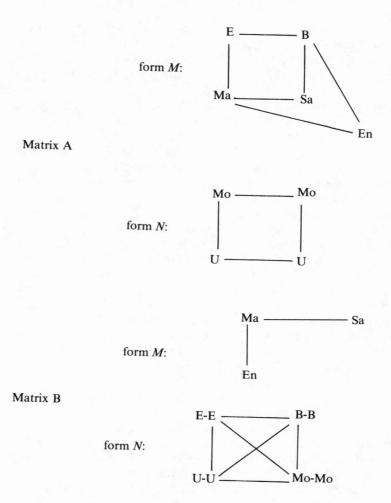

Figure 2.1.
Prisoners' Dilemma Matrixes

e.g., E − E. So long as these restrictions are maintained, the joint outcome most preferred by each player is successfully realized. Form N is a
society of unrestricted liberty of association. One individual can interact with any other individual (other or same-principle associations)
and still produce a joint outcome ranked best on the preferential ranking of each individual. Both M and N provide rational continuity between individual choice and joint outcome, but M gives up liberty of
association to do so. We can interpret these forms in two ways. One is
that M is a regulated society sacrificing one value, liberty, in order to
secure Pareto. Since N does not require such a sacrifice, Pareto and
liberty are secured when citizens share certain types of values. The second interpretation is that M is rational in terms of the segmented orderings that establish local conditions of rationality. On this interpretation, M is a society marking off zones of rationality that specify
conditional associations; if rationality is to be achieved, then certain
associations must be avoided. The N form, on this understanding, represents the compatible rationalities of "enlightened" orderings (morality, benevolence, utilitarianism), plus egoism on occasion. Unrestricted
liberty is given up in M (and maintained in N), but free association
among individuals may still be allowed in M in local areas where only
compatible individuals are clustered.

The thought that only certain types of individuals can produce
rational associations is not generally developed in theories of the moral
or just society. But it is a common enough conviction. In Plato's
Republic, a society of thieves is dismissed as internally divisive even
though one of shared values. Individuals can, in general, highly prize
goods that are scarce, thus creating conflict (and frustration of rational
demands) in efforts to acquire the goods. Individuals can even agree on
the same particular goal, when the goal is accessible only to a subset of
that set in agreement over it. Thus, I can want to make love to my mistress, but if you agree on the particulars—also wanting to make love to
my mistress—then we are in disagreement through both wanting the
same thing. Such divergencies between shared values and harmonious
pursuits are well-known. The game of Prisoners' Dilemma illustrates
the special incompatibilities between various principles of choice.
Compatible principles may still yield conflicting demands. But one
general condition for a rational association seems to be the presence of
principles that are rationally compatible; and in coordination and
assurance failures, the existence of a set of meta-rules that establish
compatible principles by structural change (social partitioning).[5]

Look more closely, however, and a better moral can be seen. The compatibility and rational success of different principles are functions of the payoff matrix. The change from the coordination to the assurance game dramatically transforms the interactions among the players. Egoism, for example, becomes as rational and socially congenial as benevolence, morality, and utilitarianism in the assurance game. Two types of individuals (from the seven introduced to Prisoners' Dilemma) can associate with each other rationally in the coordination game. All but the envious, masochistic, and sadistic players (who, poor things, have only each other to engage rationally in the assurance game) can produce a most preferred outcome from self-association in assurance matrices. The lesson here is intuitively known in the question asked by every bright student first encountering Prisoners' Dilemma: who sets up the matrix of payoffs? The power to bring about rational conditions is in the control of the matrix. This simple point is nowhere better illustrated than in matrix C (above), where no outcome rational to both players is possible in a non-iterated game unless the payoff structure is changed. Indeed, the recalcitrance of this game to simple resolutions expresses a more general need for structural change in the social practices represented by Prisoners' Dilemma games. Individuals must be members of institutions or basic structures that permit rational cooperation if the dilemma is to be resolved.

Turn back now to the levels of preferences elaborated by Sen and Baier. A higher order preference, which might reasonably be called a moral point of view, would rank the first-order preferences as Mo > B > U > E > En > Ma > Sa (on the grounds, roughly, that morality and benevolence are better than social utility, which is better than egoism, with self-interest superior to envy, which in turn is better than self-harm, and self-harm is better than harming others sadistically). Other first-order preferences can, of course, also claim a moral point of view. But any such ranking would have no reference to the game of Prisoners' Dilemma, for higher order preferences provide only a ranking of preference orderings, not a principle with which to choose alternatives in Prisoners' Dilemma games. Nor can higher preferences even rank game outcomes (as first-order preferences do), so there is no measure of success in game play even if a principle of choice could be derived from a higher order preference. Higher-order preferences seem to be drawn from meta-principles that can rank rational partitions, which in Prisoners' Dilemma are generated by the principles that produce first-order preferences.

A ranking of partitions drawn from the ranking above of first-order principles and appreciative of liberty would order rational societies as matrix A—form $N > M$; matrix B—form $N > M$; and N in matrix A $> N$ in matrix B. The moral point of view expressed in higher order preferences seems by its nature to be a background principles for evaluating social forms.[6] This type of evaluation, moreover, is parasitic on the activity of first-order principles competing with each other and generating the social forms to be ranked. The principles for higher order preferences do not affect the formation of rational forms, but can rank such forms when they appear as clusters of compatible first-order principles.

3

The close relationship between individual choice and structures that these three exercises demonstrate—the two effects of (a) payoff matrices on resolution efforts and (b) the size of the social unit on the rationality of defection, and the almost symbiotic connections of individual principles to structural arrangements—affirm the obvious: that the rational discontinuity represented by Prisoners' Dilemma is a failure of compatibility between individual parts and the collectives the parts are assumed to constitute. This failure, moreover, is a failure to fulfill the expectations of methodological individualism that wholes equal the sum of their parts.

Look at the type of rational breakdown that Prisoners' Dilemma represents. The breakdown is not a simple failure of individuals to get their most preferred outcome. That individuals fail to see their preferences realized in collective outcomes is a commonplace, hardly a candidate for a rational problem. Nor is Prisoners' Dilemma a breakdown in criterial continuity between individual and collective. Arrow's theorem, for example, demonstrates that criteria employed by individuals—transitivity, pair-wise methods of comparison, and universal domain—cannot be successfully transferred to the collective level if certain collective conditions are to be maintained (especially Pareto and nondictatorship). Prisoners' Dilemma does not represent this type of problem, for it is exactly the criteria and principles of choice used by individuals that function at the collective level to signal a suboptimal outcome. Prisoners' Dilemma represents instead a violation of well established composition rules. The two individuals in the original Prisoners' Dilemma agree on the equity outcome of 2,2 as second best. But unanimity on an alternative does not select the alternative for the collective outcome. Pareto is violated.

Pareto is fulfilled by outcomes that increase the welfare of at least one individual without lowering the welfare of any others (weak version) or outcomes that increase the welfare of all individuals (strong version). It is a composition rule with impeccable credentials, satisfying intuitive notions of both equity and rationality. Arguments against the rule as an ideal are difficult to contrive. How can anything oppose a rule that justifies outcomes with benefits and no losses? The rule also draws on widely acceptable philosophies of parts and wholes. The philosophy of methodological individualism maintains that wholes are no more and no less than the sum of their parts. Unanimity among the parts ought to be represented in the whole. But unanimity in Prisoners' Dilemma fails to be reproduced in the joint outcome. An emergent, the third-best outcome, is the result. Prisoners' Dilemma represents a situation where all individuals choose rationally, but everyone loses. For everyone to lose when there is unanimity on an equity outcome requires the violation of a composition rule, Pareto, that cannot be violated if equity, rationality, and established views on wholes are to be maintained.

4

It is in the close connections between Prisoners' Dilemma and methodological individualism that the types of solutions to the game can be catalogued and properly identified. Methodological individualism is a philosophy that Lukes (1968) sees as containing five distinct theses. The first is truistic social atomism: the claim that collectives consist of people. The second is the claim that all statements about a group or relations in a group either are, or are reducible to, statements about individuals. The third is the ontological thesis that only individuals are real, while wholes are not. The fourth is the claim that sociological laws are impossible. The fifth is the view that social ends are, or ought to be, in the welfare of individuals.[7] Theses four and five do not bear on the problems of rational continuity represented by Prisoners' Dilemma and other games and theorems in collective choice. But the first three versions of methodological individualism state some of the guiding assumptions in game theory and collective choice, and also express the philosophy of wholes on which the tests of individual-collective continuity are framed.

Any number of arguments elaborate methodological individualism. Three are especially prominent. First is an argument for the historical precedence of individuals, that individuals had to be in place earlier than wholes. A second argument is that individuals have causal precedence over wholes; individuals produce wholes, wholes do not produce individuals. A third consists of a variety of assertions that individual attitudes are the conceptual origins for wholes. The third argument is developed on the indisputable locus of attitudes in individuals. Whatever claims may be made on behalf of holism, no one seriously entertains the thought that social wholes have attitudes or intentions or anything like intelligible dispositions in general. It seems to follow that the meanings of social entities like laws, prices, passports, are traceable to individual human beings. A passport, for example, may be a physical unit, a book of bound paper with ink on it. But it is a passport only as the result of the attitudes of individuals. From this view of meaning, champions of methodological individualism conceptualize wholes as derivable from, and reducible to, individuals.[8]

Wholes, in methodological individualism, are formed by composition rules that act on individuals. The simplest type of composition rule is addition. Look, for example, at the statement, "The crowd is angry." For methodological individualism, the holistic state—an angry crowd—is a summary statement of individuals in the crowd who are angry. Theses one, two, and three obtain: the crowd is a collection of individuals; the description of the crowd as angry is derivable from and reducible to angry individuals; and the angry individuals are real while the angry crowd is not (except as a composition of real individuals).

Game theory and collective choice are well within the philosophy of methodological individualism. The fields start with discrete and countable individuals, and produce joint or collective outcomes by means of arithmetical composition rules. Arrow's theorem defines the problem of collective choice in a standard way: how to produce collective outcomes from aggregating separate individual preferences. The individualism of game theory and collective choice is celebrated in testimonials. Riker, for example, explicitly affirms the individualistic premises of his own body of work.[9] The traditions of game theory and collective choice could not exist in the absence of the thought that wholes are arithmetical compositions of individual units. Nor is the ontological thesis alien to the fields. There is little point in starting with in-dividuals unless wholes have a derivative status.[10]

The intimate associations of methodological individualism with game theory and collective choice present interesting opportunities to broaden and deepen our understanding of rational breakdowns be-tween one and all. The breakdowns, first, occur as failed expectations of methodological individualism. Put simply, rational wholes are not derivable from rational individuals. An attribute of individuals, ration-ality, does not sum to a holistic state with the attribute (as anger does in angry crowds). But, second, critiques of methodological individualism as a proper philosophy of wholes are also critiques of the assumptions of game theory and collective choice. Alternative premises for these fields can be identified by exploring the alternatives to methodo-logical individualism.

Two main lines of criticism can be directed at methodological individualism.

The first is that aggregates are not always derivable from, or reduc-ible to, individual parts. "The jury is hung," for example, suggests pre-liminary complications. The indecisiveness of a jury is inversely related to the decisiveness of individual members of a jury.[11] Inverse relation-ships may still be producible from composition rules, although more complicated ones than addition. "The crowd is dangerous," however, is more difficult to accommodate. A crowd can be dangerous (as a whole) without any individual in the crowd being dangerous. The holistic state is a demarcated whole. Like "The surface of the lake is calm," or "The ground is soft," the danger of the crowd is a state of affairs (a) produced after a threshold of individual values is exceeded (aggregation is non-monotonic), and, (b) not found in any of the individual parts (the whole is an emergent).[12]

The second criticism of methodological individualism is that some wholes are not aggregations. Relations among parts are not always arithmetical products. They can be structures or practices that express arrangements, not totals—furniture and social strata, for example. Or consider mass nouns. Some nouns individuate into items that form sets—for example, person, cat, house. These are "amount" or "count" nouns and can be prefixed by the articles "a," "few," "many." Whatever the value of the items covered by count nouns, only one equivalence relation holds among sets containing the same number of members (ten persons ≃ ten cats ≃ ten houses). Other nouns, like coffee, gold, water, do not individuate in the absence of external measures. They are mass nouns, divisible only into quantities. There is more or less water and gold, but not ten waters or ten golds, unless particular measures are imposed on the quantity. When a noun is both count and mass, its sense seems to shift with the shift in use: coffee *is* to ten coffees *are,* some fish *is* to some fish *are.* Various equivalence relations hold among quantities, depending on the measure employed. The same volumes of water and sand are not equivalent in terms of weight.[13]

The first line of criticism predicts the breakdowns demonstrated in game theory and collective choice. In simplest terms, rational individuals aggregate to irrational wholes. In Prisoners' Dilemma, a counter-intuitive threshold is quickly reached: any combination of two choices on the Prisoners' Dilemma matrix can produce an emergent holistic state not only different from, but antagonistic to, the descriptions of each individual's preference ordering of outcomes. The reality of holistic states is at least credible on such outcomes.

The second line of criticism, however, suggests those alternatives to aggregate wholes that define solutions to Prisoners' Dilemma problems. Social theory is replete with mass nouns. A public good, for example, is a nonindividuating noun. And, like many social nouns, a public good extends to individuals viewed as countable by different concepts. Prisoners' Dilemma seems to represent a parallel tension. Any number of nouns describe the players in game theory as countable units. But the dilemma produced from viewing individuals as countable items is resolved by describing individuals in terms of mass nouns and, in effect, abandoning methodological individualism in favor of one form or another of holism.

5

The transformation from countable to mass forms of association can be more accurately documented by introducing formal expressions of methodological individualism and its alternatives. It is easy to mislead with the phrase "additive composition rules." There is addition and addition. In its simplest form, an additive outcome, Y, is expressible as $Y = a + b + c + \ldots + n$, where a, b, c, are integers. (This is the form in which we all first learn to add.) Additive rules, broadly construed, can also cover linear relations among variables. A linear equation producing outcomes as a function of two variables—$Y = a_0 + b_1x_1 + b_2x_2$—is an additive calculation. The introduction of exogenous influences—$Y = a_0 + b_1x_1 + b_2x_2 + b_nx_n$, where $x_n =$ an exogenous variable—still maintains basic addition rules. Even the development of regression equations is a variation on addition (as is any basic arithmetical combination rule, such as subtraction, multiplication, division). The additive rules used in Prisoners' Dilemma are narrowly conceived. First, and trivially, only ordinal scales, on the whole, are used to rank outcomes. Second, no interactive terms are found in the rules. The model used in Prisoners' Dilemma combines discrete units with no common terms distributed among the units.

Two other models offer intelligible accounts of social wholes. One is a "practice" model. Here interactive relations among individual parts (e.g., rules, social practices, patterns, arrangements, etc.) constitute the whole. Social theories of class or strata exemplify such wholes. "Corporate" models are a third type. A corporate whole is a collection of nondiscrete parts, and holistic outcomes are (a) produced through systemic relationships, or (b) expressed as nonindividuating units.

An elaboration and refinement of these models is provided with some quasi-formal differences among additive, interactive, and what can be called unitary relationships among variables. Let Y = a whole, and $x_1, x_2, x_3, \ldots, x_n$ = parts. Two simple sets of relations represent the numerical model:

(1) $y = x_1 + x_2 + x_3 + \ldots + x_n$

(2) $y = a + b_1 x_1 + b_2 x_2 + b_3 x_3 + \ldots + b_n x_n$

The first equation defines the whole as an additive product of single units. In the second equation, y is the outcome of a regression equation with two or more variables. The introduction of a linear relationship with multiple variables (the second equation) merely expresses the relationships of the whole (y) to several units. But y is still an additive outcome. Equations (1) and (2) represent numerical wholes and express the composition rules of Prisoners' Dilemma.[14]

Wholes can also be expressed as the result of interactive relationships. In simplest forms, any partially distributed terms are interactive:

(3) $y = a + b_1 x_1 + b_2 x_2 + (b_3 x_2) x_3 + (b_4 x_2) x_4 + \ldots + (b_n x_2) x_n$

Here y is an outcome of interactive relationships, $(b_3 x_n)$, $(b_4 x_n)$, etc. Holistic values depend on the value of the distributed term, x_n. An example of x_n is the history of a social unit, which can interact with a number of relationships. Note that, like additive relationships, a change in any of the variables can affect the value of y. And, again, like additive relationships, a change in the distributive terms changes several relationships. Equation (3) represents a practice whole if the distributive term is not universal (autonomy of some relationships is maintained). Seen in this way, practice wholes are special types of numerical wholes—those where discrete units are relational terms partially interacting with one another (interaction defined as those relationships that change as the values of terms in the interactive set change).

Interactive relationships can also be total, where some term is distributed throughout the set of relationships:

(4) $y = a + x_n(b_1x_1 + b_2x_2 + b_3x_3 + \ldots + b_nx_n)$

In equation (4), any change in x_N changes the values of all relationships. Interactive relationships of the type represented by (4), whether formed by distributed terms or any other device, are systemic. Any variance in a distributed term affects both the value of the whole (y) and the value of every other relationship.[15]

The use of exogenous costs and benefits and the establishment of social practices are both attempts to transform the conditions of Prisoners' Dilemma into interactive relationships. In the first, a common incentive is provided for all individuals to cooperate (choose as one). The distributive term is the artificially created incentive. The value of the whole is changed if the incentive is distributed throughout the set of individuals (or nearly so in N-person games). Note this: the cost or benefit need not be distributed (applied in fact) to be effective. For example, the oldest closure device, coercion, allows the players to do that which they rationally want or need to do but cannot do in the absence of guarantees that others will act in certain ways. If coercion is effective as a guarantee, it is never employed within the game, a point Hobbes expresses by suggesting that a sovereign who generally uses force is not functioning as sovereign.[16]

In the second case, social practices are to close the distance among individuals. Again, interaction must be total, or nearly so, if the dilemma is to be avoided. It is instructive that practices permitting individuals to remain isolated invariably fail. "Signaling," for example, one of the oldest of modern solutions to Prisoners' Dilemma, fails to break the dominance of defection; for in a sequence of games, the simple allegiance to defection is superior to a tentative departure every now and then to signal a willingness to cooperate.[17] The interaction is incomplete. A cohesive society, Taylor's (1976) face-to-face world is needed if Prisoners' Dilemma solutions are to succeed on the original conditions. This tight sense of community, moreover, must extend to future as well as temporal selves. Unless individuals have modest discount rates—in effect, rating future selves as equal to present selves on an assumption of similarity among those separated by time—defection again dominates cooperation.[18]

The wholes represented by y in equation (4) are weak corporate wholes. Corporate or, in this case, organic wholes are sometimes defined as those which change when parts are deleted.[19] For example, Rawls' difference principle represents social arrangements as organic on such terms.

	x	y
a	10	10
b	5	6
c	4	3

The difference principle favors society x above, for the worst off representative figure, c, is better off in x than in y. But if c is removed, then society y is favored because the new worst off figure is b, who is better off in y than in x. The danger in using such simple organic wholes is that many quite different types of measures can produce inversions of value. Utilitarian formulae, either maximum total or average utility, mandate rearrangements of social rankings if the right number of units is subtracted (dropping average or total utility below some rival society). Even voting, clearly a numerical cluster, requires reversals of outcome if critical voters are subtracted from the majority side. It would be better to reserve the term corporate for descriptions of relations that are at least systemic in the way represented by equation (4).

A stronger sense of corporate whole is represented by interactive relationships dominated, or at least strongly influenced, by the outcome. Let the systemic relationships from equation (3) be reproduced with the following changes:

$$(5) \quad y = a + b_1 x_1 + b_2 x_2 + (b_3 x_3) y_n + (b_4 x_4) y_n + \ldots + (b_n x_n) y_n$$

In equation (5), y is an outcome of interactive relationships that include y (where N = levels of y) as a variable. Two patterns are possible: (a) the interactive units are a mixture of y's and x's; (b) the interactive terms are only, or predominantly, y's. In (b), the corporate whole is obviously a stronger concept since y is the main variable. Population density, for example, might be an interactive outcome of marriage rates, birth rates, death rates, educational levels (etc.). If, however, the density of a population is itself the influencing factor in each of these interactive units, then density is a variable in a corporate whole.

Finally, two other types of corporate wholes are possible. Suppose:

(6) $y = a + y_n(b_1x_1 + b_2x_2 + b_3x_3 + b_nx_n)$

(7) $y = y$

Equations (6) and (7) are unitary forms of wholes. In the first case, the whole is defined in terms of a regression equation where the variation in the independent variables is mediated throughout by the whole, y. The whole in (6) may even dominate its parts. In Prisoners' Dilemma, the influence of the matrix of payoffs on the rational calculations of individuals is represented by equation (6); for, as we have seen, the matrix can be decisive in settling the rational interactions of individuals.

Equation (7) represents collective nouns or nonindividuating wholes. The whole is not a product, additive or interactive, of individual units. Equation (7) is roughly illustrated by singular collectives ("The tennis association is" instead of "The tennis association are"). Collective wholes are described with terms referring to the whole rather than its constitutive parts and the parts are not separable as individuals. Equation (7) also represents mass nouns, which do not (as we say) individuate without an extrinsic measure. (They are not "internally" decomposable.) The structural reforms that avoid Prisoners' Dilemma are represented by equation (7). Partitioning structures by means of complementary pairs is a nonadditive method for reaching collective outcomes. Harmony is established by constructing society from dyadic or N-person complements. This arrangement of parts is a holistic effort, designed to bring into accord the two levels of rationality, individual and structural, without the composition rules of methodological individualism.

Resolutions of Prisoners' Dilemma thus represent more basic changes in conceptions of society. The problem Prisoners' Dilemma expresses is a failure of the model of social wholes set out and justified by methodological individualism to reach outcomes consistent with its own requirements. The model assumed in Prisoners' Dilemma is numerical: rational individuals are discrete and countable units, and outcomes are produced by means of additive composition rules. Collective rationality is a summation of individual rationality. But the summation does not fulfill the expected continuity. The succession of parts into wholes without essential change is interrupted. A rational discontinuity occurs. The restoration of rational continuity then takes

the form of movement toward one or another forms of holistic conceptions of society.

The isolation of individuals is vital to the demonstration of the
Prisoners' Dilemma. Imagine, for example, mirror image Prisoners'
Dilemma, where one individual faces his symmetrical alter ego in the
game. Only two outcomes would be possible, (2,2) and (3,3), and
cooperation would dominate defection. The Prisoners' Dilemma occurs only on the possibility of divided choices—opposition between individuals who are distinct and capable of choosing differently. Solutions, in turn, establish communal ties among individuals. Exogenous
costs and benefits distribute holistic values among individuals through
the provision of rational incentives. Voluntary associations that mandate cooperation through proximate relations (increased contacts, per-
manent membership, high awareness) establish mutual effects among
individual actions. Structural change joins individual pairings and
collective arrangements. In all cases, resolutions of Prisoners' Dilemma
are efforts to replace numerical models of association with corporate
models.

6

The numerical model has been a fixture on our intellectual land-
scape at least since the seventeenth century. The basic form of this type
of rationality is found in Hobbes, Bentham (and utilitarianism in
general), Mill, and, more recently, Nozick. The state of nature in the
Leviathan is constituted by isolated individuals at war with one another.[20] Bentham's utility calculus is made by single individuals; the social utility is a summation of individual utilities.[21] Mill assumes that individuals are separate units, able on the whole to function independent
of one another. When they collide harmfully, government regulation is
warranted.[22] Nozick's elaborate tract depends heavily on the isolation
of individuals. (At one point, he suggests the image of adults living on
desert islands as a metaphor for society.)[23] Though different features of
the numerical model are emphasized by each proponent, the basic
device survives remarkably well.

But corporate views of society also have a distinguished pedigree.
The main idea in the corporate model is that society and its products
are collective, not collections of separate parts. Aristotle, for example,
defines the polis as an arrangement of shared understandings among

equals. The political society is not, for Aristotle, a combination function. It is logically coextensive with individuals, and individuals are embedded in the polis. The question raised by Hobbes, How to derive the political society from individuals? cannot be raised in Aristotle's political theory because individuals are inseparable from the polis. Corporate models, however, are not confined to classical theories of the political society. Any common interest version of the public interest, for example, is a corporate form of association.[24] In recent traditions, the model is developed in terms of unrestricted rationality—Rousseau's general will, Kant's noumenal agent, Adam Smith's impartial spectator.

If (as argued here) Prisoners' Dilemma demonstrates one type of breakdown in the numerical model, and if (as also argued here) efforts to avoid this breakdown usher in corporate forms of association, then the changes in social thought demanded by Prisoners' Dilemma are substantial indeed. The surface change seems minuscule. A primitive term, "individual," is recast as mass; numerical composition rules are abandoned. But, like the physicist's acceptance of quarks instead of hadrons as the more basic particle, the implications of change at elementary levels can be profound. Sealing the fissures between one and all exposed by representations like Prisoners' Dilemma may require substituting one tradition of political thought for another. Unlike anomalies in physics, however, the resolutions do not have to be invented, but rather retrieved from materials either discarded or (until recently) underused. The individualism of game theory and collective choice has only recently become fixed in political theory. Longer traditions routinely accept individuals as mass rather than discrete.

The recognition of a deeper level of change in Prisoners' Dilemma resolutions, from numerical to corporate models, also discloses the need to rethink a number of concepts vital to understandings of a political society. In addition to recasting the protean concepts of individual and whole, the concept of time must be reconstructed. Game theory and collective choice often view time as a sequence of discrete intervals. A common expression of a utility function over time is $U = u(c_1, c_2, c_3 \ldots, c_n)$, where $1 \ldots n$ represents the periods of time broken down (often arbitrarily) to accommodate logarithmic functions. Such expressions attempt to represent the rational calculations of individuals in one temporal location viewing the future as a state separated from the present by other discrete events. The notion of discount rates fits this metaphysic. But the metaphysics may be faulty. Collectives do not coincide with any temporal location, since societies consist of multiple and overlapping generations. If past, present, and future are contained within social units, perhaps the concept of time assigned to individuals establishes yet one more chasm between one and everyone that must be bridged to provide an intelligible account of a rational society.

NOTES

1. Exogenous costs and benefits are usually developed in coercive terms, as in Hobbes' *Leviathan* and Mancur Olson's *The Logic of Collective Action* (Cambridge: Harvard University Press, 1971). See, for social practices, the efforts at institution building cited in some of the experimental literature, such as Hayward R. Alker and Akihiko Tanaka, "Resolutional Possibilities in Historical Prisoners' Dilemmas," paper presented at the Annual Meeting of the International Studies Association, Philadelphia, Pennsylvania, March 18, 1981; the cooperative patterns recognized in Robert Axelrod, "Effective Choice in the Prisoners' Dilemma," *Journal of Conflict Resolution* 24 (March 1980): 3–25, "The Emergence of Cooperation Among Egoists," *American Political Science Review* 75 (June 1981): 306–18, and *The Evolution of Cooperation* (New York: Basic Books, 1984); and the intriguing, more general experiments in cooperative collective action, e.g., Alphons van de Kragt, John M. Orbell, and Robyn M. Dawes, "The Minimal Contributing Set as a Solution to Public Goods Problems," *American Political Science Review* 77 (March 1983): 112–22. Modifying the structural context is analogous to the reforms stressed in, e.g., recent Marxist traditions, where social relations are viewed as the conditions on which individuals choose and the objects to be transformed as a way of changing alternatives.

2. Coordination failure is introduced by the original Prisoners' Dilemma game, elaborated early by R.D. Luce and H. Raiffa, *Games and Decisions* (New York: John Wiley & Sons, 19858), ch. 5. The assurance failure game is proposed by Amartya Sen, "Isolation, Assurance, and the Social Rate of Discount," *Quarterly Journal of Economics* 81 (1967): 112–24. Andrew Schottes describes the game of matrix C in *The Economic Theory of Social Institutions* (Cambridge: Cambridge University Press, 1981), pp. 22–23.

3. Michael Taylor, *Anarchy and Cooperation* (New York: John Wiley & Sons, 1976), in one of the most frequently quoted passages in the book: "This requirement of a high degree of awareness on the part of the conditional cooperators is itself 'more likely' to be met in a small group of players than in a large group—and even more likely in the sort of small community in which people have contacts with and can observe the behavior of many of their fellows and which is fairly static, in the sense that there is little mobility in or out. This is the sort of community which is the ideal of many anarchist writers" (p. 93).

4. I mean "principle" to refer to those more basic standards that order alternatives. Equality, liberty—these are examples of political principles. The principles in Prisoners' Dilemma are less elegant, covering primarily egoism, morality, etc., or those criteria that rank joint outcomes. Principles are unlike decision rules, e.g., Bayesian, maximin, dominance (used in conditions of uncertainty generally and in Prisoners' Dilemma in particular), which produce a decision or choice after principles rank outcomes. See

Ronald Dworkin, *Taking Rights Seriously* (Cambridge, Mass.: Harvard University Press, 1978), for some additional thoughts on principles versus rules, pp. 14–80.

5. So it is with benevolence, altruism, morality: changing only the principles of choice to make the players better will not solve coordination or assurance problems. This is important to know in order both to dispel common notions, e.g., Taylor in saying, "if they [the players] are sufficiently benevolent, then it is rational for them to cooperate in the Prisoners' Dilemma *ordinary* game (and *a fortiori* throughout the Supergame)," p. 93, and to establish the need for a structural guarantee against defection *even among moral figures*. Or, the matrix of payoffs, not egoism, is the heart of darkness in Prisoners' Dilemma. See, however, the elaborate treatments of types of preferences in Kurt Baier, "Rationality and Morality," *Erkenntnis* 11 (August 1977): 197–223; Sen, "Rationality and Morality: A Reply," *Erkenntnis* 11 (August 1977): 225–232; John Harsanyi, "Morality and the Prisoners' Dilemma Game: Comments on Baier's Paper," *Erkenntnis* 11 (November 1977): 441–46. The exercise here elaborates Amartya Sen's efforts in "Choice, Orderings and Morality" by (a) expanding the variety of players, and (b) introducing different players to two different payoff matrices. See also J.W.N. Watkins, "Comments: 'Self-Interest and Morality'"; and Sen, "Reply to Comments," all in Stephen Korner, ed., *Practical Reason* (New Haven: Yale University Press, 1974).

6. Which, curiously enough, is exactly the role John Rawls claims for his principles of justice. See Rawls, "Basic Structure as Subject," *American Philosophical Quarterly* 14 (1977): 159–165.

7. Steven Lukes, "Methodological Individualism Reconsidered," *British Journal of Sociology* 19 (1968): 119–129. Lukes is sceptical about the dispute between holists and methodological individualists, although he admits that he intends only to clear up confusions. See, however, Alan Ryan, *The Philosophy of the Social Sciences* (New York: Macmillan Publishing Co., 1970), who argues that a distinction between "actual" and "typical" individuals renders the dispute meaningless, since the latter are logically interchangeable with holistic entities. Ryan's arguments seem to me so clearly to beg the issue ("typical" individuals being defined in terms of social roles or positions, which presumes holistic terminology) that I leave it to the reader to judge whether I have missed something in his argument. But, also, see Michael Martin, "Explanation in Social Science: Some Recent Work," *Philosophy of Social Science* 2 (March 1972): 61–82, especially pp. 66–70; Michael Hyland and Martin Bridgestock, "Reductionism: Comments on Some Recent Work," *Philosophy of Social Science* 4 (June–September, 1974): 197–200; and Martin, "Reduction and Typical Individuals," *Philosophy of Social Science* 5 (September 1975): 307–308. The dispute between holism and methodological individualism may be one of those discussions where recent age *has* withered and custom staled the infinite variety of interesting ideas found in the earlier literature.

8. One can pass over the first two arguments. Neither is much help to methodological individualism. Even if historical precedence could be established, the claim does not address priority, e.g., fire predating electricity says nothing about the priority status of either. Causal precedence, more successful for methodological individualism if true, does not seem always to be true. Holistic states can serve as psychological causes (for example, the thought of systemic unemployment discouraging individuals from seeking work); and they can even serve as external causes (for example, population density as a cause of mental states whether perceived or not). The causal effects of wholes on individuals are so pervasive that the term "individual" may be a residual category, taking on meaning only within social practices. See, for a defense of the historical precedence of individuals, J.W.

N. Watkins, "Ideal Types and Historical Explanation," in Herbert Feigel and May Brodbeck, eds., *Readings in the Philosophy of Science* (New York: Appleton-Century-Crofts, 1953), especially pp. 729–33. For a defense of causal precedence, a stronger statement is unlikely to be found than Watkins' assertion that "no social tendency exists which could not be altered if the individuals concerned both wanted to alter it and possessed the appropriate information," in his "Methodological Individualism and Social Tendencies," in May Brodbeck, ed., *Readings in the Philosophy of the Social Sciences* (New York: Macmillan Publishing Co., 1968), p. 271. To my relief, Watkins admits that this assumption is both "counterfactual and metaphysical," although how it can be seriously maintained after such an admission is difficult to understand. Ernest Gellner, in "Holism vs. Individualism," in Brodbeck, ed. (1968), points out that de Gaulle was motivated in many of his actions by a view of France as a living whole. Then, of course, Marx argued that to be a cause or originator is superior to being acted upon. See the interpretation developed by Eugene Kamenka, *Marxism and Ethics* (New York: St. Martin's Press, 1969), especially pp. 8–30. For a successful defense of individual ascription of meaning (or attitudinal priority), see Watkins, "Ideal Types and Historical Explanation." See also the discussion of these issues in J. Roland Pennock, *Democratic Theory* (Princeton, N.J.: Princeton University Press, 1979), pp. 59–120.

9. For example, William Riker and Peter Ordeshook, *Positive Political Theory,* p. 37.

10. Reduction, the converse of derivation, is unavoidably ontological. The explanation of the phenomena of one field in terms of the phenomena of another, e.g., chemistry in terms of physics or psychology in terms of physiology, is reduction. But the phenomena thus explained are then dissolved into the explanation. They are no longer real. See, for example, John G. Kemeny and Paul Oppenheim, "On Reduction," in Baruch Brody, ed., *Readings in The Philosophy of Science* (Englewood Cliffs, N.J.: Prentice-Hall, 1970), pp. 307–18, where on p. 309 the authors state that when T_1 can explain T_2, and T_2 is no more complex, then "we drop T_2 from our body of theories, and strike out all terms in Voc (T_2) [Note: Voc = the theoretical vocabulary] which are not in Voc (T_1). Then we say that T_2 has been reduced to T_1."

11. Discussed in Paul Lazarsfeld and Herbert Menzel, "On the Relationship Between Individual and Collective Properties," in Amitai Etzioni, ed., *Complex Organizations* (New York: Holt, Rinehart & Winston, 1966).

12. Another example of an emergent whole is the well-known case of the compromise candidate. Suppose a three-member group with preferences for A, B, C, and D. The ranking according to vote and weight for each of three voters is as follows:

	First Voter	Second Voter	Third Voter
(4)	A	C	D
(3)	B	B	B
(2)	C	D	A
(1)	D	A	C

An electorate arranged in terms of these preferences will give candidate B 9 votes, candidates A, C, and D 7 votes each. Candidate B is the first-place "choice" of the group, even though no member of the group has chosen him for first place.

13. For the classic statement on the distinction between "count" and "mass" nouns, and the case for the individuation of mass nouns by measure, see Helen Cartwright,

"Quantities," *Philosophical Review* 79 (January 1970): 24–42. For an earlier and different account of roughly the same distinction, P. F. Strawson, "Particular and General," *Proceedings of the Aristotelian Society* 55 (1953–54): 242.

14. Herbert Simon's "decomposable" systems are variations on numerical models (systems of individual elements that can be treated as if they were independent of one another), in *The Sciences of the Artificial* (Cambridge, Mass.: MIT Press, 1969), pp. 84–118.

15. I am grateful to one of my colleagues, Jeff Stonecash, for suggesting interactive relationships. See, for a different expression of interaction, Stonecash's "Local Policy Analysis and Autonomy: On Intergovernmental Relations and Theory Specification," *Comparative Urban Research* 5 (1978): 5–23, and "Politics, Wealth, and Public Policy: The Significance of Political Systems," in Thomas R. Dye and Virginia Grey, *The Determinants of Public Policy* (Lexington, Mass.: D.C. Heath, 1980). Statisticians tend to see interactive terms as primarily explaining residual variations instead of establishing systemic relationships. See John Neter and William Wassermen, *Applied Linear Statistical Models* (Homewood, Ill.: Richard D. Irwin, 1974). An especially graceful treatment of interaction, although still lacking a strong contrast with additive relationships, are chapters three and four of Lawrence H. Boyd, Jr. and Gudmund R. Iverson, *Contextual Analysis: Concepts and Statistical Techniques* (Belmont, Calif.: Wadsworth Publishing Co., 1979).

16. *Leviathan* (Liberal Arts ed.), p. 145, where Hobbes warns that if "any one or more" of the sovereign's subjects challenge authority (speciously—"pretend a breach of the covenant"), then all revert to the state of nature. The sovereign's authority must be accepted generally, not be chronically enforced, for the civil society to work successfully. The correspondence between N-person Prisoners' Dilemma games and Hobbes' state of nature has been noted by several commentators: J.W.N. Watkins, for example, in "Imperfect Rationality," in R. Borger and F. Cioffi, eds., *Explanation in the Behavioral Sciences* (Cambridge: Cambridge University Press, 1970).

17. Luce and Raiffa, ch. 5.

18. Given the asymmetries of power and uncertainty toward future values chronic to all calculations across time, identifications with future selves are heroic efforts. But unless the assumption of similarity is made, that present and future individuals will be (roughly) the same, discount rates are impossible to set. These points are developed in the literature on justice-across-time. Among the interesting pieces in this literature (in no special order): John Rawls, *A Theory of Justice* (Cambridge, Mass.: Harvard University Press, 1971), pp. 284–303; R. M. Solow, "Intergenerational Equity and Exhaustible Resources," *Review of Economic Studies* (1974): 29–45; Edwin Delattre, "Rights, Responsibilities, and Future Persons," *Ethics* 82 (April 1972): 254–58; Kenneth Arrow, "Rawl's Principle of Just Saving," *Swedish Journal of Economics* 75 (1973): 323–35; Peter Danielson, "Theories, Intuitions and the Problem of World-Wide Distributive Justice," *Philosophy of Social Science* 3 (1973): 331–40; Partha Dasgupta, "On Some Alternative Criteria for Justice Between Generations," *Journal of Public Economies* 3 (1974): 405–23. See, however, for special attention to the two points in the text, Brian Barry, "Justice Between Generations," in Sikora and Barry, eds., *Obligations to Future Generations* (Philadelphia: Temple University Press, 1978).

19. Robert Nozick, *Anarchy, State and Utopia* (New York: Basic Books, 1974), p. 209.

20. *Leviathan* (Liberal Arts ed.), especially ch. 13. Hobbes, ever the hybrid case, also works with mass terms in the assumption of security needs. All persons require security against physical attack; and, like any public good, if security is effective (available) at all,

it must be effective for all. Individuals are as one, therefore, in their need for, and consumption of, security.

21. A representative statement in the tradition of the numerical society by Jeremy Bentham: "The community is a fictitious body, composed of individual persons who are considered as constituting as it were its members. The interest of the community, then, is what?—the sum of the interests of the several members who compose it. It is vain to talk of the interest of the community, without understanding what is the interest of the individual." *An Introduction to the Principles of Morals and Legislation*. (London: Oxford University Press, 1923), p. 3.

22. Mill, *On Liberty,* ed. by David Spitz (New York: W.W. Norton & Co., 1975), especially ch. 3, 4.

23. *Anarchy, State and Utopia*. The entire work is developed on the assumption that society is a cluster of separate individuals with rights that cannot be morally overridden by the state. The desert island metaphor is on page 185.

24. Survey in Virginia Held, *The Public Interest and Individual Interest* (New York: Basic Books, 1970).

3

Liberal Models
in Collective Choice

1

The high standing of methodological individualism in collective choice is maintained and celebrated throughout Arrow's theorem. The starting conditions of the original proof require discrete (non-overlapping) individuals. The collective, in turn, is a combination of separate orderings. Arrow extends a tradition of thought which assumes that the definitive question in collective choice is how to aggregate the values of separate individuals to reach a collective outcome. The theorem develops a rational breakdown between individual and whole that questions this tradition and the influence of methodological individualism on collective choice.[1]

The formal nature of Arrow's theorem seem at the outset cause for celebration. One of the attractive features of formal theory is that conditions and axioms are stated explicitly and relationships among basic concepts are demonstrated. The explicit and demonstrable nature of such theorizing provides a clarity and generality of thought that can extend from one level of theory to another, and can even extend to substantive areas sharing the same abstract calculus. But formal theory succeeds only if all of the terms needed to understand a problem are disclosed; and it is by no means certain that the most important conditions, axioms, and relationships are treated in Arrow's proof. If one inspects a deeper layer of assumptions, a different and more general set of components can be uncovered and used to demonstrate conflicts of a different order. These conflicts, moreover, may require languages that do not meet the requirements of formal systems.

One background set of assumptions in Arrow's theorem, for example, defines a liberal model of a political society: individuals are (a) moral equals who are (b) separate from one another and (c) free to pursue their own goals without institutional impediments or interference by others. Yet only the second and third of these three features of liberalism are explicit in the theorem. The first—moral equality—must be inferred from the formal conditions of the proof. If one began and ended an understanding of Arrow's theorem with the surface conditions and axioms, moral equality would never be encountered. Yet, the concept of moral equality helps us to understand both the logic and the meaning of the theorem as an exercise in social theory.

One indication that there is a deeper layer of concepts in Arrow's theorem is that the demonstration of the problem is not completely describable in logical or rational terms. Three of Arrow's original five conditions are influenced by moral or equity concepts: Pareto, nondictatorship, and universal domain. Each of these three conditions is an effort to fulfill autonomy: Pareto in ensuring that unanimity will be represented at the collective level, nondictatorship in ruling out the dominance of one over all, and universal domain in prohibiting the manipulation of alternatives. If moral concerns are dismissed, no rational problem occurs in the theorem, for transitivity and the independence condition can be satisfied with a violation of any one of the three equity conditions.

The moral concerns of Arrow's theorem define a common grid on which are found a number of theories that appear disparate and even contradictory on surface considerations. Both Rawls' theory of justice and Nozick's libertarian state share the same liberal model found at a background level in Arrow's theorem. Rawls' liberalism, like Arrow's, is concealed and must be discovered, in Rawls' case, through an understanding of the social contract. But Nozick's market justice begins with the foreground assumption of a liberal community. What is especially intriguing about these three theories is that each is an attempt to reconcile the moral concepts and radical individualism of liberal theory. The two theories that use arithmetical composition rules fail consistency tests (Arrow and Nozick). The theory that transforms all into everyone (a holistic noun) remains consistent (Rawls). The more interesting observation, however, is that a general understanding of collective choice is gained by elaborating the liberal model as it strains to accommodate arithmetic. Since aggregation and exchange both fail only on the acceptance that individuals are moral equals free to set their own goals, an inspection of the liberal model should identify in a more general way what concepts must be modified to avoid contradictions in collective choice.

2

The surface, or explicit, axioms and conditions of Arrow's theorem tolerate many forms of inequality. Entries to the aggregation machine (any device for aggregating preferences) can be counted more than once, so that a social state in which one individual has, say, one hundred votes and another only one vote is not ruled out by Arrow's theorem. Also, the individual actors, though required by the conditions to be discrete, do not have to be singletons. They can be sets, collectives, blocs, lumps, or whatever. Both United Technologies and an individual citizen of an upstate New York village can be individual actors in the theorem.

The theorem is also silent on any number of other equality measures and criteria. The ratio of participants (those individuals introducing preferences to the aggregation machine) to nonparticipants is not an issue in Arrow's theorem. So, like Aristotle's views on citizenship, exclusionary rules may keep most individuals from participating; and whatever equality exists among individuals in an Arrow society (and in an Aristotelian one) may apply only to a very small subset of individuals. The theorem also says nothing about equality within sets or blocs, so that even if the actors in Arrow's theorem are in some way equal, the members of such units may be unequal to each other and to members of other units. The absence of overlap among actors reinforces whatever inequalities may exist within units, for the possibility of multiple memberships vitiates the more extreme effects of inequality within collectives (allowing individuals to be unequal in one setting while equal in another, as church vicars may find themselves low on the club tennis ladder). Finally, all but one of the theorem's conditions permit inequalities in the distribution of goods (nondictatorship, see below, is the exception). Pareto, for example, is a concept used by Arrow mainly as a device to guarantee that unanimity will be honored. But the concept itself does not require any distributive equality.[2] If equality is to be found in Arrow's theorem, it must be located in the context of an assemblage of concepts that, on the whole, tolerate a variety of inequalities.

The presence of a concept of equality is suggested by the strong evaluative language in which many of the rational problems of collective choice are typically described. The "free rider," for example, is an individual who benefits from the collective production of public goods without contributing to the collective effort. The phrase, free rider, suggests the stigma that helps form the rational problem. A free rider is a cheat, someone who gets something he doesn't earn. In broader terms, an individual who fails to contribute to a cooperative enterprise in which he is a member does not meet minimal tests of fairness. The free rider is someone who ought to contribute, but does not; and as a noncontributing member, the free rider is a moral as well as a rational failure. The individual who deserves the public good without contribution—one who is very ill or very young, for example—is not a free rider. The rational problem of suboptimal provisions of public goods would look entirely different if noncontributors were justly excused from group participation. Arrow employs evaluative language in an even stronger and more explicit sense. The decisive set consisting of a singleton is a "dictator," one whose orderings are the orderings of all. In Prisoners' Dilemma, the cell in which one individual secures optimal returns at the expense of the other player is routinely labeled the "exploitive" cell or the "sucker" outcome.

Much of the explicit evaluative language in collective choice, is, of course, window dressing, except for Arrow's formal use of the nondictatorship condition. But the language is still formed by expectations that collective outcomes must fulfill Aristotle's definition of numerical equality as equal shares to and from all relevant individuals; for none of the rational problems is represented by a canon of claims that might rank individual claims on, and obligations to, collective action in some distributive pattern. Instead, unequal outcomes, by virtue of being unequal, are viewed (for different reasons) as failures of collective action. The free rider, the exploitive Prisoners' Dilemma cell, and Arrow's dictator are regarded as pathologies of collective choice. Now, it is an axiom of equality that inequalities in the social unit may be needed to ensure equalities among individuals. If, for example, patient *1* needs 3 units of an antibiotic for a restoration of health and patient *2* needs 5 units to achieve the same result, then, in the table below,

	1	*2*
a	3	3
b	3	5

social state b is a more authentic expression of equal treatment of patients 1 and 2 than is social state a.[3]

Arrow's theorem can permit distributions of goods in collective outcomes. But the distributions are not fixed or justified by the language of the theorem. For example, alternatives in the theorem can represent different and unequal distributions of goods. A selection of one alternative over another in the collective outcome can then result in unequal distributions of goods. But the theorem does not contain a language to justify unequal distributions. Unequal outcomes are simply the result of applying various composition rules to preferences.

The individuals in Arrow's theorem are also without a language of claims. No information of any sort is provided on individuals. No interpersonal value comparisons are conducted (except at a late point in the development of Arrow's theorem, and then with "extended sympathy"). Individuals in the theorem are no more than isolated devices to order preferences. Nothing in the theorem permits them to make claims on the collective outcome beyond the orderings that they feed into the aggregation machine. On the expectation that individuals *can* make claims for distributions of goods, a theory that views inequalities of outcomes as unsatisfactory without a language to evaluate claims must assume that the individuals producing and consuming the outcomes are equal. Or, above, if a is preferable to b, 1 and 2 must be equal in their claims (effect, need, desert, etc.) on the shares distributed.

The nondictatorship condition expresses such a dissatisfaction with unequal outcomes. The condition rules out a decisive set consisting of a singleton, which ruling means only that no individual's ordering can be the ordering for all others in the society. The question is, why not? An individual endorsing a more just social distribution can dictate legitimately to others without being a dictator. A judge (in a nonjury trial) can dictate the outcome of court proceedings. The decisiveness of single individuals can be denied only on the assumption that no individual has an authoritative claim over all others.

The point can be taken further. Arrow's theorem proves that local decisiveness is contagious. If a set, S, of individuals is locally decisive for x against y, then, with Arrow's conditions, that set is also globally decisive for x against y. Or if any individual, i, dictates on some pair of alternatives,

$$x >_i y \text{ for } i \in s \text{ and}$$
$$y >_j x \text{ for } j \in s \text{ then}$$
$$x \in v \Rightarrow y \notin \mathrm{Cu}\,(v)$$

that individual, i, is decisive for any pair of alternatives.[4] Thus any inequality of effect can extend to dictatorship.

Arrow's individuals are equal to one another on the conditions of the theorem; for if any one is decisive on a single pair of alternatives, that decisiveness extends over all pairs of alternatives. Nondictatorship is a condition assigned to the rules for reaching collective outcomes, and maintaining it in the context of the theorem requires that individuals be morally equal to one another. No one can be authoritative over others on any set of alternatives.

The equality assumption in Arrow's theorem seems to be an amalgam of equal effects and equal claims. The contagion effect of decisiveness requires that no individual can dictate locally; and this prohibition of unequal effects on any alternative is intelligible morally only if individuals are equal in their claims over the alternatives. Collective choice theories often assume that justice is settled prior to the stage of decision making.[5] Arrow's theorem is no exception to this expectation. But the theorem restates background languages of equality in ruling at dominance patterns. A moral equality (equal effects, equal claims) is set against other conditions of equity (Pareto) and ordering rules (universal domain, independence, rationality). Note (again) that nothing in the theorem prohibits a distribution of goods or resources in the collective outcome. It is simply that arithmetical composition rules provide no criteria for justifying distributions save the fact that individuals prefer one distributive alternative or another; and, as an added indictment of aggregation, the theorem itself is a proof that all such composition rules can fail equity and rationality tests. But the main point is that the absence of a language of social justice to address, and warrant, inequality compels the theorem to regard individuals as equal.

3

In its reliance on equality as a background concept, Arrow's theorem is similar to Rawls' theory of justice. The theorem and the theory are, of course, unlike one another in several important ways. Arrow's starting conditions of choice contain discrete and countable individuals who have ordinary knowledge about themselves (their abilities, needs, interests) and their probable locations in a collective outcome. Rawls' individuals choose governing principles in an "original position" where they are denied knowledge of their assets and liabilities, their locations in the social practice formed by the governing principles, and a theory of the good. One effect of this veil of ignorance is to suspend the information that ordinarily allows individuals to demarcate themselves from others. Rawls' original position individuals are not discrete and countable, for each is identical to every other. (One is equivalent to everyone.) A second effect of the veil is to set aside aggregation. Arrow's individuals express preferences that are combined by means of arithmetical composition rules. Individuals in the original position have preferences (for distributive principles) that are logically unanimous. The two principles of justice in Rawls' theory, liberty and equal opportunity conjoined with the difference principle, are composed or logically derived from the conditions of the original position. They are not produced from aggregation.[6]

Nor is it clear that the rule governing individual preferences and collective outcomes are congenial in each case. Arrow's four conditions and two axioms fit Rawls' original position only in part. One condition, universal domain, is comfortably joined to Rawls' theory. Individuals in the original position can survey all logically possible distributive principles (including those of utilitarianism) without any restrictions (except those built into the features of rational choice in the original position, a point which can be directed against any conditions in rational choice). The domain of social choice can then be seen as consisting of every logically possible combination of individual orderings of the alternatives surveyed (thus satisfying universal domain). Two of the other three conditions, however, do not bear on the original position. Pareto and nondictatorship are useless when applied to the conditions of the original position, for each requires more than one discrete individual for its primary effect. Where, as in the original position, individuals are not rationally distinguishable and, as a consequence, unanimity is logically assured, Pareto and nondictatorship are worthless standards.[7] The independence of irrelevant alternatives, however, is important. It is always worthwhile to ensure that collective choices will not vary on static preferences, even where outcomes are derived rather than aggregated.[8] One axiom of individual choice, binary comparisons, is not used in the original position. (Rawls allows global comparisons of principles.) The other, transitivity, is not mentioned in Rawls' account, but it can be reasonably expected to apply to the means-ends deliberations he endorses.

But in spite of these disjunctures and only mild overlaps, Arrow's theorem and Rawls' theory of justice share a common set of assumptions. These assumptions are disclosed in an inspection of the deeper model of a political society in Rawls' method of theorizing. Recall that intuitionism—the establishment of a rank ordering of basic principles without benefit of publicly accessible criteria for ranking—is abandoned by Rawls in favor of the social contract. Intuitionism (as in Plato's *Republic*) permits authoritative accounts of political arrangements insulated from challenge by those who have not had the critical intuitive experience or who do not have access to the ranking criteria. Contract theory, on the other hand, presumes that individuals are equal in the formation and ranking of political principles. The deep assumption in Rawls' theory is that all individuals, regardless of their status, have a right to be given an equal regard in the establishment of social practices (Dworkin 1978).

The assumption of rights to an equal regard is itself part of a larger set of assumptions. Rights depend on critical separations among individuals and between individuals and the political society. A right, as commonly understood, is not a constraint on the individual to whom it is assigned; it is a constraint on others not to impede the actions of the one who has the right. Thus, a right to vote is a constraint on registrars (and the like) that forbids interference with an individual's effort to vote, but that does not require of the individual with the right to vote that he or she do anything (even vote). Similarly, rights against the state restrict the state from interfering in the areas protected by rights. It follows that rights presume that individuals are separate and capable of adversarial relationships with each other and with the political society. It also follows that freedom is assigned to individuals, for in the absence of freedom there are no rights at all (Hart 1955).

When this larger set of assumptions is described, we see more clearly how the original position functions in Rawls' theory. It is an intermediate device that represents and transforms a model of discrete individuals into a hypothetical community of identical rational agents. This hypothetical community is a moral society that fulfills tests of fairness. These tests (primarily impartiality) allow us to view the two derived principles as principles of justice. That the derivation fails to produce a substantive outcome from a formal procedure has been adequately documented (Barry 1973; Wolff 1977). The list of primary goods strongly biases the theory toward liberalism; the "general facts about society" condition sets historical limits on the generality of the theory. But this failure only reaffirms Hume's dictum that nothing can be found in the conclusions of a deduction that is not present in the premises. Once the deeper assumptions are produced, the theory is properly seen as an expression of a liberal model filtered through the mechanism of an original position. Nowhere is this implicit liberalism clearer than in the derived principles of justice. Liberty is the first principle chosen, and it is shielded through a lexical ordering from economic practices (set by the difference principle). This version of justice is as strong an expression of the liberal ideal of a political society as one is likely to find.

Arrow's theorem is also developed on a deep assumption of equality, though the equality is more deeply embedded. The possibility of contagion in decisiveness sets forth the strictest type of equality of effect; and both the general acceptance of equal distributions and the denial of authoritative claims by means of nondictatorship require equality of claims. Liberal ideals of autonomy are expressed by these conditions. Indeed, all four of Arrow's explicit conditions—universal domain, Pareto, nondictatorship, and the independence of irrelevant alternatives—are features of a liberal society. They suggest a well-known account of autonomous individuals originating social practices without constraints from any external source (natural law, institutions, procedures, or other individuals).

A liberal society is developed on two distinct moral perspectives (Dworkin 1978A). One is that the state must be neutral on the values that individuals ascribe to their lives. Another is the view that all members of the political society are to be given an equal regard, without reference to their circumstances. Though these two perspectives can lead to quite different and frequently contrary conclusions on the proper role of the state in regulating the lives of its citizens, both are congenially represented in Arrow's equity conditions. The uses of universal domain and Pareto express the first form of liberalism—neutrality. Universal domain, in particular, ensures state neutrality in the availability and ordering of alternatives. Pareto grants legitimacy to those alternatives, and only those alternatives, that have unanimous support from individuals (not support from the state). Both conditions depend on a standard justification for state neutrality: a noncognitive theory of value. Any theory of value that ranks moral principles or statements on truth criteria would immediately (a) dismiss universal domain by restricting the range of acceptable alternatives for individuals to order, and (b) address Pareto from the perspective of a critical morality that would not necessarily accept unanimity as the satisfaction of moral demands (Little 1952). The current labeling of preferences as "tastes" (Riker 1982) is thus no mere convenience but an expression of the belief that values make no truth claims. In the absence of a noncognitive theory of value, Arrow's theorem could not be developed. But the other moral perspective on liberalism is also represented in the theorem.

Nondictatorship sets up a procedural condition that expresses, through a logical guarantee, the thought that each individual is to be given an equal regard in, and even have an equal effect on, the collective outcomes of society. Taken together, these two moral perspectives amount to the more complex liberal view that individuals are self-legislating creatures who are morally equal to one another, and that the political society in some way originates in the expressed preferences of these individuals.

The complex liberal view begins to break down in Arrow's theorem with the use of arithmetical methods to reach collective outcomes. The methods are justified by the individualism of liberal theory. "Counting heads" is a way of ensuring that social practices originate with descriptions of individuals. This individualism is elaborated in the philosophy of methodological individualism: wholes are arithmetical compositions of, and reducible to, their parts. Two features of Arrow's theorem represent this philosophy. The first is the separate and countable status of individuals. Atomism is not too strong a metaphor. Individuals are not, as in Aristotle's polis, conceptually embedded in the political society. Nor is society temporally or conceptually prior to the individual. The opposite is assumed: individuals are the independent variables from which social states are derived. The second feature, complementing the first, is that collective outcomes are no more and no less than an arithmetical combination of individual orderings (a requirement that finds one expression in the independence condition). The liberal need for nonemergence is met by an arithmetical approach to collective choice.

Rawls' theory, however, is closer to meeting the liberal need for nonemergence than is Arrow's theorem. Rawls' early work attempted to produce more than the premises allowed—substantive principles from formal procedures. His later, more developed theory of justice (1971) introduced substantive conditions to the procedures of choice (e.g., primary goods, the general facts about society) that are necessary if the principles of justice are to be derived. But these substantive conditions compromise the effort to maintain the procedures as purely formal devices. The full theory was presented as a general theory of justice. But liberal principles appear in the premises and make their way through the filter of the original position to emerge as (justified) principles of justice. Everything that emerges in Rawls' theory is present in the premises, and the assumptions become principles that are consistent with procedure once the liberal status of the theory is acknowledged. Arrow's assumptions, in contrast, lead to emergents that are self-contradictory: the collective state does not successfully represent individual values. The different methods employed in each approach to collective choice explain the different outcomes. Rawls mediates the arithmetical language of liberalism with a Kantian representation of equal regard. The original position reconciles the atomism of liberalism with its moral needs, ensuring equal regard not through the requirements of methodological individualism, but by means of that collective state formed by the veil of ignorance. Arrow's theorem, in contrast, tries to produce a collective state by arithmetical means in aggregating separate preferences. The effort fails to meet its own conditions for success.

The contradictions disclosed by Arrow's theorem, however, do not occur within the set of arithmetical assumptions. The production of, say, a nontransitive ordering from a collection of transitive orderings is logically intriguing. But such events are natural features of arithmetic and logic and often avoidable with extension or manipulation of the formal systems. In Arrow's theorem, for example, a decisive set satisfies transitivity at the collective level. Rational problems occur only if the theorem is viewed as a representation of social conflict and allocation. The representation must stand for outcomes that are, in Rawls' phrase, "burdens and benefits" to members of society.

Such representations are indeed found in collective choice. Look again at the free rider problem. Imagine a group of individuals who cooperate to produce some collective good—musicians, say, who voluntarily provide a concert every Sunday for the neighborhood. If some individuals take up a collection to help the musicians with expenses, contributions would be nice but could not be obligatory even for those who live close enough to the site of the concerts to hear the music without any effort. The concert is produced without benefit of a collective agreement, explicit or tacit. If an individual has not consented to a joint effort, and indeed does not care if the good is provided or not, the evaluative force of the phrase "free rider" and the logic of the free rider argument are meaningless. A fairness principle is needed for the free rider argument, and a cooperative community is needed for the principle. If all have consented to a jointly beneficial project, then each person has a reason to cooperate. In the absence of a consensual community and the sense of fairness drawn from it, the formal proof of the free rider dilemma cannot be developed.[9]

Arrow's conditions require a similar sense of community. Nondictatorship suggests that the community must be a moral community. Unless individuals are taken to be moral agents, the dominance of one over all is not describable as dictatorship. Imagine a faulty roulette wheel that always produces the same number, ensuring the dominance of that number over all the others on the wheel. If the wheel is demonstrated as a curiosity, we would not say that such numerical decisiveness is dictatorship. Dictatorship is the way we would describe the use of the wheel by a flawed dealer to dominate other (human) gamblers by taking their money. Or imagine a decisive star, one whose luminosity is so bright as to render all rivals practically invisible. Or think of a decisive solution to a mathematical problem, or a decisive experiment in science. None of these are dictatorial events. Nondictatorship is a condition that rules out the dominance of one agent over all other agents, a dominance that is without reason or agreement from those dominated.

The two other equity conditions support this moral sense of community. Universal domain ensures that all possible alternatives can be considered. One point to this condition is to avoid manipulation of preferences. The attempt fails, of course. Even with universal domain, the theorem and its many successors demonstrate that manipulation is possible; for outcomes are not independent of the paths to them. But the attempt is senseless if moral agents are not the victims of manipulation. Pareto follows the same logic. The nonperverse expression of unanimity in outcomes is empty as a purely mathematical condition. It does not bear on the social representation of the theorem. Pareto, as a moral concept, guarantees that the unanimous preferences of reasoning agents will be fulfilled at the collective level. Moral agency is, in general, needed to establish the equity conditions without which the rational problem of Arrow's theorem does not occur.

A community of moral agents, whatever else it is, consists of individuals who self-legislate, ordering alternatives on reasons. This is a moral condition of liberalism. Such a community is not consistent with an arithmetical community. Prescription is a feature of all reasons. A reason to do *a* rather than some rival alternative is a rational appeal for all to do *a*. A reason for an action prescribes for a class of relevantly similar agents, never just for a particular person or situation. Moral agents are thus never entirely distinct units but always have normative effects on each other by means of the reasons employed for orderings. A moral accord is based on reasoned argument, not aggregation. And reasoned deliberations permit emergent values. For example, a juridical proceeding, one device to accommodate reasoned orderings, is normally seen as defective unless (a) individuals are viewed not as discrete units but as members of classes, (b) outcomes are produced from rational deliberation rather than arithmetical combinations, and (c) decisions can establish new precedents from conventional rules and evidence. The second sense of a community, also present in Arrow's theorem, is holistic rather than numerical, in the sense that individuals are constituent members of social practices established on shared values, and in the additional sense that collective outcomes can routinely produce emergent values.

The problem is that the theorem contains no device to express this second community. Rawls' theory of justice uses the original position to represent a moral community. Rational agents are transformed into moral agents, choosing for everyone, by the veil of ignorance. But unlike Rawls' theory, Arrow's theorem has no filter (like the original position) to mediate between the disjointedness of the liberal model and collective outcomes. Collective outcomes are instead produced directly by aggregating the separate preferences of discrete individuals. This uninterrupted transformation fails to be completed. One or more of the features of liberalism conflict with each other. The equality engraved in Arrow's theorem by logical contagion never leads to a warranted inequality. All dominance is therefore unjustified. Rawls' theory, in contrast, justifies distributions that (in complex ways) favor the worst-off representative person. The original position uses equality as the basis for justifying inequalities. The force and elegance of this hypothetical condition can be appreciated anew. The absence of such a mediating device in Arrow's theorem aggravates the natural tensions in liberal societies between equality and inequality or, more broadly, between arithmetical and moral needs. Aggregation and the moral conditions of liberalism are articulated throughout Arrow's theorem, with no instrument to render them consistent with each other. There is no reason to think that anything resembling an original position would resolve Arrow's problem. But the impossibility result is a failure of consistency between aggregation and morality that Rawls' theory, whatever its liabilities, avoids.

4

The liberal community of rational and autonomous moral agents is prominently displayed in exchange theory. Arrow's theorem demonstrates that separate and countable individuals cannot be joined arithmetically to produce collective outcomes meeting simultaneous tests of rationality and equity. The same type of problem occurs in markets, where again efforts to map a collective outcome from discrete individuals fail to fulfill the moral and rational expectations of liberalism.

Let a market be defined as a collection of exchanges.[10] A thought experiment can identify the range of problems both addressed and raised by exchange theory. Think of two rational individuals, each with a supply of goods which they freely exchange for whatever reason (though, presumably, each benefits). The first thing to notice in the exchange is that transitivity seems to be maintained through the fulfillment of Pareto. Since, in a free exchange, everyone is better off after the exchange (or some are better off and no one is worse off), a handy altimeter is provided. Each successive social state, if brought about by exchange, must be "higher" (better) than its antecedent. The cycle of cyclical majorities, or the general failure of transitive orderings, is thus avoided. If A (exchange state 1) $> B$ (exchange state 2), and $B > C$ (exchange state 3), then with the altimeter of Pareto, $A > C$.[11]

The two individuals may also believe that they avoid the other failures of collective action prominently displayed in various theorems and proofs. Certainly their preferences are transformed without interruption into collective outcomes. Each individual gets exactly what he prefers in an ideal exchange. Equity tests also seem to be met by the condition of liberty found in exchanges. If individuals are truly free to exchange goods, nondictatorship is realized. The liberal model of a political community is maintained by introducing its defining features directly into an idealized view of markets.

But the requirements of liberalism are not met in market institutions. Theories about institutions can be criticized from two standpoints. One might say that, as applied to reality, they have (logically, empirically) anomalous or contradictory implications. Such a critique of Plato's *Republic,* for example, would concentrate on the general problems of implementation and the effects of partial implementation on one or another of the state's features. (What happens, say, to the ideal status of Plato's arrangements if one part fails—i.e., there is no common property for the upper guardians—and all other parts are intact?) A second line of criticism might concentrate on the theory as an ideal and trace out problems and inconsistencies in terms of its internal logic. Both lines have been developed in the literature on exchange. An inspection of this literature will suggest (a) how markets, like aggregation machines, fail tests of rationality and equity, and (b) what changes in the general concepts of collective choice might be needed to avoid these failures.

The failures of markets, however, must also be measured against our expectations. An especially optimistic and persuasive case for the rationality and fairness of exchange is drawn up by Robert Nozick (1974). Nozick's account is important in several ways, not least because the moral community fixed at the background level in Rawls' theory of justice and in Arrow's theorem is an explicit and richly described society in Nozick's story of justice. We are asked to imagine a collection of separate and rational individuals in conditions of no authority (a state of nature). Lockean problems occur in these conditions, primarily overestimations of harm that lead to excessive retributions in an endless series of retaliations. Mutual protection associations develop to address these problems. Eventually a dominant association emerges that provides protection to all who pay for its services.

The statelike entity providing protection to its clients is limited by the moral endowments of individuals in conditions of no authority. Nozick suggests a hyper-plane of moral space around each individual which can only by crossed if the individual consents. (If the state must cross such a moral border in protecting its clients, compensation must be paid to the individual.) The unauthorized crossings in the state of nature are precisely what occasion protection associations. The moral status of individuals, as separate from each other and with rights to pursue their own goals without interference from others, is unchanged when authority is established. Limitations on state authority are thus set by the starting moral features. The state cannot redistribute resources but only carry out the protective functions for which it was created.

The contrasts between such a limited state and interventionist accounts of authority are well-known.[12] Collective distributions are just on Nozick's theory if the individuals are entitled to their shares of the collective product, not if the distribution satisfies some time-slice principles that is indifferent to the way the distribution occurs (e.g., Rawls' difference principles). Put simply, a distribution is just on Nozick's tests if it arises from another just distribution by legitimate means (prior steps that are just). Legitimacy in this case follows the pattern set by the original moral community. Liberty must be maintained in the acquisition and transfer of holdings; and liberty, according to Nozick, is best secured through local exchanges of goods. The liberal model of discrete and autonomous individuals is maintained consistently throughout

Nozick's theory of justice by accepting only those social conditions—in particular, exchange—that do not affect its defining features.

But exchange fares no better in maintaining the liberal model than aggregation does. Even the basic distinctions between power and exchange on which market justice is developed cannot always be drawn clearly. Power is an unreasonably complex term. It can be expressed as an actual occurrence,[13] an ability,[14] the successful achievement of intended results,[15] and many other things. When distinguished from exchange transactions, the asymmetry of power is seized by analogy: "A has power over B" is like "A causes B" to do something, where the flow is in one direction, A to B. (If A has power over/causes B to do a, then B does not have power over/cause A to do a).[16] Power is also unlike exchange in its capacity to be assigned to environmental or ecological control; for example A can effectively get B to do a by affecting some set of conditions, C, without any communication or direct contact with B; or $A - C - B$ (a).[17]

An exchange transaction is, by contrast, a relation between A and B characterized by a transfer of items (goods, behaviors, etc.). The customer buying a dozen eggs with ready cash has engaged in a social exchange characterized by a medium of general value (money). When set apart from "power," the symmetrical nature of exchange is stressed: equity in outcome, volition, effect is characteristic of social exchange. The flow of action is reciprocal, from A to B and from B to A. Economics is frequently said to be concerned with social exchange and politics with power relations; a division of labor is assumed on distinctions between the two types of events.[18]

Critics, however, have pointed out a rich area of overlap between power and exchange. In general, each concept seems robust enough to include almost all members of the other: (a) Coercion (or negative sanctions), long a defining component of power, can successfully be viewed as a feature of social exchange in which B does a in order to avoid the sanctions (in other words, he exchanges his behavior for the non-occurrence of the sanction). (b) The nonvolitional nature of power, in which the respondent acts against his will (preferences, interests), is uninterpreted in the absence of opportunity costs. Thus, the provision of sufficient rewards can at once get B to do a against his will and also complete an exchange transaction. (c) An imbalance in outcome, volition, or effect can also be found in social exchanges; for an exchange unfavorable to one or some of the parties (non-Pareto in outcome) is nonetheless an exchange.[19] Or, power can be viewed successfully as an exchange; and exchange looks remarkably like power. One intriguing effort to transform exchange to power fragments exchange into a series of power relations: A gets B to do j (hand over a dozen eggs), and B gets A to do k (hand over the ready cash), so that A and B each temporarily occupy the role of power authority versus respondent.[20]

The only clear distinction between the two concepts might be drawn up on differences between actions that are direct (individuals act on each other) and those that are oblique (individuals act on attendant conditions or collateral agents). Authorities who control through positive or negative sanctions are exercising power in a direct fashion. When control is consummated by restricting the agenda of choices or by failing to make decisions for alternative social arrangements, then power is oblique, and thus distinct from exchange.[21] Note that the condition of universal domain—one guarantee that agendas will not be controlled by authorities—is embedded in a satisfactory definition of liberty.[22] So to the degree that exchanges fulfill liberty, oblique power will be excluded from exchange. But direct forms of power are less easily demarcated from exchange.

Suppose, however, that the critics can be satisfied with criteria demarcating exchange from power. Even then the concept of exchange falters in decisive ways on a settlement of the rational problems surveyed here. Imagine now in the thought experiment that a third party, though not involved directly in the exchange, is part of the social practice of exchange between the first two individuals involved directly in the exchange. Suppose also that the exchange results in a loss to this third individual, that some of the costs of the transaction are passed off to him. Then Pareto is an illusion maintained only by ignoring the external effects of an exchange. And transitivity is lost when the wider effects of exchange are calculated. Shifting costs to those outside a transaction is a violation of equity, however conceived, since the outsiders are neither responsible for, nor benefit from, the exchange. But the rational point is more important: a comprehensive perspective on exchange can deny one of the principles—Pareto—that justifies exchange as superior to power or authority. The altimeter that cyclical majorities deny in majority rule is also missing in exchange when externalities occur.[23]

Nor are coordination and assurance failures necessarily avoided by exchanges. Experimental efforts at institution-building in game theory frequently use bargaining and side payments—the introduction of exchange as a solution to coordination problems. Let a simple case be part of the thought experiment on exchange. Two individuals consider alternatives a and b. Let each individual assign a utility to the alternatives, represented by the integers below:

	a	b
1	10	0
2	0	10

If each alternative requires the support of both individuals to be realized, then a cooperation dilemma occurs with advantage going to the player whose preferred alternative is considered first. Since exchange depends on the realization of a and b, the conditions for successful exchange may be exactly those avoiding coordination and assurance dilemmas: either a cohesive social unit established by stable players, repetitive alternatives, a continuing framework of rewards and penalties, small, face-to-face social relations, and so on;[24] or an external guarantee of compliance with agreeements (e.g., the coercive state, long accepted as the guarantor of property rights and contracts). Exchange theory, in short, does not so much solve the problems of coordination and assurance as restate the conditions needed for a solution.

If we maintain in the thought experiment the image of numerous individuals exchanging goods to be aggregated into a collective outcome, another version of the fallacy of composition can occur with exchanges. A decision to exchange items in individual transactions is not equivalent to, or the condition for the derivation of, a preference for the distribution resulting from the aggregated transactions. Professors can consistently (a) choose to pay $10 to see their favorite soccer team play, while (b) not preferring the inequitable distributions of moneys to star players that result (e.g., $1 million per year salaries). Champions of the market (like Nozick) inevitably point out that a modification of the aggregate distribution will restrict the liberty of individuals to dispose of, and accumulate, their resources as they wish. But this observation does not touch the point on rationality: what is rational for the individual in single transactions can be irrational for the individual in aggregate form.[25]

What does touch on liberty, however, is a widely held point on the empirical operations of markets. Exchange transactions are notorious for producing inequitable distributions of resources. Even the most cursory glance at the operations of the free market will reveal enormously unequal distributions. Again, however, the logic of exchange suggests why unequal patterns are possible. Repeating an exchange over time while maintaining liberty provides no check on the pattern of resource distribution. Outcomes can, and empirically do, result in unequal accumulations. And unequal outcomes affect the premises of exchange. Full freedom to exchange goods depends in the most obvious ways on equality of starting resources. If individual *1* is wealthy and individual *2* is not, it is a matter of little dispute that coercive results are both possible and likely. And if dictators, those who dominate others on the disproportionate accumulation of wealth, are the products of free markets as well as of political institutions, then exchange cannot be a solution to the equity problems of collective choice.[26]

These brief points on markets are, of course, compressed critiques of a complex set of theories. To be reasonable, they have to be joined to empirical studies of the market, and, of course, expanded. Even in compressed form, however, they state what only blind advocates of the market can deny: that markets do not fulfill the rational and moral criteria drawn from the liberal model on which markets are developed. Markets may fail to transform preferences into collective outcomes (assurance and coordination failures can occur), and they may fail both consistency tests (the fallacy of composition holds for markets as well as for aggregation devices) and equity criteria (Pareto and nondictatorship). Markets, in short, seem as vulnerable to rational and moral breakdowns as aggregation machines, and so markets are members of that species of rational problem represented by the Prisoners' Dilemma and Arrow's theorem. It is important to note that market failures occur because there is no feature of exchange that will guarantee the conditions set out by the rational and moral criteria of collective choice theory. The logic of exchange, although altering several of the conditions found in collective choice (successfully substituting, for example, various cardinal scales for Arrow's orderings), still permits rational breakdowns between liberal premises and collective outcomes.

The failure of markets, moreover, is due to the same conflict between arithmetical and moral languages found in Arrow's theorem. Nozick's unexamined assumption is that individuals are self-legislating creatures. Yet markets provide no institutional arrangements to address individual claims or justify aggregate outcomes. Like aggregation machines, markets accept only reasonless entries; and market outcomes are ungoverned collections of such entries. The absence of reasons has a double edge in exchange theory. On the one hand, there are advantages. Exchange is effective in reaching joint outcomes in large measure because shared reasons are not required to reach an agreement. (Even the definition of a gain or loss can vary with each in-dividual in an exchange.) Outcomes satisfactory to all parties that leave intact the variety of reasons contributing to dispute are obviously less demanding than those requiring an agreement on reasons. Indeed, to demand that each individual in an exchange agree on reasons may be pathological, rupturing the selective compromise that is distinctive of exchange. A Pareto optimal outcome can be reached with each in-dividual having a different reason to support the outcome.

On the other hand, however, the absence of reasons makes rational agreement difficult, perhaps impossible, on a number of issues. If reasons are entirely excluded from settlements among individuals, then those issues requiring a reasoned resolution, such as moral issues, can-not be included in such settlements.[27] This limitation is generally recognized in the use of exchange. In ordinary language, items are sometimes "priceless." One import of such thoughts is that certain goods are regularly excluded from the marketplace. Children, it is fre-quently noted, are not bought and sold as exchange commodities. They are allocated, when allocation is needed, on reasoned grounds by adop-tion agencies. Although the items that are uncomfortable with ex-change settlements vary with conventions, those items with moral status resist market transactions (moral language requiring reasoned orderings). Thus life-maintenance items and basic rights are often out-side the pale of exchange in Western societies. Technical resolutions, since they require reasoned outcomes, cannot be settled by exchange. The limited usefulness of exchange as an instrument to resolve moral and technical issues is the natural consequence of reasonless orderings. And these limitations restrict the capacity of markets to represent that liberal community of reason-giving individuals that provides rational and moral criteria in collective choice for evaluating institutions.

The limitations of exchange are generally recognized in the devel-opment of regulating devices that meet liberal tests. Dworkin (1981), for example, introduces the liberal model in order to elaborate theories of equality. A hypothetical collection of immigrants (rational, autono-mous, and discrete individuals) is faced with the problem of distribut-ing bundles of resources among themselves. A distribution is equal if no one prefers anyone else's bundle of resources to his own. An auction is the device that Dworkin suggests to effect an equal distribution of resources: prices are set so that all lots (resources) clear the market (there is only one purchaser). The auction addresses the problem of dis-satisfaction with resource bundles, due to different tastes or needs, by distributing each lot in terms of how important the resource bundle is to all individuals in the community. The auction thus assigns importance to each individual preference by comparing it to all other preferences.

Unequal talents require additional devices, however. Nozick's noninterventionist state must permit any inequality that might follow from the initial conditions of equality. Dworkin also allows inequality in the distribution of resources. But, unlike minimal-state theories, Dworkin's account requires that inequalities be ambition sensitive (reflecting industry and effort) but not endowment sensitive (reflecting luck and genetics). The state must permit the first type of inequality and compensate for the second. The device used to reestablish a distributive balance is the progressive income tax at rates set by a hypothetical insurance market. Suppose each individual knows his own talents and the income distribution but not his location on the distributive matrix. He can then choose an income level and pay the premium set for that level. The insurance would then pay the difference between the actual and chosen income levels. Devices such as these are designed to compensate for unequal distributions of talent without penalizing unequal expenditures of effort. Nozick's star athlete, Wilt Chamberlin, will in this way be taxed progressively at rates deemed fair by a theory that marks off warranted and unwarranted inequalities.

An inspection of exchange tells us that, as with aggregation, additional devices must be introduced if the moral features of liberalism are to be successfully represented in institutions. If the liberal model is interpreted simply in terms of numerical units, integers to be arithmetically combined, nothing compels us to compensate for inequalities. But the liberal community of moral agents in a hypothetical setting of autonomy both guides and justifies the combination rules designed to extend liberalism to institutional forms. The transformation by markets is incomplete without regulating devices to ensure that the moral conditions of the hypothetical community are realized in the actual conditions of society.

5

A general view of aggregation and exchange submits this to our understanding: that the surface and background assumptions of collective choice fail to generate an arrangement of individual parts that is comprehensible in terms of the assumptions.

The failure of the assumptions is traceable to a basic incompatibility between moral and arithmetical languages. A liberal model of society is a background assumption in Rawls' theory of justice and Arrow's theorem; it is a foreground description in Nozick's market version of justice. This liberal model sets out certain moral conditions that are to be fulfilled in collective outcomes, but these conditions cannot be fulfilled with the use of arithmetical composition rules. The moral language of Arrow's problem surfaces in conflicts between rationality and equity. Arrow's dictator, for example, satisfies the requirements of rationality as set out in the conditions of the theorem. Indeed, decisive or dominant individuals violate no rule of rationality known to collective choice theory. Equity, however, is offended by dictatorship or exploitation. As we have seen, the rejection of decisive individuals requires that no individual override any other on any preference ordering; and this avoidance of inequality in all areas of collective choice requires that individuals be absolutely equal. No collective outcome can then be generated without violating at least one of the theorem's other conditions. The starting point for this eventual paralysis is the same liberal model of morally autonomous individuals that leads to the failures of exchange.

The moral conditions of liberalism seem to be incompatible with any procedural or technical effort to forge social institutions. Imagine two individuals. Now, combine by counting some set of values discovered or ascribed to the two individuals, or witness the two individuals transferring a unit of value. Suppose that either event starts and stops with the physicalist fact (a description of aggregation or transfer). Nothing can be inferred from the physicalist fact that will establish moral and rational criteria. The individuals might be machines, the action a mechanical process. Now imagine that the two individuals have been invested with moral and rational qualities (they are autonomous; they feel, suffer, think, calculate; they are moral equals). Neither aggregation nor exchange has the capacity to address the claims (reasoned preferences) these individuals might make on the outcomes of their joint actions or even on the practices within which their actions occur. Both aggregation and exchange fail moral and rational tests because each is a numerical form of interaction and the tests are drawn from moral conceptions of human life. The conflicts in each case occur between counting rules, emergent outcomes, and the moral conditions of a liberal community.

It is a truism that all theories depend on assumptions. It is another truism, though a more profound one, that there are two models of a political society that order and interpret even the most basic of assumptions. One is holistic, the other arithmetical. Aristotle, developing his political theory on holistic terms, fuses items that arithmetical models maintain as separate: individual, state, society. One consequence of this fusion is that a number of concepts and theories characterizing liberal and libertarian political theory cannot be developed on the Aristotelian version of the polis. Among these are individual rights, anarchism, and civil disobedience—each of which requires an adversarial relationship between the individual and society that is impossible to conceive in Aristotle's political society. Hobbes, in contrast, separates individual, state, and society on a more nearly numerical model of association. From the separation follow theories of individual rights, the intelligibility (though not rationality) of anarchism, and the possibility of civil disobedience.

Concepts change in their sense from one model to the other. Liberty, for example, is a communal fulfillment in Aristotle, a negative freedom from state regulation in Hobbes. But the stronger effect of the two models on political thought is seen in the realization that some concepts exist only in terms of one or the other. Anarchism, for example, is not rejected by Aristotle (as it is by Hobbes). The question asked by Hobbes, Ought there to be any authority? is simply excluded on the conditions of Aristotle's political theory. Anarchism is literally unintelligible on Aristotle's organic model of civil society.

The contradictions of aggregation and exchange are more fully understood if framed in terms of a conflict within liberalism between the holistic needs of morality and the discrete logic of arithmetical languages. The liberal model accepts individuals as separate and countable units, yet endows them with moral features that are more comfortably elaborated in holistic political theories. The failures of collective choice represented by Arrow's theorem and exchange theory are the result of contradictions within liberal theory. These contradictions are produced because there is no mediating device to transform the disjointed features of liberalism into the type of moral community liberalism seeks. The analysis of background concepts tells us in general that the formal terms and conditions of collective choice do not cut deeply enough, and that there is another layer of conflict where theories with competing needs (in this case, liberalism) must be amended to produce noncontradictory collective outcomes.

Perhaps the original flaw in liberalism is that it is best elaborated as a series of shields that insulate individuals from collective regulation. Certainly the failures of aggregation and exchange testify to the difficulty of extending the hypothetical community of moral agents into the area of social practice. Yet the very minimalism of these two combining forms, which at first seem congenial with liberal communities, is the source of failure. Neither form is robust enough to express the moral and rational criteria that liberalism seems to require. More substantial structures are needed to move the liberal assumptions in collective choice to the explicit level of a rational political society. In Prisoners' Dilemma the structure, or payoff matrix, controls solutions to coordination and assurance failures (even demarcating several types of rational problems). In combination-rule failures a conflict between arithmetical and holistic structures creates the rational problem, and the development of institutions that meet moral and rational tests is needed to avoid the failure.

It is important to see the problems of aggregation and exchange as a conflict between two different kinds of languages in order to recognize those institutions that do meet liberal needs. MacKay (1980), for example, views Arrow's theorem as an infinite regress paradox requiring a familiar resolution: introduce a first cause, in this case a dismissal of unlimited scope, through a restriction on the pattern of preferences. Since it is well-known that single-peaked preferences avoid cyclical majorities (Black 1958), transitivity can be achieved and the paradox dissolved. But if the breakdowns originate in background moral expectations, unlimited scope cannot be dismissed without first in some way preserving autonomy, one of the features of moral agency that creates the problem in the first place. The identification of background assumptions tells us that some reconstruction of basic concepts is needed for a satisfactory solution to the problems of collective choice. The prime candidates seem to be the concept of rationality, the primitive term "individual" (currently both a count noun and a holistic unit in collective choice), and the composition rules producing collective outcomes.

NOTES

1. Kenneth Arrow, *Social Choice and Individual Values* (New York: John Wiley & Sons, 1963). The cyclical majority, for example, demonstrates that individuals can have transitive orderings that will, when summed, lead to an intransitive collective ordering.

2. In the arrangement

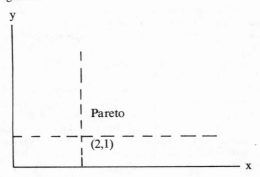

the upper right quadrant contains all distributions Pareto superior to (2,1). These distributions can be radically unequal, for example (900,3).

3. Or, individuals sometimes have to be treated differently in order to be treated equally. Douglas Rae, *Equalities* (Cambridge, Mass.: Harvard University Press, 1981). See also the discussion by Felix Oppenheim, "Egalitarian Rules of Distribution," *Ethics* 90 (January 1980): 164–79.

4. If xSy (local decisiveness), then suppose U restricted to the set $\{x,z\}$ where $x >_i z$ for all i in S,

$$S{:}xz$$
$$N_1{:}xz$$
$$N_2{:}zx$$
$$N_3{:}(xz)$$

and then U' from inserting y's, where

$$S{:}xyz$$
$$N_1{:}yxz$$
$$N_2{:}yzx$$
$$N_3{:}y(xz)$$

Now by xSy, $xP_u'y$; by Pareto, yP_uz; transitivity then produces $xP_u'z$. Thus C_u' $(\{x,z\}) = \{x\}$. The independence condition yields C_u $(\{x,z\}) = \{x\}$. So xP_uz and thus $x \in V \Rightarrow z \notin C_u$ (V), or the set S is globally decisive for x against z ($x\bar{S}z$). Thus $xSy \Rightarrow x\bar{S}z$. This exercise can be carried out to show that S will be decisive over every alternative if decisive for x over y. Extensions of this point can be found in Arrow's *Social Choice and Individual Value* and numerous secondary sources, but I have found especially helpful Jerry Kelly's *Arrow Impossibility Theorems*.

5. See Dennis C. Mueller, *Public Choice*, ch. 14, for an overview discussion.

6. John Rawls, *A Theory of Justice*. The principles are produced from a bargaining game in the first model of justice, in Rawls' "Justice as Fairness," in Peter Lasslett and W.

G. Runciman, eds., *Philosophy, Politics, and Society,* second series (New York: Barnes & Noble Books, 1962). But the later amendments to this first model bring out Kantian features of the original position, which make bargaining inappropriate and indeed impossible. See Eric Von Magnus, "On Modeling the Original Position," *Reason Papers* 6 (Spring 1980): 25–35.

7. This is true even though the formal requirements of Pareto and nondictatorship are satisfied with a single individual. Pareto is met when x, y X (the set of all alternatives), and the set of all N is decisive for $x > y$. Nondictatorship states that no individual is decisive for x against y for all x, $y \in D$ (D = profile). Now a set, S, is decisive for x against y (x, $y \in X$) if, for every profile D in which (1) $x >_i y$ for all $i \in S$, (2) $x >_i y$ for at least one $i \in S$, we have (3) $x \in v \Rightarrow y \notin C_u (v)$. So both Pareto and nondictatorship formally apply to a singleton set. But since Pareto seeks to ensure that unanimity is reflected in collective outcomes, and nondictatorship rules out a single individual dominating all others in the collective outcome, the use of each condition in Rawls' original position would be otiose.

8. The independence condition requires that two distinct profiles, whose restriction to an agenda are the same, must also have choice functions that act the same, at least on that agenda. Or, put less formally, collective outcomes are to remain the same if individual orderings do not vary. Any theory of collective choice that derives principles from individual choices would be concerned to ensure such noncreativity of composition rules.

9. See Robert Nozick's examples and discussion in *Anarchy, State, and Utopia,* pp. 93–94, where he develops the modest point that the benefits of collective action to an individual must be more than his own calculated costs in contributing (in order for fairness to apply); and pp. 267–68, for a recognition that some may legitimately refuse to contribute even if all others give to collective action ("they don't care about the ride at all").

10. Theories of the market routinely use a number of other defining conditions but rarely agree on these conditions. Neo-classical economics, for example, develops markets on perfect information, while the tradition identified with Ludwig von Mises, in *Human Action—A Treatise on Economics* (London: Hodge, 1949), abandons conditions of perfect information. I know of no theory of the market, however, that does not contain as a core concept the minimalist definition I offer here.

11. Douglas Rae, "An Altimeter for Mr. Escher's Stairway: A Comment on William H. Riker's 'Implications from the Disequilibrium of Majority Rule for the Study of Institutions'," *American Political Science Review* (June 1980): 451–55. Rae views the altimeter of neoclassical markets as a device "to underwrite the rights-utility bond" in liberal thought.

12. Among the fine anthologies elaborating and criticizing Nozick's theory is the symposium "Robert Nozick's *Anarchy, State, and Utopia,*" *Arizona Law Review* 19 (1977).

13. Robert Dahl, "Power," *International Encyclopedia of the Social Sciences* (New York: Macmillan, 1968).

14. Quentin Gibson, "Power," *Philosophy of Social Science* 1 (1971): 101–12.

15. Stanley Benn, "Power," in Paul Edwards, ed., *The Encyclopedia of Philosophy* 6 (New York: Macmillan, 1967), 424–27.

16. For example: James March, "An Introduction to the Theory and Measurement of Influence," *American Political Science Review* 49 (June 1955):   431–51; Robert Dahl,

"Power;" Jack Nagel, *The Descriptive Analysis of Power* (New Haven, Conn.: Yale University Press, 1975).

17. The first recognition of "ecological" power was, so far as I know, by Dorwin Cartwright, "Influence, Leadership, Control," in James March, ed., *Handbook of Organizations* (Chicago: Rand McNally & Co., 1965): 1–41.

18. Harry Eckstein, "Authority Patterns: A Structural Basis for Political Inquiry," *American Political Science Review* 67 (December 1973): 1142–61, for a slightly different rendition.

19. For a review of recent literature (and some helpful contributions to it), David Baldwin, "Power and Social Exchange," *American Political Science Review* 72 (December 1978): 1229–42.

20. Baldwin, "Power and Social Exchange"; Felix Oppenheim, "'Power' Revisited," *The Journal of Politics* 40(August 1978): 589–608.

21. Peter Bachrach and Morton Baratz, "Two Faces of Power," *American Political Science Review* 56 (December 1962): 947–52.

22. Universal domain ensures only negative liberty, or the absence of obstacles to free choice. No condition in the theorem guarantees or even refers to positive liberty, which requires the provision of those conditions in the absence of which effective liberty is impossible. I refer here to Isiah Berlin's famous distinction in *Two Concepts of Liberty* (Oxford: Clarendon Press, 1958), and *Four Essays on Liberty* (New York: Oxford University Press, 1969). See also the synthesis of negative and positive liberty by means of the concept of "constraint," in Gerald MacCullum, "Negative and Positive Liberty," in Alan de Crespigny and Alan Wertheimer, eds., *Contemporary Political Theory* (New York: Atherton, 1970). The theorem's concentration on negative liberty indicates yet again the liberalism of the view that individual autonomy depends on noninterference. The possibility that a different, and perhaps more robust, sense of autonomy occurs in communal arrangements, especially those guaranteed by the state, is simply never considered.

23. William H. Riker and Steven J. Brams, "The Paradox of Vote-Trading," *American Political Science Review* 67 (December 1973): 1235–47. The technical literature on this issue, as with the others treated here, is vast. See, for example, Thomas Schwartz, "Vote Trading and Pareto Efficiency," *Public Choice* 24 (1975): 101–109 for one among several qualifications to the claim that externalities can make everyone worse off in exchange (in this case, vote trading).

24. Peter Bernholz, "Prisoners' Dilemma, Logrolling and Cyclical Group Preferences," *Public Choice* 29–32 (Spring 1977): 73–84.

25. This is a well-known critique of Nozick's main argument in *Anarchy, State, and Utopia*. The recent discussion of vote trading in William H. Riker, *Liberalism Against Populism* (San Francisco: W.H. Freeman & Co., 1982) establishes in more general ways that exchange will not avoid composition fallacies, on pp. 157–67. See also the discussion of market disequilibria by Norman Schofield, "Instability and Development in the Political Economy," in Peter C. Ordeshook and Kenneth A. Shepsle, eds., *Political Equilibrium* (Hingham, Mass.: Kluwer-Nijhoff Publishing, 1982).

26. This last point is an irresistible observation on the empirical operation of markets that is much disputed in the literature. The conceptual point, however, is indisputable: liberty in exchange is strongly conditioned by the prior distribution of property rights; and no continuing system of exchange can guarantee equity in the distribution of property. Indeed, markets provides no criteria for the normative task of assigning property

rights, which nonetheless is required prior to the operations of the market. An especially helpful discussion of these points is Charles Lindblom's *Politics and Markets* (New York: Basic Books, 1977). See also the nice summary in Charles Schultze, *The Public Use of Private Interest* (Washington, D.C.: Brookings Institution, 1977).

27. An idea expressed first (and best) by Marx. See, for example, the lovely phrases in the opening pages of "Needs, Production, and Division of Labor," in T.B. Bottomore, ed., *Karl Marx: Early Writings,* (New York: McGraw-Hill, 1964). See also the classic study by Charles Titmuss, *The Gift Relationship* (London: George Allen & Unwin, 1971). The tradition of excluding items from markets on moral grounds is long and varied. Even libertarians join in. Mill, in *On Liberty,* rules out slavery as a possible outcome from exchange.

4

Individuals and Groups

Collective choice in Prisoners' Dilemma and Arrow's theorem instructs us in some of the ways that numerical associations can fail to realize the moral conditions of liberalism. Separate and countable individuals cannot on a variety of conditions combine to produce an outcome that satisfies rational and equity tests. At the center of such failures seems to be a conflict between two models of a political society—numerical and holistic. The combination rules of collective choice do not comfortably express the holistic language of that morality represented by the liberal model on which collective choice theory is developed.

The tension between arithmetical and moral languages is concentrated on interpretations of the primitive term "individual" in Arrow's theorem. The type of individual required by the arithmetical composition rules of the theorem fails to fit the moral assumptions needed to prove the theorem. Imagine two individuals constituting a society requiring a distribution of goods. Suppose further that the only information available on this society is that the two individuals are separate, countable units with preferences. How, using Arrow's conditions, can a just distribution of the goods be determined? Since no claims on behalf of either or both individuals are known, the answer to the distribution problem is, on no basis.[1] Or, transform the society into a decisive pattern, where individual *1* secures goods at the expense of individual *2*. Is individual *1* a dictator? Or an exploitive figure? It is impossible to say without more information; for individual *1* may (or may not) be the one

73

with greater claim to society's goods on the basis of need, merit, desert. Yet it is precisely such determinations that must be made for nondictatorship to be accepted.

The separate and countable nature of individuals seems at once fixed by the requirements of aggregation, yet anomalous in accommodating the moral conditions that are also introduced with the liberal model of a political society. Two observations follow. First, since the moral language of collective choice is unintelligible unless "individual" is modified beyond the sense in which the term is used in the theorems and proofs, a hermaneutic circle begins to appear: the theorems and proofs are developed on certain equity conditions, and the equity conditions require a transformation in the term "individual" that is hostile to the aggregation needs of collective choice. Second, given the formal needs that collective choice has for discrete individuals, any change away from a concept of the individual as a discrete unit is bound to have profound effects on recent traditions of political thought.

2

Many of the failures of cooperation in collective action are traceable to the isolation of individuals from each other. Hardin (1982) overviews and extends Olson's (1965) early theories on why groups fail to organize or persist when individuals have an interest in the collective outcomes such groups can secure. Among the major considerations in recent explanations are what I have called structural considerations. Such considerations include the matrix of payoffs in Prisoners' Dilemma that subdivide cooperative problems into those in which (a) noncooperation is a dominant strategy no matter what the other individual does, and (b) cooperation is rational if others cooperate (the assurance game). Other considerations that bear on the success of group efforts are efficacy, in the narrow sense of how many others and how much effort may be required to produce a collective good, and the features of the outcome that is sought, such as its value (magnitude of benefit). Other considerations that bear on success are: whether the collective product is a divisible or indivisible good; whether a good is being provided or a bad is being eliminated; whether the good is a step-good (binary, for example) or one that can be provided continuously;

and whether provision is internal or external (by group members or with the help of others outside the group).

Some recent considerations amend the conditions of Olson's original arguments. Asymmetries, such as divisions among individuals over the value of the collective product, obviously are important factors in group success. But they are also deviations from the original conception of cooperation problems, in which individuals find it rational to defect even when all agree on the value of the collective outcome. It is hardly surprising that individuals may rationally not cooperate when they disagree over the value of the collective outcome (costs and benefits are asymmetrical, demand is unequal, benefits are heterogeneous, etc.). Noncooperation in such circumstances lacks the counter-intuitive force of Olson's original formulation of collective action problems.

But the main contribution of recent studies is to introduce a dynamic analysis to the mainly static conceptions of earlier studies of collective action. The value of the contribution is not only its greater realism (social action being clearly dynamic), but also the importance it assigns to overlapping group activities in successful collective action. Both Prisoners' Dilemma and Arrow's theorem are developed on a view of individuals as atomistic units who interact in discrete intervals. The interaction fails in well-known ways. If failures of cooperation and combination rules occur on the same non-overlapping conditions, and if successful cooperation requires that individuals overlap in various ways, a more general view of collective action, its problems and solutions, is suggested. An extended sense of individuals may contribute to a solution generalizable to several different types of rational breakdowns between individual and collective.

Any effort to find a general solution to these rational breakdowns, however, must proceed sequentially in examining each of several factored problems of collective choice. The third of our representations is efficacy failure. Though not elaborated in formal theory, efficacy failure is nevertheless an important problem in collective action. First, a failure of efficacy nullifies any rational connections between one and all established on other grounds, so long as a means-ends version of rationality is maintained. (If one has no effect in securing an end, no incentive exists to act toward that end.) Second, an understanding of efficacy failure and what exactly avoids such failure is helpful in seeing the broad conflicts between numerical and holistic models that are found in all representations of rational breakdowns.

3

Efficacy is the power to produce an effect. What is meant by an effect and how efficacy fails vary with whether individuals are countable or holistic, or—more generally—whether numerical or corporate wholes are models for the social unit. The story of efficacy failure is typically told on the conditions of numerical associations. The simple core of the story is that efficacy fails if (a) individual participants are singletons, and (b) the number of participants is large. A conjoining of (a) and (b) leads to the observation that efficacy is a proportional measure represented by the fraction, 1/number of participants. Though this conception of efficacy is without interesting complications, it still provides a core understanding of effects as dispersed in large numerical groups and preserved in small numerical groups. The rational force of the dilemma is seen clearly in large electorates. When many individuals are voting, no single vote will likely have an effect on outcomes. Thus no individual should vote. But if no one votes, there is no election. And this conclusion follows even if elections are rational and moral ways for reaching collective outcomes.

This simple story has its own complications. If no one votes, then any one vote can determine the election. Thus any one individual should vote. But if one should vote, then all should vote (on identical rational calculations). But if all vote, then no one should. One learns to sympathize with Alice in her conversations with the Red Queen.[2] One also discovers yet another rational breakdown to place alongside the failures of composition rules represented by Prisoners' Dilemma and Arrow's theorem. If efficacy is pushed beyond these simple dimensions, however, a more complex story emerges with any number of lessons for collective choice. Among the more intriguing of these lessons is how efficacy failure and resolution are conditioned by numerical and corporate models of association.

Begin with a distinction between efficacy and decisiveness. Barry (1980) defines a decisive individual as one whose probability of success increases when he tries, and a lucky individual as one who is successful without trying. Efficacy is obviously not related to luck. Nor, less obviously, is efficacy equivalent to decisiveness. An efficacious action, as one that has an effect on outcomes, may not increase the probability of success. The voter in small electorates (e.g., committees) may be guaranteed that his vote counts for something in a numerical sum—he has the power to produce an effect—yet he may not necessarily succeed in increasing any probability that his preferences will be reflected in the collective outcome. (The winning coalition may be set against him.) Efficacy, seen in this way, is a necessary condition for, but not equivalent to, decisiveness. It is also more accurately seen as a capacity that individuals have, a dispositional term that is realized in certain conditions.

The striking feature of the simple story of failed efficacy is that the moral, "do not participate," can be drawn regardless of the preferences of others. In large electorates, for example, the majority of voters may be for or against the preferences of any single voter. But whether for or against, the voter is still rationally advised to abstain; for his vote will not increase in any appreciable way his probability of success because it (the vote) has no appreciable effect on outcomes. The size of the electorate, in and of itself, is a condition that prevents the dispositional, efficacy, from becoming an actual feature of individual actions.

Even the simple story thus tells us that efficacy can be fully elaborated only by examining the ways in which individuals and structures (a term to be used to describe political societies, with no implications for structural theory in any of its forms) affect one another. Indeed, the first solutions to efficacy failure simply change some of the conditions of numerical association. The simple story of efficacy failure assumes that singletons are the acting units. Relaxing this assumption provides the first exit route away from the failure: assume that individuals can and do form coalitions. Individuals acting in tandem with others is a commonplace in both causal models and group theory. When, for example, $p \& r \rightarrow q$, $p \& s \rightarrow q$, but $r \& s \rightarrow \rightsquigarrow q$, then p causes q, but only with r or s. Individuals in social life typically coalesce in groups, or with other individuals, to make demands on the political system. And their efficacy is improved as a consequence of finding allies.[3]

Coalitions in hierarchical societies can transfer the problem of efficacy to the subunit level in a way consistent with the features of numerical associations. If subunits are small enough to permit each individual to affect outcomes, then a federal structure can transfer effect through stages to collective outcomes at the social level. Imagine now not a 1,000-member but a three-person subunit, where each unit joins in a "higher" three-unit arrangement until a collective outcome is reached.

A less than unanimous vote in each collection of subunits (a vote of two to one) rules out the transformation of the minority member's vote into the outcome at the next highest level. But efficacy, like rational continuity, does not require that individuals win. Only the possibility of an effect is needed, and effects are secured within each subunit. If the alternatives are modest in number, minority views may be represented by other subunits at higher levels. But the main advantage gained from federalizing effects is in the creation of subsets small enough to permit individual efficacy. Partitioning is the solution, in this case hierarchically through progressive joinings of subsets.

The importance of structures in efficacy is even clearer when impediments to efficacy are examined. Think of a path between the single individual and an outcome, o, of her choices. Let efficacy stand for a positive effect on o. In addition to the dilution of effect that other single individuals bring, there are (a) the shielding effect of mediating institutions, and (b) the diffusing effect of multiple alternatives. On (a), shields can be so strong in some institutions, like authoritarian governments, that no ordinary participant has an effect on collective outcomes. Some voting rules are better than others in permitting positive effect—majority rule, say, over a rule requiring two-thirds support.[4] But, also, any number of institutions can absorb individual efforts, fixing political action at points well short of their aims. On (b), a large number of alternatives can reduce the effect any individual has on joint outcomes.[5] Both (a) and (b) are intervening effects, structural devices that interrupt the path between effort and outcome.

The thought can be sketched in even broader terms. Mediating institutions can deflect individual effort from its goal. But mediation can also facilitate. Institutions like the family, organized religion, neighborhoods, etc., can be particularly powerful devices to channel private efforts into public effects.[6] Like social partitioning in the management of coordination dilemmas, subcultures of shared value can exist in larger heterogeneous settings. The individual is efficacious through the framework of the mediating institution which, by virtue of common value, proximity, and relative size, is more responsive to individual effort. The rational connections between local and national are expressed in theories of federalism. Each social unit is an efficacious member of progressively larger units, with meta-rules at the national level providing direction and autonomy at the local level.

A number of social practices solve efficacy problems by defining individuals as vital members of larger units. Suppose, for example, that individuals are members of a social practice that distributes efficacy to each individual. One method that is particularly effective in doing this is a rotation in power.[7] The failure in efficacy represented by voting is produced when all individuals act at once and the outcome is a summary of individual actions. Suppose now a system in which each individual rules by turn, and each is even decisive for the period of time in office; and suppose further that each individual performs a necessary function while in office that can be performed by no other individual who holds office in turn. On such conditions, efficacy is guaranteed to every person; for the participation of all is needed for the continuation of the social practice and the production of outcomes. The well-known practical problems in establishing such a system limit its usefulness. To be feasible, a rotation system requires (as a self-evident truth about time restriction) a relatively small social unit. But the type of social practice, not the size of the unit as such, is again decisive in resolving efficacy problems.

Each of these efforts to solve efficacy problems is aimed at the social practice within which participation occurs. The dependence of efficacy on social contexts is more fully disclosed with the simplest formula for ensuring efficacy—reduce the size of the social unit. The controlling logic is arithmetic. If efficacy is measured by one over the number of participants, a decrease in the denominator will increase the efficacy of each individual participant. But the effects of social practices belie the simple arithmetical formula. Like the more elaborate management of defection in N-person iterated Prisoners' Dilemma games, social cohesion is the controlling variable (Taylor 1976). If individuals are units embedded in social practices, in the sense that they have effects on others and are themselves affected by others, then efficacy is achieved by definition. Cohesion can occur in very large groups. Or, better, the numerical size of a society is secondary to the presence or absence of those social practices that do increase cohesion among individuals. Again, a reconstruction of the structure (or social context) of choice is needed to restore rational continuity.

Structures also condition, and even create, the possibility of negative efficacy. Suppose that individuals want to affect an outcome in the negative sense of preventing a change in the status quo. The efficacy of these individuals will be realized only by denying the successful effects of others on any of the collective outcomes that change the status quo. It follows that precisely those structures that prevent efficacy—large numbers of participants, shielding and diffusing institutions, the isolation of individuals from coalitions—can permit negative efficacy.[8] There is another variation on negative efficacy. Sometimes individuals can, as singletons, be effective in preventing a collective outcome. Suppose the existence of a good desired by a, b, c individuals and only concerted action by all three individuals can provide the good. Now each individual is efficacious in a negative way (one defection prevents the production of the good) and in a positive way (each person can produce the good on the condition that the other two cooperate). The individual in this second sense of efficacy has an effect on outcomes as a unit in a group (not as an isolated figure). Negative efficacy is created through the special features of the social unit.

Structures may compete with individual efficacy. Here a further refinement of efficacy is needed. It is possible that efficacious structures may prevent individuals from having an effect on either the structures or the outcomes produced by means of the structures. Dahl and Tufte (1973) suggest that a conflict exists between institutions accessible to individual influence and institutions capable of effective action. Local social units, those that are small and accessible, are more amenable to effective individual participation. One of the possible reasons is the greater likelihood of reciprocal communications between citizens and leaders in small social units. But such units may lack the capacity to produce effective outcomes. Systemic effectiveness may depend on concentrations of power and knowledge, and a level of organization, that may not be optimal for individual effectiveness. Efficacy is in this way dichotomized. Individual efficacy requires one set of structures; system efficacy is possible only with a different set of structures. There may not be any structures that satisfy both senses of efficacy.

The one clear possibility of individual effect on large numerical associations is also conditioned by structures. A threshold voter is one who is decisive in turning an election toward one alternative or another. But whether any single individual will be a threshold voter is a function of the size and closeness of the election. Brams, in an earlier contribution, maintains that the expected number of decisive voters in presidential elections may be related to the square root of the size of the state because (in the United States) there is a larger number of electoral votes to influence.[9] Even a sequence of elections may affect efficacy, as voters in early primary elections are more efficacious in selecting presidential candidates than those in later primaries. Thresholds are themselves captives of social practices. Whether there is a threshold, and how many, will depend on practices. Radiation exposure is continuous in its harmful effects, with no threshold that inverts the value of each rad. Teaching has two thresholds—a very small number of students and a large number of students both reducing the quality of instruction in lecture classes.

4

Thresholds illustrate in yet different ways how structures are decisive in interpreting efficacy. A threshold is an outcome brought about by an action that would not have caused the outcome had not other events accompanied the action. Suppose, for example, a case of sequential and open (nonsecret) voting. In a set of ten voters, where majority rule determines a winner and where the ballot is unanimous, the sixth vote is the threshold action. It causes an outcome (the election of the unanimous choice) because accompanied by other, in this case antecedent, actions (the first five votes).

Utilitarian theory has for some time accepted thresholds as nonlinear functions of individual (or simple) and collective (or general) utility (Lyons 1965). Linearity of effect (in Lyons' formulation) is achieved when $T = n \times E$ (where T = total, or collective, outcome; n = number of acts; and E = the effect of each individual act). A threshold is a nonlinear relationship of T to $n \times E$. For example, when lying occurs in great numbers, a loss of confidence in communication can result, so that $T \neq n \times E$. A breakdown between simple and general utility follows; for $G \neq n \times S$ (where G = general utility, n = number of acts; and S = simple utility) when collective outcomes sum to more than the effects of combined individual acts (given that simple utility is assigned to individual effects, general utility to collective effects).

Among the many types of thresholds are those in which the collective effects cumulatively occur in a step-by-step fashion up to the threshold, and then, at some critical point, the collective state assumes a value discontinuous with the previous effects. Lying, one may assume, harms a social group in incremental steps and may, at some frequency level, damage a group at some higher level discontinuous with individual lies below the critical frequency (see Figure 4.1).

In contrast to this is the case of individual actions accumulating with no collective effects (along the value represented by the y axis) until a threshold point is reached at which a collective outcome occurs that is discontinuous with the antecedent individual actions (see Figure 4.2).

This second type of threshold is represented by the tragedy of the commons (Hardin 1968). In this well-known story, individuals calculate whether to increase or maintain their use of a common resource when (1) the costs of the commons are shared, (2) the benefits of use are

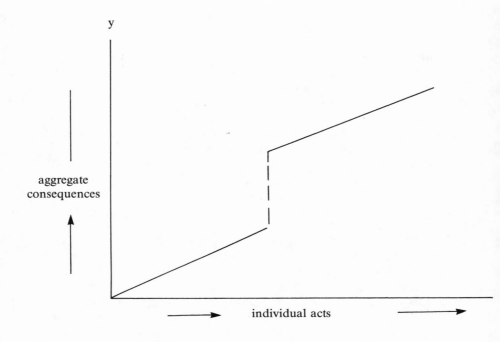

Figure 4.1.
Step Discontinuities

private, and (3) the commons has a threshold point of use beyond which it is (eventually) destroyed. (The conclusion of the story, its "tragedy," is that the individuals will always rationally increase use beyond the threshold point.) But if individuals use the resource at a point before the threshold is reached, individual usage has no deleterious effect. The commons can replenish itself and the collective outcome (the tragedy) does not occur.

Thresholds are far more common than the language here may suggest. Rubber bands snapping, water boiling, metamorphic change—the world is filled with discontinuous sequences of events. A separate branch of mathematics, topology, states discontinuities in formal terms (Thom 1975). Even the problems targeted in utilitarianism for examination are (it seems to me) an exploration only of "fold" changes—those that have only one control factor and thus only one behavior axis (as set up in the figures drawn here to represent thresholds). Nothing es-

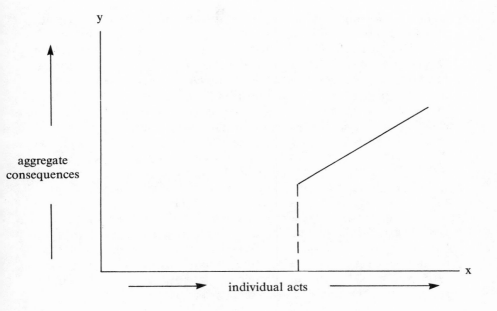

Figure 4.2.
Abrupt Discontinuities

pecially interesting for mathematics should be expected to follow from such explorations. Nor are the methodological problems unique or even odd. Discontinuities are cases where a monotonic relationship between an independent and a dependent variable—expressible as "an increase in X brings a proportionate increase in Y"—ceases, and the dependent variable varies without explanation. Such problems are common in the study of empirical relationships, and efforts to remedy them fill introductory textbooks in methodology. Among the standard approaches to such phenomena are searches for intervening or fresh antecedent variables. The case of lying seems almost to beg for such treatment; for breakdowns in whole systems of communication seem likely to be caused by changes in attitudes that intervene between individual lies at high frequency levels and collective consequences.

The commonplace status of discontinuities suggests that thresholds are worth our attention only if they address more profound issues of rational discontinuities. And so they do, although indirectly. The instructive contribution is Lyons' (1965) solution to threshold problems. The solution Lyons offers is at once ingenious and conservative. He suggests that the flaw in admitting thresholds to utility calculations is in the description of individual actions. Thresholds occur as events within a social practice. Yet the relationship of individual act and collective outcome is expressed on the assumption that acts occur in a vacuum, each isolated from all others. This mistake can be corrected by describing acts in terms of their social context, in particular by including in the description the effects of the acts on threshold events. For example, individuals walking across a lawn can bring on a threshold event if the number and frequency of crossings are high enough. (The threshold in this case is the ruin of the lawn.) A correct description of individual acts of walking across the grass must include the effects of each act on the lawn as part of the practice of lawn-crossing. Then causal continuity (which Lyons calls linearity) is reestablished "within classes of acts the members of which are exactly similar in all causal respects" (Lyons 1965, p. 91). And continuity between simple and general utility is restored within the newly separated classes of acts.

Lyons' solution is seductive in large part because of its simplicity. Problem: Collective outcomes have an emergent effect, one not traceable to the descriptions of individual acts and the arithmetical composition rules that combine these acts. Solution: Redescribe the individual acts to include the threshold effects that emerge. Consequence of solution: Simple and general utility are reconnected on the causal continuity between various classes of acts and the collective effects these acts produce. Although rule utilitarianism is the eventual casuality of vesting individual acts with the sole authority to originate wholes, a reductionist goal is sought in explaining macro events in terms of individual acts. Discontinuities suggest that wholes can be independent of parts, and this suggestion offends the strong individualism of recent social theory. Lyons' solution attempts to affirm the soundness of methodological individualism by maintaining individuals as independent variables, and redescribing the independent variables to include the collective variance that occurs after the threshold. In this way, wholes remain no more and no less than the sum (arithmetical product) of their parts. Few would deny that this effort is worth our close attention.

Lyons' solution is at once an exemplar of common strategies used toward rational discontinuities, stated simply now as an extension of individual acts, and a measure that (intentional or not) protects existing expectations in social inquiry. Scientific inquiry is chronically faced with events that do not seem to square with the paradigm of a given age. There are two basic responses to such anomalies. One is to stretch the available conceptual framework to accommodate the anomalies. The most intriguing example of conceptual stretching is probably the seemingly endless production of epicycles to maintain the Ptolemaic system. Another is to view the anomaly as a sign that there is something wrong with the paradigm, and that a revision of basic concepts may be required. Any study of science will show that there are no hard and fast rules to guide us in deciding which response is appropriate.[10] But Lyons has clearly chosen the first of these responses, especially as it protects the philosophy of methodological individualism.

The thoroughgoing individualism of Lyons' solution can be seen immediately in the mathematical formulation of effects and totals. For $T = n \times E$ to be true, each individual must have an equal effect on the total outcome; for if effects are unequal, the total could not accurately be represented as $n \times E$. A stronger premise on individualism, however, is found in the assignment of priority to individual acts in explanations of collective events. Continuity between individual and collective action is restored in Lyons' approach by reestablishing individuals as the origin of social outcomes. But even in an effort so strongly individualistic as this one, the competition between numerical and holistic models occurs.

Imagine first the commons tragedy as a demographic pattern without individuals who can calculate rationally. Say that cattle are simply increasing naturally in a grazing area. In this case, continuity at the threshold is satisfied by a description of the consequences of some increment at the threshold—a numerical effect. Now, second, imagine that rational actors are threshold figures (the farmers in the commons tragedy). Then the establishment of continuity requires that the individuals at the threshold consider collective consequences as part of their utility calculations. A rational dimension has been added to what are otherwise numerical descriptions.

The distinctions between primarily numerical thresholds and those that involve rational actors suggest differences in what we mean when we say an individual act is redescribed to include threshold effects. A redescription of purely demographic effects leaves the threshold event as a discrete phenomenon—one unit that, because accompanied by other units, has an effect that would not have occurred were the act to have occurred in isolation. When the acts of rational individuals are redescribed, however, the individual's calculations are invaded by collective considerations. Rational continuity is reestablished when individuals think of the effects of their actions on others and on social practices. The social context is incorporated within individual calculations. In this mentalistic or intentional sense, individuals are holistic rather than discrete. The problem that this invasion causes for methodological individualism is that such individuals may not be discrete and countable; and, as a consequence of this shift in the meaning of an individual, wholes may not be arithmetical sums of parts. This distinction between arithmetical and holistic versions of wholes interprets Lyons' solution in more radical ways. It raises questions about what is meant by the unexamined term "individual" and by "continuity" between individual acts and collective consequences in different types of social practices.

It is, in any case, arrogant to proceed as if wholes are nothing more than collections of parts. Suppose that the authentic independent variable in frequency of lying is a feature of the social system, say population density, in the sense that this condition makes it rational for people to lie. A step-by-step correlation between individual lies and population density can then occur, but the causal direction is reversed. For each incremental increase in density (y axis), another individual tells a lie (x axis). Now suppose that at a certain threshold of individual lies the uncertainty of institutions makes it rational for individuals to increase dramatically the size of their families. Again, the event can be successfully graphed as a discontinuity. But a reliance on purely individual effects will not restore continuity, for the collective state is not a consequence of individual acts but is rather caused by other, macro, events. Some macro events, for example nuclear war, have no correlates in, nor even emerge from, micro events. They "exist" only at the upper quadrants of the graphs. A threshold can thus be explained by methods that do not resort to redescribing individual effects; and any general solution to these patterns that does reduce collective states to individual consequences celebrates the philosophy of methodological individualism, but risks a misidentification of the independent variable and the direction of influence. Holistic models are not reduced to numerical models by utilitarian solutions to threshold problems. And what we mean by individual effect will be different in each model.

5

The deeper distinctions between social models, however, are the main structural conditions on efficacy. The relative success of some famous solutions to efficacy failure will draw out the points. There are three solution sets: (1) deontological instead of teleological rewards; (2) byproduct theory; and (3) entrepreneurship.

Suppose first that the intrinsic merits of action replace the merits of consequences, avoiding the problem of efficacy by denying efficacy as the effects of individual action on group outcomes. In Book II of Plato's *Republic,* Glaucon tells the story of Gyges, possessor of a magic ring that renders him invisible at will. Thus empowered he is able to act without fear of reprisals. Glaucon asks Socrates for reasons to act justly when all coercive incentives are missing, when a person can do anything without fear of penalty. Plato develops justice in terms of internal rewards, reflective satisfactions that would bind Gyges because they express a good-in-itself. Efficacy for Gyges is turned inward.[11]

More pragmatic internal rewards, the "private consequences of choice," have lately been stressed. Inner feelings like self-esteem, fulfillment of social obligations, status, prestige, altruism, legal sanction, etc., are proposed as rational incentives for participation.[12] Many doctrines of traditional democratic thought emphasize the benefits of political participation in and of itself, separate from the act of participation on political outcomes. All of these approaches are variations on a basic theme, which is that action may be valued for its intrinsic merits or internal effects as much as for its consequences on group outcomes.

Internal rewards can be seen as special types of incentives. Moe (1980) has suggested that purposive incentives (internal benefits) introduce a new benefit curve that may exceed all of the costs of participation. An opponent of abortion, for example, may be willing to invest considerable effort in right-to-life groups, even if the effects on abortion laws are minimal, because of the moral satisfaction such investment brings. Conversely, an individual who opposes the goals of a group, who receives negative internal returns, may still support the group effort. But he will do so only if economic incentives are considerable and/or the effects of support are marginal. In both cases, internal rewards provide a measure of support/nonsupport that is traded off against efficacy.[13]

A second solution is developed in terms of byproduct theory.[14] The central thought here is that cooperation failures can be avoided if interest groups act not only toward other groups and the political society, but also toward their members. The oldest action is coercion. The justification is Hobbesian—that even when individuals share the same goal, they may not have a rational incentive to cooperate unless some coercive guarantee is present; and, like the argument applied to Prisoners' Dilemma, the assumption is that the existence of common goals renders the actual use of coercion improbable (so long as it is credible). Another action is more benign. Groups may provide additional benefits to render participation rational. Low-cost travel and insurance, discount prices on items, gift bonuses, lottery prizes, convention trips—the lists typically offered to illustrate the incentives could not be less Hobbesian.

Look at the general statement of selective incentives as developed in Moe's (1980) helpful discussion. Let B (X) represent the benefits accruing to individuals from the provision of a collective good, C (X) represent the costs of such provision. Let, further, S = selective incentives, D = dues, d = the amount of D assigned to S, and X = the amount of the collective good provided by others. Moe suggests that a nonefficacious supporter of a group's goals will join if and only if $S + [B (X_{D-d}) - B (X_o) > D$ or $S > d + \{[C (X_{D-d}) - C (X_o)] - [B (X_{D-d}) - B (X_o)]\}$. A nonsupporter will join if S is high enough even when $(BX_{D-d}) - B (X_o) < 0$. (If the individual is efficacious, then he or she will make the more economical calculation to join when the point at which the marginal benefits of the collective good minus marginal costs is less than X—though S can also complement, add to, or shield the collective good incentive in participation decisions.) In general, byproducts can substitute for efficacy failures in groups by making it rational to participate even when the individual has little or no effect on joint outcomes.[15]

The third type of solution is entrepreneurship. Olson's (1965) early discussion of the free rider problem recognizes two patterns of voluntary (no byproducts) cooperation: (1) all produce the collective good, or $(x > y) > z$ (where x = benefits to the group, z = gain to one or more individuals in the group, and y = total cost of producing the good); and (2) one or a few produce the good, or $z > (x > y)$. The latter pattern of voluntary cooperation is found where leaders are willing to bear the production and organizational costs of producing collective goods and where leaders attempt to convince the rank and file that individual contributions do count. Two types of leaders do this. One is an elite whose main efforts are aimed at producing the good because the benefits to this elite are more than the total costs of the good. Entrepreneur theory stresses a second type of leader—one who produces the good, but also allocates selective incentives to maximize grass roots participation.[16]

Hardin (1982) presents the solution in especially clear terms. A group is privileged (likely to succeed in securing the collective product) if the benefits of collective action are greater than the costs for some (k) efficacious set of individuals in a group. A group is latent (likely to fail) if costs are greater than benefits for all individuals in the group. The critical variable in group success seems to be the actions of the subgroup for whom the good is worth securing, which actions may be independent of the size of the (general) group. Of course, if $k = n$ (the number of individuals in the group), then it is rational for all to cooperate, though in such a case (as Hardin points out) the benefits may be too small to make individual participation rational. One (among several) limitations a cooperating k-group faces is that the subgroup cannot credibly threaten noncooperators not to produce the good (if the good is of real value to them), for nonprovision would hurt the subgroup most of all. But the main point is that collective action can succeed if the ratio of benefits to costs is large enough for some subgroup, even if it remains irrational for most of the remaining members of the group not to contribute to the provision of the good.

Each of these three solutions to efficacy failure finds some measure of success when applied to interest groups. But notice what happens when they are applied to electorates. Consider deontological values, for example: If voters go to the polls primarily to satisfy internal needs, then the outcome of the election is, proportionately, a matter of indifference to them. An election, however, is a method for determining winners from among alternatives. With the ballot a voter supports the alternative he prefers (for whatever reasons, including strategic) as the collective outcome. Internal reasons for voting cut away at the very meaning of an election as a decision rule to settle among alternatives by counting the preferences for these alternatives in the electorate. Citizens moved to participate by internal reasons are missing the main reason to vote in the first place—to support a preferred alternative so that it may win over its rivals. Would, for example, internal rewards even occur if the voting machines were turned off in a district (a failure of efficacy)? Internal rewards are parasitic on the reality of individuals having an effect on joint efforts.

Or consider byproduct theory. Suppose first that coercion is applied to voters. Several countries—Costa Rica, Brazil—administer fines to those who do not vote. Set aside the interesting issue of how coercion restricts the voter's choice to abstain. Are coerced voters efficacious? Obviously not, if they were inefficacious when voting voluntarily. If I have no effect on an outcome, forcing me to participate does not change that fact. Or consider inducements. Individuals in interest groups may find it rational to participate because of benefits provided by the group, not because of their effects on the collective good. Again imagine turning off the voting machines for singleton voters (efficacy failure dramatically illustrated). Is it then rational for individuals to "vote" if the selective incentives provided by, say, the district captain outweigh the costs of going to the polls and pulling the lever (any lever, in this case)?

The answer may be yes, but the yes answer still does not affect the failure of individual efficacy. Electorates are not like interest groups. Voting is a social practice that is consequentialist by definition; and if an individual has no effect on the electoral outcome, there is no point assigning byproducts as quantifiers for support of the collective effort. Byproduct theory in general transforms participation into exchange transactions: benefits provided for services rendered. On the assumption that a critical number of participants is required to produce a collective good, it is rational from both the group and individual perspectives to ensure enough participants through selective incentives. In this sense, byproducts function for interest group supporters in roughly the way coercion does in Prisoners' Dilemma: as providing the conditions needed to allow individuals to cooperate successfully in producing collective benefits. But elections do not produce collective goods. Their purpose is to disclose collective sentiments, either preferences for alternatives (a classical sense of democracy) or checks on leaders (a Madisonian view of democracy). Since no good is produced, there is little logic in inducing any single individual to vote if he has no practicable effect on the election outcome.

The strong consequentialism of voting also sets aside entreprenurial theory as a solution. Suppose once more that efficacy has failed and a leader aims to set things right. The leader cannot absorb the costs of the election and produce the outcome on his own. The thought is absurd on its face. An election result produced by an entrepreneur is not an election result, no matter how beneficial such an outcome might be for an elite. Nor do the imaginative pleadings and inducements of entrepreneurs transform efficacy failure into efficacy success. An electorate mobilized into activity still faces the reality that size diminishes the effect of any single vote on the election outcome.

The differences between an electorate and an interest group are the differences between an unorganized and an organized collective. An electorate is composed of discrete individuals who come together numerically at one point in time. All are in principle equal. No hierarchy divides responsibility or importance. The practice of voting consists of rules (like the secret ballot) that maintain, rather than collapse, the independence of individuals from each other. An interest group, by contrast, is a collection of individuals organized to produce outcomes that are beneficial to at least some, and often all, of its members (as opposed to an election, which produces one of several competing outcomes that is useful primarily, if not exclusively, to the winning faction). Members of an interest group are typically arranged hierarchically. The organizing rules assign different responsibility or importance to different roles and specify how individuals are to be interdependent.

These differences tell us how resolutions of efficacy problems that are successful in organized collectives fail in unorganized collectives. An organized collective can provide or rely on incentives tangential to the purpose of the group (D-terms, coercion, selective incentives, elite needs) that are justifiable if the intended goals are secured. The point of the group is to produce a good that is a consequence of the actions of the group; and the organizing rules need not assume equality of effect and responsibility. An unorganized group like an electorate has no point except to disclose collective preferences. Measures that do not meet the rational needs of this narrow point are senseless; and efforts that deny the starting assumptions of equality do so without the justification that hierarchies provide.

6

The importance of different types of association (organized versus unorganized) in interpreting efficacy and in establishing the success of efforts to avoid efficacy failure discloses a recently well-worn truth: that the size of a group is, in itself, not a decisive consideration in collective action, while the type of group *is* crucial. If we assume that structural considerations do not rule out cooperation, then ongoing relationships are the typical source for the reciprocity in action that makes noncoercive cooperation rational (Hardin 1982). As in iterated Prisoners' Dilemma games, the important contribution of continuing interaction is the establishment of rules and conventions that close the distance among individuals. Put simply, individuals who see each other frequently and continuously will typically establish commitments that noncoercively assure reciprocity. Numerically large societies may make such ongoing relationships less likely. But this is an empirical matter and varies with any number of other factors, such as the kind and extent of communications systems in a society. Numbers alone are not decisive. Social practices are, especially as they form a network of mutual interactions that do not permit individuals to be isolated from each other.

These points locate efficacy in a more general discussion of the forms of association appropriate for various types of collective action. Numerical (unorganized) associations are the conditions on which efficacy failure develops; and so long as collective outcomes are the results of aggregating the separate values of separate units, efficacy remains a problem. Organized associations permit strategies that avoid efficacy failures, mainly because such associations are defined in terms of social practices (shared interests, hierarchies) that connect individuals to one another. Imagine, for example, a political system that represents interests rather than individuals. The effect of discrete individuals on outcomes is no longer a measure of efficacy in such a system. Success at the collective level is a matter of representing those values—in this case, interests—within which individuals are embedded.

Embedding individuals in shared values is a common strategy in addressing efficacy failure. Indeed, the purpose of at least two ameliorative strategies—byproducts and enterpreneurship—is to coalesce individuals by a common effort to appeal even to their own idiosyncratic needs. (Deontological responses can claim group unity on private and perhaps quite different internal incentives, although the public response must be substantially uniform for the strategy to succeed.) Numerical associations are not easily dismissed. Some social forms— voting in modern Western democracies, for example—require discrete entries and arithmetical composition rules. But efficacy failure is an unavoidable consequence of such forms when they are numerically large. Organized associations can solve efficacy problems because they nullify the effects of large numbers by means of social practices.

If a broader perspective is applied to collective choice, we can see that social practices in general address (perhaps natural) separations among individuals. It is easy to see that individuals occupy different time-space locations (though ordinarily these differences are very fine);

and that these different locations can provide different amounts and types of information on which to make rational choices. Conditions of uncertainty can, in general, present different worlds to consider, in the sense that individuals with diminished knowledge can command different slices of information. It seems that, at both abstract and concrete levels, our expectations are that individuals are in asymmetrical relations with one another.

These asymmetries are expanded when different selves apply perspectives to each other. Consider concepts of self and others. At the most rudimentary level, an individual has a concept of himself and of others. Let A and B now stand for any two individuals, suspending for the moment how even facts and basic laws can vary with the locations of individuals. Then the following table represents conceptions in individual identity (the term "identity" distinguishing only the self from its surroundings).

	A	B
A	A's concept of A	A's concept of B
B	B's concept of A	B's concept of B

The rock-bottom content of individual identity is represented by the rows, which contain a concept of self and a concept of other. Now notice how the individual identity expands with the columns, where each individual now has a concept of the self. The expansion produces a new table.

	A	B
A	A's concept of A in terms of B's concept of A	A's concept of B in terms of B's concept of A
B	B's concept of A in terms of A's concept of B	B's concept of B in terms of A's concept of B

The rows represent a concept of self and other enriched by the other's concept of self. But now there is nothing to prevent turning again to the columns and getting a further enrichment, where (1) A's concept of A is mediated by B's concept of A in terms of A's concept of B, and (2) B's concept of B is mediated by A's concept of B in terms of A's concept of A. And so on.

This infinite regress of conceptions is paralleled in game theory. Individual A must calculate what individual B will do, which calculation by A includes what B is thinking about A. So A's thoughts of B must include B's thoughts of A. But then B's thoughts of A must include A thinking of what B thinks of A. And so on, ad infinitum. Suppose that it is rational for A to defect from cooperative action only if B and C cooperate. If the three individuals are rationally identical, then the expected symmetry requires B to defect only if A and C cooperate, and C to defect only if A and B cooperate. Such rational calculations are infinitely regressive because the individuals are separate minds each trying to encapsulate the others. But the efforts to encapsulate others fail. Reflective and separate individuals elude the conceptual specifications placed on them by others.[17] Even perfect information fails to provide identical or uniform perspectives among isolated individuals who are self-defining and (the language here is inadequate) other-defining.

It is in the context of such asymmetries that efforts to identify individuals in networks of associations must be understood. Those social practices that lead to successful collective action reduce the natural asymmetries among individuals. Social exchange theory, for example, is often (Hardin 1982) distinguished from markets by the presence of continuing encounters, which are sharply contrasted with discrete market transactions. The continuity in social exchange is the resource for rendering individuals in symmetrical terms, or, in simpler language, for making oneself like the other. This symmetry is sometimes represented by the provision of reciprocal sanctions, where one allows sanctions over the self in order to have sanctions over the other. One acquires through such practices a confidence that the other will act in predictable ways. The rules so generated provide a concept of self not controlled by the other, but expressed in the practices shared by individuals.

7

One of the most intriguing features of participation problems is the importance of decisive individuals in resolution patterns. Prisoners' Dilemma fulfills the rational requirements of the decisive (or, in this case, dominant) individual in the exploitive cell. Arrow's decisive individual is a formal satisfaction of transitivity. Efficacy is no problem for any individual dominating electoral outcomes. If Arrow's "dictator" appellation is expanded to its full use in ordinary language, a decisive figure in any group will successfully avoid rational breakdowns between at least *one* individual and *all* by effectively enforcing his own values as the group outcome. It is one small irony that decisiveness is, for the dictator, even more generalizable than unanimity as a solution to rational problems; for agreement in Prisoners' Dilemma still produces a suboptimal outcome, and individual voters in unanimous elections will still find efficacy a function of the size of the electorate.

Decisiveness, however, is faulty on two grounds. First, it is a fractured resolution of rational discontinuities, successful for the decisive figure while still denying rational continuity for dominated individuals. Second, it fails the tests of morality drawn from moral concepts found (in a more or less unexamined state) at the background level in the problems. Think, on the second point, why the discontinuities represented by large-electorate voting, Prisoners' Dilemma, and Arrow's theorem are problems. At one level, more clearly represented by Prisoners' Dilemma than by Arrow's theorem, the problem is that a rational choice produces an irrational outcome. But a deeper explanation is also possible. All individuals are morally equal in the starting conditions of the problems: each has identical rational capacities and no individual has an overriding claim on the collective outcome (though individual entries can be counted more than once in Arrow's machinery). The problems are failures of this equality. The ineffectual individuals in large-electorate voting have no rational incentives to vote because all are equal (and thus inefficacious). The exploited individual in Prisoners' Dilemma games and the individuals dominated by Arrow's dictator are victims of inequality. In all cases, the sub-rosa moral concept of equality is either the source of the problem or the standard against which the problem is defined. The simple decisiveness that solves the problems is dismissed because it violates equality assumptions. (Otherwise, dictators would be a satisfactory solution.)

The moral tests of collective choice, however, require a different type of individual. Moral agents are autonomous and rational individuals who choose on a concept of interests that extends at least partially to others. This expanded sense of an individual is well-developed in both contract theory and utilitarianism. Harsanyi (1975) employs such identification to justify on Bayesian calculations the utilitarian decision rule of maximizing average utility. Kohlberg (1980) uses the extended individual in reverse-role morality, elevating to stage six the individual who decides collective outcomes by giving an equal regard to each individual's interests. Hare (1965, 1981) specifies the meaning of utility in terms of reverse-role morality. And Rawls's "original position" individuals are collective creatures deciding for the well-being of everyone, because the veil of ignorance denies them status as discrete individuals with isolated interests. The problem for collective choice is that such extended individuals do not easily fit aggregation rules, an anomaly represented by the commonly held thought that moral choices are not *counted* to reach an outcome. Put simply, a preponderance of preferences from separate, atomistic individuals is not necessarily a moral result.

Solutions to efficacy failure redefine the relationships of individuals to collective outcomes. Individuals in organized associations are no longer countable, discrete units. They are embedded in the constitutive rules that establish reciprocity among individuals. These changes shift the metaphor of *caused* effects in efficacy to one of reciprocal and even simultaneous actions. Like the relationships among functional variables (e.g., the solar system, the ratio of gas to temperature and volume expressed in $v = t/p$, economic events in general equilibrium theory), individuals in organized associations are no longer antecedent units combining to produce an effect. They are rather constituent members of a social practice within which individuals are as easily effects as causes, and may even be no more than the residual categories of social structures. It is easy to see that the atomism of methodological individualism has given way to a more holistic view of individuals. It is also clear that this expanded sense of an individual is more comfortably attuned to the extended demands of moral reasoning. Individuals defined by the rules of social practices are bound to each other by the defining categories of organized association. They are no longer the discrete units that ordinary egoism requires. It is at once encouraging and intriguing that the exit routes away from efficacy failure are the entrance paths to the moral discourse suggested by background concepts in collective choice.

The most interesting implications of efficacy success, however, are in the effects such success has on aggregation. If efficacy can be resolved only by defining individuals in terms of social practices, it is not clear that arithmetical composition rules can be used to reach collective outcomes. Organized associations, unlike random collections of individuals (e.g., pedestrians on a street corner), are governed by rules and interests; and, to the degree that individualism is subordinated to the organized unity of a group, counting heads is less important than expressing interests. It is easy to exaggerate the point. But one of the casualties of efforts to ensure efficacy may be the arithmetical composition rules on which preference-aggregation democracies are founded.

8

The problems of rational continuity in collective choice revive the issue raised by the contract theorists of the seventeenth and eighteenth centuries: how to justify authority on the acceptance of individuals as moral equals. None of the contract theorists addresses the specific failures of combination rules and efficacy, though Hobbes discusses assurance and coordination problems. But the moral problem of conflict between rational individuals and collective authority (suggested in collective choice theory by the rejection of exploitation and dominance) is treated in all contract theories of the state.

Each of the three main contract theorists—Hobbes, Locke, and Rousseau—negotiates the relationships between individual autonomy and collective authority in different ways. Hobbes assigns virtually complete authority to the sovereign (reserving to each individual only the right to preserve the self). The sovereign represents by definition the interests of each citizen; for the sovereign has authority to define right and wrong, truth and falsity. Liberty depends on the absence of law. Locke tells us that all individuals have rights to freedom and property. These natural rights are carried into the political society and prohibit state regulations in the areas they delimit. Rousseau reconciles individual liberty and authority through the general will, which is (among other things) an instrument to render collective regulation morally identical to self-direction. The liberty of individuals is in this way compatible with authority so long as the authority is that of the general will. Such authority is without limits.

The breakdowns of collective choice seem to combine—unsuccessfully—a number of ideas in contract theory. The negative liberty assumed by Hobbes and Locke is especially influential. Individuals are free so long as they are unimpeded by others or the social structures in which they act. This sense of liberty complements the isolation of individuals found in the states of nature elaborated by Hobbes and Locke and in the starting conditions of collective choice theory. The Lockean use of natural rights is also found in collective choice theory, although without the language or even (perhaps) an awareness of the influence. The values assigned to individuals remain unchanged in all variations of the games and theorems, and any violation of the assignment is considered a failure of collective action. In Arrow's theorem, for example, the descriptions of individuals found in the background assumptions (autonomy, equal regard, equal effect) and in the theorem itself (rationality) are fixed, not to be changed under any circumstances. That these values may reasonably be given a different interpretation by virtue of establishing collective life is never considered. This Lockean view of individuals leads to effective checks on collective regulation and is represented by the partitions that solve Prisoners' Dilemma problems: it shields certain practices from collective action. But that there are problems in combining such values should hardly be surprising, for the point to natural rights is to remove certain values from collective action.

Rousseau suggests the exit routes away from these problems. The general will requires a distinction between public and private selves (Barry 1967; Dagger 1981). Individuals expressing preferences in terms of self-interest cannot produce a collective outcome that can legitimately regulate individual action. If, however, individuals identify themselves as members of the political society, then they will express the common interest or general good in their preferences. This public state of individualism is not balanced against self-interest. The individual is instead redefined as collective; and as a member of the collective, the individual is (logically) equal to all others. This public equality is communicated in laws that are impartial, giving all individuals an equal regard.

Note that the general goods which individuals select as collective units in Rousseau's theory are best viewed as laws or procedures. Even public goods are not comfortable with Rousseau's solution; for any public good can in some circumstances fail tests of impartiality. One can, for example, exclude individuals from many goods, such as natural defense, sea lanes, etc., that are regarded normally as nonexcludable; or one can imagine social changes that will make even rigidly nonexcludable goods as divisible, and thus marketable, items, such as bottled air instead of "natural" air in severely polluted regions. Rousseau's attempt to reconcile liberty and authority requires that the outcomes of collective choice be in the interests of all members of the political society. Many laws meet this test. But the more likely candidates for a collective interest would seem to be the rules by means of which individuals act as members of the collective state. The promise in Rousseau's political philosophy is that individuals can be redefined in terms of some set of criteria that can address the claims of rational agents already defined as members of a liberal community.

NOTES

1. Economists have a variety of market solutions to this problem; although based on conditions unlike those found in Arrow's theorem. Microeconomics, for example, on the assumption of individual indifference curves, offers the Edgeworth-Bowley box for two individuals.

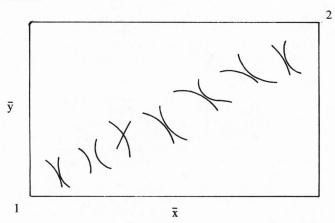

Any point of tangency between individual 1's indifference curves and individual 2's indifference curves (plotted within the feasibility space of x and y, or the amount of x and y available) is Pareto optimal. The contract curve is the collection of Pareto points in the box.

2. One also sees another point to Alice's complaints to the caterpillar about her expansions and contractions in size. "'I'm afraid I ca'n't put it more clearly,' Alice replied, very politely, 'for I ca'n't understand it myself, to begin with; and being so many different sizes in a day is very confusing.'" In Lewis Carroll, *Alice's Adventures in Wonderland* (New York: W. W. Norton, 1971), ch. 5.

3. Georg Henrik von Wright, *Explanation and Understanding* (Ithaca, N.Y.: Cornell University Press, 1971), ch. 2, for a helpful discussion of conditional causality. See also von Wright's intriguing and controversial case for retroactive causation, same chapter. Brian Barry outlines the importance of allies in being able to affect outcomes in "Is it Better to be Powerful or Lucky?" *Political Studies* (1980).

4. Douglas Rae, "Decision-Rules and Individual Values in Constitutional Choice," *American Political Science Review* 63 (1969): 40–56.

5. A helpful discussion of this point can be found in Peter Fishburn and Steven Brams, "Efficacy, Power and Equity in Approval Voting," *Public Choice* 3 (1981): 425–34.

6. Peter Berger, "Mediating Structures: The Missing Link of Politics," *Commonsense* (summer 1978); Berger and Richard Neuhaus, *To Empower People* (Washington, D.C.: American Enterprise Institute, 1977).

7. The rotation may be by lot. See Robert Dahl, *After the Revolution?* (New Haven, Conn.: Yale University Press, 1970), pp. 149–53. Though, as Dahl and others have pointed out, rotation involving any significant number of people wil require an unreasonable length of time to complete.

8. Thus, as Riker has always maintained, creating cyclical majorities is a rational strategem if one wants to maintain the status quo. See Riker and Ordeshook, *Positive Political Theory,* and Riker, *Liberalism Against Populism.*

9. Steve Brams and Morton Davis in "The 3/2's Rule in Presidential Campaigning," *American Political Science Review* 68 (March 1974): 113–34. Barry, in "Is it Better to be Powerful or Lucky?", argues persuasively that pivotal individuals are not decisive individuals. But the argument is not entirely successful. An individual can be decisive, indeed powerful, because of circumstances, finding himself, say, in the position (through no effort on his part) of being able to determine an election by his vote. Though power is, in general, best conceived as a capability rather than as a pivot, surely we would allow for the possibility of circumstantial power. Perhaps pivotal individuals are momentarily powerful because lucky.

10. Ponder the well-known cases of Uranus and Vulcan. Throughout the nineteenth century, it was known that, because of its shape, the planet Uranus had an orbit that was wrong according to Newtonian mechanics. But these data were not taken as a falsification of Newtonian astronomical principles. Rather Adams and Leverrier postulated the existence of Neptune as the unknown factor causing Uranus' eccentricities. Telescopic observations later confirmed the existence of Neptune, thus vindicating Newtonian principles. But when irregularities of Mercury's orbit were later explained by postulating Vulcan, the postulated planet never appeared. Though Newtonian mechanics were maintained with other explanations (until micro events were observed), it is in general not at all clear how rational decisions are to be reached on retention or abandonment of basic principles, in large part because verifiability, falsifiability, and confirmability each have substantial flaws. See, on many of these topics, Anthony O'Hear's wide-ranging discussion in *Karl Popper* (Boston: Routledge & Kegan Paul, 1980).

11. Plato, *Republic,* Bloom translation (New York: Basic Books, 1968), pp. 37–44.

12. Riker and Ordeshook, *Positive Political Theory,* p. 109, for what the literature has come to call "D-terms."

13. Terry M. Moe, "A Calculus of Group Membership," *American Journal of Political Science* 24 (November 1980): 593–632. Some have assumed that preferences exist for political action as such, and involvement satisfies these preferences. See James B. Kau and Paul H. Rubin, "Public Interest Lobbies: Membership and Influence," *Public Choice* 34 (1979): 45–54. But, again, this assumption ignores the strong consequentialism of many political practices. Changing the decision rule from expected utility to other rules, such as Hurwicz's coefficient of optimism or a Savage regret criterion, faces the same objection. For example, a rational use of the regret criterion that includes awareness of nonefficacy will surely minimize the regret of not participating. See, for an attempt to salvage voting through a regret criterion, John Ferejohn and Morris Fiorina, "The Paradox of Not Voting: A Decision Theoretic Analysis," *American Political Science Review* 68 (June

1974): 525–36. I see nothing in value change—from teleological to intrinsic, from self- to other-directed—that will avoid efficacy failure. As Olson puts it in considering whether egoism is the source of efficacy failure, "A man who tried to hold back a flood with a pail would probably be considered more of a crank than a saint, even by those he was trying to help." In *The Logic of Collective Action,* p. 109.

14. Developed by Olson, *The Logic of Collective Action*.

15. I am avoiding the path of easy virtue represented by "subjective efficacy" pursued most recently by Moe in his otherwise admirable piece, "A Calculus of Group Membership." Here the problem of efficacy is avoided by relaxing the assumption of perfect information to produce believed, but not real, efficacy. Since I am concerned to discuss the reality of rational continuity and do not try to explain why individuals participate in groups, efficacy will be maintained as objective.

16. Norman Frolich, Joe A. Oppenheimer, and Oran R. Young, *Political Leadership and Collective Goods* (Princeton, N.J.: Princeton University Press, 1971). See also the overview in Frohlich and Oppenheimer, *Modern Political Economy* (Englewood Cliffs, N.J.: Prentice-Hall, 1978).

17. George Herbert Mead, *Mind, Self, and Society* (Chicago: University of Chicago Press, 1934). See also the regresses delineated by R. D. Laing in *Self and Others* (London: Tavistock Publications, 1969).

5

Rationality and Reasoning

1

The vast literature commenting on Arrow's theorem has at one time or another taken on each of the conditions and axioms. Nondictatorship was rejected early on with the observation that all moral choices are dictatorial (Little 1952), then abandoned again with a later attempt to justify the dictator on Rawls' difference principle as the individual who has more to lose in the collective outcome (Strasnick 1976). Pareto, that most innocuous of conditions, has been judged inadequate when morally oppressive values are represented (Little 1952). Any cognitive theory of value will dismiss universal domain. The independence condition has been set aside by a tradition of exchange theory as rich and interesting as the literature within Arrow's conditions (Buchanan and Tullock 1962). And binary comparisons have been replaced (although Arrow's problem has not been avoided) by any number of alternative scales (Riker 1982, for survey) and even a form of global comparison (MacKay 1980).

The one condition that has escaped close and sustained examination is rationality. This neglect is understandable in a number of ways. There is first the minimalist form of the concept. Connectivity and transitivity specify rationality in Arrow's theorem, and a less substantive specification is hard to imagine. Then there is the cogent force of the components. Surely individuals must prefer one of two alternatives or be indifferent as to which is selected (*aRb*, *bRa*, or *aIb* for all *a,b*). And surely in any triplicate of ordered pairs, transitivity must obtain (if *aRb*, and *bRc*, then *aRc*). The entire tradition of neoclassical economic theory is based on such a version of rationality (and other similarly minimal conditions, e.g., nonsatiation). Arrow's concept of rationality, in short, seems to be the least objectionable of his conditions and axioms. Indeed, the concept of rationality used in the theorem has achieved paradigmatic status, remaining fixed as a background principle while other components of the theorem are tested and varied.[1]

Yet the rationality axioms are among the components that prove the impossibility results by demonstrating how individuals are unlike collectives. An individual ranking alternatives on binary comparisons can always produce reflexive, connected, and transitive orderings. It follows that collective orderings can also be reflexive, connected, and transitive if collectives are like individuals (which the theorem assumes in applying these conditions to collective orderings). But this paradigm of rationality cannot be successfully transferred from the individual to the collective level through any known aggregation device (or collective choice rule) without violating one of the equity conditions of the theorem. Given the importance of the rationality axioms in establishing the proof, it is reasonable to ask if rational choice is itself a concept that ought to be addressed as a way of elaborating and solving the problem that Arrow's theorem represents.

The version of rationality accepted in the theorem, moreover, contributes to the contradictions in liberal democracy that the proof exposes. Rational choice for Arrow is always individual choice, an ordering of alternatives from the isolated perspectives of discrete individuals. The theorem demonstrates the logical breakdowns that occur when these separate orderings are combined arithmetically. One of the lessons communicated by the proof is that separate preferences cannot be aggregated on the equity conditions of liberalism while maintaining the minimalist rationality found in the theorem. Any examination and reconstruction of Arrow's concept of rationality must be sensitive to the natural hostility between liberal impulses to shield individuals from collective influence and the needs of preference-aggregation democracies to combine individual orderings to reach a collective outcome. There is no reason to anticipate that both liberal shields and arithmetical composition rules can be maintained in any theory of collective choice. Arrow's concept of rationality, however, may be the best place to begin exploring these contradictions in liberal democracy.

2

One of the first signs that the Arrow rationality axioms may be flawed is found in the difficulties that all ordering models of rationality have in using moral values. The failure of ordering rationalities in moral discourse is especially important in Arrow's theorem, for the proof depends on a number of moral statements framed within liberal perspectives. If the version of rationality used in Arrow's theorem cannot express moral values, then changes in rationality may be demanded as a way of accommodating the moral expectations found in the proof.

The anomalous effects of moral values on standard models of rationality are encountered first in Pascal's wager. Recall that an individual is asked to consider two alternatives. In one, God exists. In the other, He does not. The wager is developed on the supposition that the value attached to the existence of God so far surpasses the negative alternative that, no matter how low the probability of God's existence, the bet that he exists is the better wager. In more recent language, we would say that the extremely high expected value of one alternative overrides the probabilities assigned to each alternative, thus nullifying the equilibrium sought between expected values and probabilities in rational decisions. Or, consider von Neumann-Morgenstern tests (Luce and Raiffa 1957) when peremptory values are introduced. The tests were conceived as a way of settling on cardinal scales unique to an individual. The individual is asked to choose between the certainty of b versus variable probabilities of receiving a or c when he orders the three alternatives as $a > b > c$. An equilibrium value of p is defined as $BI(p)$ a, $(1 - p)$ c, which then can define the intervals between a, b, and c. (When an equation is solved for p, numbers are assigned to each alternative.) If the preference for a is strong enough, however, an individual may always prefer a chance for a (no matter how small the probability) instead of the certainty of b. The absence of an equilibrium point because of a strong endorsement of one's preference is one way of stating the overriding character of some moral commitments, and perhaps even the incommensurability of some alternatives (or, with Arrow's conditions, the absence of connectivity).

These anomalies may suggest that certain types of values, those that are moral or technical, may require a different mode of expression than that found in rational choice theory. It is instructive to see how various decision rules accommodate moral values. For example, a widely used (Bayesian) formulation of a participation decision is

$$P(O_i)\, U(O_i) - P(O_k)\, U(O_k) > 0 \text{ for } i \neq k$$
$$\rightarrow i > k$$

where the probability (P) and utility (U) differences between one action (i) and an alternative (k) affecting an outcome (O) express the efficacy and desirability of i versus k. Now, suppose concern for the morality of i versus k. Again, a standard move is simply to add a new utlity function, for example

$$P(O_i)\, U(O_i) - P(O_k)\, U(O_k) + (U_i - U_k) > 0 \text{ for } i \neq k$$
$$\rightarrow i > k \text{ (again)}$$

where $(U_i - U_k)$ represents the moral factor in calculating on i versus k.[2]

The addition of moral factors can affect (sometimes dramatically) the remaining terms in a decision rule. Moe (1980) has indicated some of the ways in which marginal cost and benefit curves can undergo a shift as a result of purposive incentives. The contributor to, say, Planned Parenthood, may be willing to incur greater net costs if he or she is receiving benefits as a moral supporter of the goals of the organization (and, as a consequence of moral support, requires less in the way of selective incentives). In the formulation above, the terms to the left of $(U_i - U_k)$ can be zero or even have a negative value, so long as the moral function is positive and greater than the negative difference between those terms and zero.

But the moral factor is nothing more than an additive function to be given some conventional weight. The same strategy for employing moral values can be expected in other decision rules, for example the rule of dominance is used in Prisoners' Dilemma. Let a_1 and a_2 represent two alternatives, and s_1, s_2, s, s_4 represent the possible futures or outcomes of the alternatives. Then if

	s_1	s_2	s_3	s_4
a_1	10	10	9	7
a_2	0	5	9	5

we say that a_1 dominates a_2 and, accordingly, is the rationally preferable alternative. The only possible way to enter a moral term in such a matrix is to assign greater weight to one of the alternatives. For example, a determination that s_3 is a moral outcome can cause a reevaluation of the weights in $s_1 \ldots s_4$ so that $a_2 > a_1$ (perhaps even on a peremptory status for s_3). One wants to a ask, however, if moral values are successfully and reasonably treated with such strategies, and if not, whether the failure to express moral values indicates how rational choice can be modified to accommodate at least the liberal morality found in Arrow's theorem and perhaps even to identify exit routes away from Arrow's conclusions.

3

One way to address the issue of moral considerations in collective choice theory is to identify formal features of moral choice and examine their effects when they are introduced to collective choice theory. Two have been elaborated and defended in moral philosophy. One is a recognition of the interests of others. A second is the use of reasons in choice.[3] The first consideration represents commonly held convictions, from Kant to Rawls, that egoism is not an entirely satisfactory expression of moral choice, that a moral choice must represent the interests of others as well as the self. The second consideration acknowledges that moral choice is not simply a preference, but a reasoned ranking of alternatives. A simple weighting of utilities will not express these two features of morality, although other formal considerations can be used to introduce this conception of moral choice to collective choice theory.

An ambitious effort has been made to express the first formal consideration, the interests of others, through "extended sympathy." The interests of others can be represented in preference orderings. Extended sympathy, however, formally expresses distinctions between self and other-oriented interests. The basic idea in the exercise is simple, although the development of the idea in collective choice theory is exceedingly complex. First, alternatives are ordered pairs of a social state and a named individual, e.g., $(x,1)$. Second, individuals rank alternatives by considering their own and others' welfare in the social states. On these larger considerations, rationality and equity are to combine successfully in collective outcomes. In one well-regarded test (Suppes 1966), a state is more just than an alternative state (to an individual) if (a) he prefers to be himself in that state rather than to be another in the alternative state, and also prefers to be the other in that state rather than the other in the alternative state; *or* (b) he prefers to be himself in that state rather than the other in the alternative state, and also prefers to be the other in that state rather than himself in the alternative state. Let x and y represent states. Then, with individuals 1 and 2, if (on a partial strict ordering) 1 = $(x,1) > (y,2)$ and $(x,2) > (y,2)$, and 2: $(x,2) > (y,1)$ and $(x,1) > (y,1)$ condition (a) is satisfied. If 1: $(x,1) > (y,2)$ and $(x,2) > (y,1)$, and 2: $(x,2) > (y,1)$ and $(x,1) > (y,2)$, condition (b) is satisfied. State x is more just than state y on either set of profiles, for both individuals 1 and 2.

Many technical problems occur in extended sympathy. Among these are that the number of profiles can rapidly rise to impractical levels (even above, with two individuals and two alternatives, there are 4! × 4!, or 576 possible profiles without counting indifference); Arrow-like cycles and the paradox of the Paretian liberal can still occur; and, given the increased number of ways to conceal true preferences, it is likely that the rules used to reach collective outcomes are still manipulable with extended sympathy. But the main difficulty is that even when individuals make identical judgments [as above: If $(x,i) P_i (y,i)$, then for all $j(x,i) P_j(y,i)$], it remains impossible to generate a collective outcome that is both rational and moral.

Look first at complete orderings. Suppose a sympathetic ranking, where 1: $(x,2) > (y,1) > (x,1) > (y,2)$, and 2: $(x,1) > (y,2) > (x,2) > (y,1)$. Then, although each individual prefers x to y when putting himself in the place of the other, making x more just than y on Suppes' test, $y > x$ on Pareto (each prefers y to x for themselves). Is this possible? Of course. Imagine (using Sen's paradox, 1970) that individual 1 is a libertarian, 2 a socialist. Say that x is a social state with moderate liberty, y is a state with effective welfare. Say also that 1 is a citizen of state y unable to benefit fully from the liberties of x, and that 2 is a citizen of x, unable to benefit fully from the socialism of y. It would be perfectly rational under these conditions for 1 to prefer to be citizen 2 in x, and for 2 to prefer to be citizen 1 in y. Yet each can also prefer their own states over being an alien in the other's state. And this conflict between sympathy and Pareto occurs on an identity axiom, where each individual puts himself in the preference structure of the other.

The way out of this difficulty has been well-traveled by moral philosophers: individuals assume the subjective features of others in extended sympathy, not just the preference structure (Hare 1965, 1981; Harsanyi 1975). Individuals then have identical extended preferences, as 1: $(x,2) > (y,1) > (x,1) > (y,2)$, and 2: $(x,2) > (y,1) > (x,1) > (y,2)$. Here the two individuals both agree on a welfare ranking, in this case that 2 is better off in his state, x, than 1 is in his state, y (libertarians may be more unhappy in socialist states than socialists in moderate libertarian states). The subjective features of each individual are successfully taken into account by the other, even though each individual prefers different states for himself (1: $y > x$; 2: $x > y$). Identical extended preferences rank social states in terms of the welfare of each individual in that social state as seen by that individual. Ordinal interpersonal comparisons of value are needed for such a ranking. But this may be a small cost to pay for consistency between rationality and equity. Arrow (1977) has claimed consistency among his (revised) conditions with the use of ordinal interpersonal comparisons (co-ordinal invariance).

But it is not clear that the costs of extended sympathy are even possible to pay, and even if paid, that they bring the desired consistency. Assuming the subjective features of the other can be interpreted in two ways: what is it like for me to be you versus what is it like for you to be you. The first is satisfied by one individual taking on the subjective equipment of another while maintaining some sense of his former self. But it is difficult to specify what is being maintained, and, in any case, the subjective transfer is incomplete and the conflict between sympathy and Pareto remains possible. The second interpretation requires that one individual lose himself completely in another to measure welfare, a submersion that may not permit cross-comparisons between the two individuals if the initial differences in subjective structure are great enough.[4]

Even if such truly strange and demanding exercises are possible, however, a unanimity on welfare orderings does not compel unanimity on welfare niches (Gauthier, 1978). Both individuals in the example above of extended preferences agree that 2 is better off in x than 1 in y. But it does not follow from this that 1 would prefer to be 2 in x. Recall Mill's observation that it is "better to be Socrates dissatisfied than a fool satisfied" (1971, p. 20). In the movie *Charly*, the recently developed genius may have suffered real distress at higher intellectual levels without wanting to be again the more contented idiot from which he emerged (example from Barry and Hardin 1982). Or, unhappy libertarians still may not want to be contented socialists and distressed socialists may not want be satisfied libertarians. For each person to be indifferent about who they are, another extension of preferences is required, e.g., 1: $(x,1,2) > (y,1,2)$, and 2: $(x,1,2) > (y,1,2)$. Individuals 1 and 2 are now completely identical, in the sense that $x > y$ and $1 = 2$ (it does not matter if one is individual 1 or 2). Welfare and preferability are collapsed to a single scale. But unanimity is purchased (at last) at the cost of individuality and on condition that the two individuals are nearly equivalent sentient beings in the first place.

Each progressive extension of sympathy is an extension of individual identity. Retaining one's subjective preferences when placing oneself in the circumstances of another fails. An acceptance of the other's subjective preferences is required. But this acceptance measures only welfare, not preferability. To secure agreement on preferability requires a complete identity of individuals. The collective sense of an individual needed to ensure rational continuity between one and everyone is in place. But the exercise not only strains credulity, it prompts a question raised by all efforts to extend individual identity—Why aggregate preference orderings if individuals are no longer identifiable as separate units?

4

The second formal feature of moral reasoning, *reasons,* discloses additional conflicts between arithmetical composition rules and moral choice. Let the logical form of a conditional represent a reasoned ordering, $x \to a > b$, where certain conditions, x, must obtain if an ordering between alternatives is to be rationally established. Two effects occur at the aggregate level with the use of a conditional form: partitioning and fusions. Arrow's theorem provides the framework for the demonstration. Imagine first a disconnected society, one where the conditions for rational orderings are segments disjoined, for the moment, simply on whatever considerations produce conditions for orderings. We can at first leave uninterpreted the ordering conditions, representing them with notations x, y, z. Then,

$$(1) \quad x \to (aRbRc)$$
$$(2) \quad y \to (bRcRa)$$
$$(3) \quad z \to (cRaRb)$$

Or each of the orderings, (1), (2), and (3), is established on the terms of each respective condition, x, y, z. Hypothetical case: a set of proposals for managing one aspect of our energy problems is introduced for collective resolution. The issue is a simple (and familiar) one. Available oil does not meet current demands. The proposals are these: a = reduce consumption; b = increase domestic production; c = increase imports. For illustrative purposes, assume what is almost never the case in the real world (but an assumption in Arrow's theorem), that the alternatives (a, b, c) are mutually exclusive. Society is now asked to settle on a policy, or social ordering, of the three alternatives without trade-offs among any of them.

The standard, unconditional outcome for such orderings in the tradition of combined collective choice is the cyclical majority: no ordering can be established for the entire society. But if the validating conditions express a warranted heterogeneity, then a way out of the cyclical majority may be available. The path out of the cycle requires the recognition of a distinction between logical dominance and rational dominance. To simplify matters, suppose two clusters of conditions warrant the orderings of alternatives. Conditions x and y each support a different ordering (as represented by the subscripts, the notational system now following from Strasnick [1976, 1977]):

(1) aR_xb, bR_ya
(2) bR_xc, bR_yc
(3) aR_xc, cR_ya

The pattern of orderings expressed by (1), (2), and (3) duplicates Arrow's combination paradox with one change: instead of individuals, the subscripts now represent justifying conditions. The orderings can also be expressed as:

$$x \rightarrow (aRbRc)$$
$$y \rightarrow (bRcRa)$$

Representative interpretations of x and y can be introduced without difficulty. Say that reduced consumption is justified ($a > c$) when alternative energy sources are readily available and weather is mild (no suffering caused by extreme cold, etc.). Increased imports are justified ($c > a$) when there are no alternative energy sources and weather is harsh. To round out the picture, assume that x and y both contain a clause that permits a priority status for $b > c$, say that new reserves of fuel can be obtained with minimum government support of industry.

The orderings in (1), (2), and (3) produce a decisive ordering when combined, in this case, a over c; for the combination of orderings in (1) is $a—I \rightarrow b$, in (2) it is $b—R \rightarrow c$ (on Pareto), and for (3) it is $a—B \rightarrow c$ (on transitivity). If x and y were individuals, x would be the dictator in standard Arrow fashion ($a > c$ dominates $c > a$ in the collective outcome.) But x and y have a rational relationship, unlike the arithmetical patterns of the combined orderings. Suppose that condition y, as a matter of general argument, is persuasive over condition x. On inductive reasoning, the evidence strongly favors condition y as the overriding set of considerations: no effective alternative energy sources exist, the winters look to be harsh, and so on, while no evidence supports condition x. Then, on rational considerations, $y > x$. But on the combined orderings, x logically dominates y as the decisive set. Since $y > x$ on inductive reasoning, and $x > y$ on logical combination, two reasoning systems exist.

Suppose now not only that $x \neq y$, but that both x and y are valid and unconnected conditions. Think now of a society heterogeneous on these two conditions, either spatially (e.g., geographical regionalism) or temporally (disjoined policy needs over time). Condition x and y express then an arrangement of conditions justifying different, separate orderings. We have, on the earlier pattern of orderings

$$(1) \quad x \rightarrow (aRb); \quad y \rightarrow (bRa)$$
$$(2) \quad x \rightarrow (bRc); \quad y \rightarrow (bRc)$$
$$(3) \quad x \rightarrow (aRc); \quad y \rightarrow (cRa)$$

Or, both $a > b$ and $b > a$ on their respective conditions; $a > c$ and $c > a$ similarly on, respectively, x and y; and only $b > c$ is a single expression of social choice. The conditions that justify the preference orderings prohibit adding or combining the orderings. Only the satisfaction of the Pareto condition (a logical expression of spontaneous as well as unanimous democracy) produces a social outcome where all choose one or another of the alternatives. Where the Pareto condition is not satisfied, the society requires a variety of different orderings, each valid on local conditions.

The social choice in such pluralistic settings cannot be a single ordering. A compound directive is required if heterogeneity is to be respected. Say (hypothetically) that the sunbelt areas of a society are rich in alternative energy sources, thus fulfilling condition x. Say also that the northern sectors have both harsh weather and restricted energy alternatives, or condition y. Then a rational rule expressing energy alternatives can be, "Reduce consumption in the sunbelt areas and increase imports in the northern sectors." Stated as a formal directive, do (or give priority to) a when x; and do (or give priority to) c when y. The policy is not simply consumer choice. It is a directive policy, variable with justifying conditions. Indeed, conditional orderings can generate social partitionings—one solution to the coordination problem of Prisoners' Dilemma.

The recognition of compound directives formed from rational, rather than logical, dominance, articulates more fully the nature and limitations of Arrow's theorem. In particular, the strong fusing effects are put into relief. The general method of aggregation aims to combine separate orderings into a single expression. In voting, the metaphor is familiar: society, thougha collection of separate preferences, speaks with a single voice. But the utilitarian collapse of multiple values to a single value is also, in Arrow's theorem, a reduction of reason to logic. The decisive set is a logical rather than a rational dominance. A society pluralistic across justifying conditions, one where different reasons support different preferences in local areas, resists a single ordering on rational grounds. That the theorem imposes one anyway reveals again the indifference of the combination rules to conditional orderings. The compound directive, on the other hand, represents the priority of rational systems in societies heterogeneous on supporting reasons.

The use of compound directives avoids combination breakdowns by avoiding combinations. Compound directives are rationally mandated when good and strong reasons divide a society; and the presence of divisive reasons can sometimes favor compound directives on rules of equity, like "Respect local values." Any beginning student of politics knows that a single policy line must sometimes be imposed on disparate views, both for rational and moral reasons. But not always. For example, the strategy of "disjointed incrementalism" contains a strong emphasis on segmented policies:

> As an illustration, we may ask again whether anyone can say that he prefers, for example, unemployment to inflation or inflation to unemployment when they confict? Some individuals think they know which they prefer, but it can quickly be shown that they cannot arrange even two such values in order of priority. Almost everyone prefers unemployment to inflation if unemployment is small enough and inflation great enough. Yet almost everyone prefers inflation to unemployment if unemployment is great enough and inflation is

small enough. One's preferences between unemployment and inflation can therefore be expressed as a set of trades or as a set of terms on
which one is willingly exchanged for the other.[5]

Or, in addition to simple trade-offs, a rational ranking of alternatives
can follow the basic form of a conditional: $x \to (a > b)$, $y \to (b > a)$.
The incrementalist strategy is not unique in accepting conditional orderings. Indeed, the unconditional rankings of Arrow's theorem seem
anomalous; the use of conditions, by contrast, appears more nearly the
rational norm. The description of collective outcomes as a package of
items that are (a) conditionally justified and (b) connected internally
on meta-rules recognizing local differences, is at least as familiar a
sight in the public choice literature as the single-ordering outcomes of
Arrow's theorem.

Note also that the strategies of bargaining, vote-trading, logrolling—
generally, those approaches that rank alternatives on payoffs from
exchanges—are also accommodated by conditional orderings. An individual, for example, could prefer $a > b$ if x and $b > a$ if y, where x and
y are items traded with other individuals. The notion of tradable items
exogenous to, and decisive for, the initial orderings fits comfortably
with the logic of conditionals. The strategy of bargaining (etc.) has been
richly explored in a literature competitive in depth and interest with
that of Arrow's theorem itself. The strategy's differences with Arrow's
approach—violations of the independence condition and binary comparisons, the reliance on cardinal scales, the problem of interpersonal
comparisons of value—have also received generous attention. The concern here has not been with the problems of this major alternative to
Arrow's methods of collective choice, except as these problems dis-
qualify markets as solutions to the rational problems discussed here.
This observation, however, is appropriate now–that much more is
given up from Arrow's theorem with exchange than with the uses of
conditionals here.

If conditions are maintained as separate justifications for orderings,
the combination rules of Arrow's theorem can be maintained. But the
outcomes may not satisfy the conditional requirements. Strasnick's recent development of Arrow's proof, still relying on the individualistic
postulates, introduces a "social unanimity condition." The condition
maintains that "For any set of individual preferences, (a) the weak
Pareto principle is to hold for any subset in a partitioning of that set.
(b) If for some partitioning, the SPF (social preference function) prefers
the same alternative in each subset, then it will prefer that alternative

for the unpartitioned set of preferences as well."[6] This condition is similar to Robert Nozick's "addition condition," which asserts that "if two distributions (over disjoint sets of individuals) are just, then so is the distribution which consists of the combination of those two just distributions. (If the distribution on earth is just, and that on some planet of a distant star is just, then so is the sum distribution of the two.")[7]

The "addition condition" requires that a predicate (outcome, value) assignable to all elements of some set, S, will also be assignable to the set consisting of the elements conjoined. The addition condition is an innocuous re-expression of the Pareto principle when interpreted in terms of unconditional orderings. But conditional orderings defy the addition condition. Suppose, for example, that aRb is a just arrangement when aRc, and bRa is a just arrangement when cRa. Now consider the following orderings.

    (1) $aRbRc$
    (2) $aRbRc$
    (3) $bRcRa$
    (4) $bRcRa$

Each of the partials, (1), (2), (3), and (4), is just on the conditions establishing just distributions. But if we combine them, then we get

    (1) bRc (on Pareto)
    (2) cIa (on the indifference condition)
    (3) bRa (on transitivity)

The combination of the partials produces bRa when cIa, an unjust arrangement under the terms set out for the partials. This exercise would be an empty demonstration in set theory were not a number of important concepts interpretable as conditional. "Justice" is among these concepts. Rawls' difference principle (DP), for example, is "lexical" in unconnected societies, and in a "simpler form" in well-connected societies. Formally, a lexical difference principle requires a sequential satisfaction of worst off representative persons, and a simple difference principle justifies inequalities in general as they benefit the worst off.[8] A society pluralistic on connectedness will tolerate sets of orderings like those illustrated above, thus requiring multiple senses of difference-principle justice. Two societies, one connected and the other unconnected, can both be just on different interpretations of the difference principle. Yet adding their distributions will not necessarily produce a sum distribution that is just because of the effects of conditionals on outcomes.

The lines of inquiry marked out by conditionals lead away from Arrow's theorem in two ways. First, conditions may represent reasons that mandate local, not collective, orderings. Such segmented rationalities promise an alternative to the collective rationality of the theorem (and, again, provide one solution to Prisoners' Dilemma). Second, the combination rules of the theorem may not dependably reproduce values maintained by conditions. Conditions may be nonadditive even when they do not mandate local orderings. The nonadditive status of conditions can restrict the power of the theorem to extend normative concepts from individual orderings to collective outcome: justice in the whole may not be identical to justice in parts still added to produce the whole.

5

The failure of Arrow's combination rules to address conditionals is a special case of a general hostility between arithmetical composition rules and a reasoned form of rationality. Aggregation machines require pure preferences. In Arrow's theorem, ordinal rankings are submitted by each individual. Utilitarian machines use cardinal rankings. Voters in single-ballot elections select a single alternative. Approval voting allows individuals to list as many acceptable alternatives as they wish. The list of preference-expressing procedures could continue. But in no procedure can individuals introduce the conditions in which an alternative is selected, neither in the local sense of "if a, then b," nor in the global sense of "all things considered, $a > b$."

Aggregation machines fail in several ways to accommodate reasoned orderings, any one of which shows why pure preferences are the only rational items aggregation can accept.

(1) A technical problem is the first failure. A reason-giving form of rationality has two levels: the ordering of alternatives and the (reasoned) conditions on which the alternatives are ordered. The two levels needed for the expression of conditional preferences can then lead to conflicts between levels. For example (where the subscripts denote individuals): $x_1 \rightarrow a > b$, $x_2 \rightarrow b > a$, $y_3 \rightarrow a > b$, $y_4 \rightarrow b > a$. Here individuals 1 and 2, and 3 and 4, agree on the reasons (represented by the conditionals) but disagree on the orderings of alternatives; individuals

1 and 3, and 2 and 4, disagree on the reasons but agree on the orderings; and individuals 1 and 4, and 2 and 3, disagree on both the reasons and the orderings. Interpretations of such patterns are easy to provide. Look at recent conflicts over abortion, where the reasons (right-to-life, right to control one's body, social needs, liberty, privacy) and alternatives (pro-life, pro-choice) are often mixed in truly imaginative ways.

It may seem that conditional orderings can be fed into aggregation machines if preferences are organized as ordered pairs. Let us say, for example, that individual 1 prefers $(x,a) > (y,a) > (x,b) > (y,b)$. This ordering can represent abortion issues in one reasonable way if x = right-to-life, a = no abortion (e.g., legal prohibitions), y = right to control one's body, and b = abortion on demand. A fervent pro-life supporter might prefer no abortion for the correct reasons, but still prefer no abortion for whatever reasons (including incoherent pairings, as in y,a and x,b) to abortion on demand for whatever reasons.

But representing conditional preferences in terms of ordered pairs cannot meet several requirements of reason-giving rationality. The first is that the representations can lead to the same rational breakdowns celebrated in Arrow's theorem, and contribute to them with the additional irrationality of undesirable and even incoherent pairs expressed as the collective choice. Look, for example, at another variation on Sen's (1970) paradox of the Paretian liberal, where (y,b) is abortion on demand on privacy rights, (p,b) is abortion on demand because the population of the underclass must be checked, and (x,a) is no abortion because the fetus has a right to life. If (a) the ordering of a pro-life individual is $(x,a) > (y,b) > (p,b)$ (preferring as a second choice the more civilized reason y to that expressed by p), and a pro-choice individual's ordering is $(y,b) > (p,b) > (x,a)$, and (b) each individual has a protected pair of ordered pairs (minimal liberalism), $(x,a) > (y,b)$ for 1 and $(p,b) > (x,a)$ for 2, then (c) on transitivity $(p,b) > (y,b)$ even though $(y,b) > (p,b)$ on Pareto. Or, not only can the same type of rational problem occur with ordered pairs as occurs with Arrow's single-unit orderings, but transitivity can force the least desirable reason for an alternative as the rational collective outcome. Since, as the earlier example suggests, incoherent pairings also can be favored strategically and perhaps be produced as the collective outcome, reasons only aggravate and do not solve the problems of aggregation.

(2) The second disorder in aggregating reason-supported (conditional) orderings is that reasons do not aggregate. Imagine a number of individuals in a state of rational disagreement, a state represented by conflicting claims (roughly, preferences or choices supported by rea-

sons). Their rational disagreements cannot be resolved through aggregation; for counting heads establishes only a preponderance of claims, not a valid settlement of disputes. A reason (whatever else it is) is a statement attesting to the normative status of a choice. The appropriate forum for a claim is a deliberative body, one where reasons can be ranked or fused. Outcomes are adjudications, not arithmetical summations.

(3) Reasons are also the source, not the solution, of the more substantial problems of aggregation. Look first at some simple (and famous) instances of self-referential paradoxes: "I am lying now" (the paradox of Epimenides); "This sentence has three erors in it"; this couplet:

The sentence below is false.
The sentence above is true.

All self-referential paradoxes contain sentences that refer back to their subjects or to themselves. A more general form of self-referential paradox is established by Gödel's proof, where it is demonstrated that a consistent system cannot be complete, a complete system cannot be consistent. Gödel's paradox is created by a closure statement that completes the list of system items but which, as a reflection on the system, is then outside of the system it closes. To bring the closure statement in (make the system consistent) requires another closure statement outside the system, and so on.[9]

Arrow's problem is a self-referential paradox of a special sort. The theorem assumes reflective individuals who survey and evaluate the outcomes of aggregation. Mind, in a more traditional language, confronts objective events (aggregation) and judges them deficient. The reflective quality of the theorem is found in the moral or equity conditions: Pareto, nondictatorship, and universal domain. Each requires a reasoned evaluation of aggregation alternatives or patterns. Take away the reasoned or reflective qualities and no contradiction occurs; for aggregation free from the reflection of individuals who are affected by the arithmetical outcomes presents no rational problem. (A decisive set, for example, is not offensive if only integers, not moral agents, are the units aggregated.) Arrow's theorem, like all self-referential paradoxes, represents a conflict between levels of activity, reflective and objective.[10] Since the background reasoning of preferences, expressed as equity conditions in Arrow's theorem, occasion the aggregation problems, it can hardly be thought that aggregation can accommodate reflection when it is introduced as the foreground, and tiered, arrangement of reason-supported orderings.

6

The use of reasons inclines collective choice toward non-aggregationist composition rules. Think now of two alternative actions, a and b, as the focus of moral choice. If supporting reasons are a defining component of moral direction, then moral deliberation on a versus b will explore the reasons supporting each course of action. Though no conclusive status may be assignable to a or b, a moral choice will select the alternative with the stronger supporting reasons. Let d and e be sets of reasons supporting, respectively, a and b. then $(a > b) \Rightarrow (d > e)$, and $(b > a) \Rightarrow (e > d)$. Example: if a = no abortion and b = abortion on demand, then the moral settlement of a or b will be negotiated through the arguments, rules, principles, utilities, physical status, and so on, which produce sets of persuasive reasons for the alternative proposals.

The introduction of reasons to orderings reveals more sharply the distinctions between types of collective outcomes. Two have been identified so far. The first is the unconditional combination of Arrow's theorem. The second is the compound outcome of conditional orderings. Reasoned orderings are also conditional orderings. But a moral choice cannot be content with the establishment of separate justifying conditions. Compound directives reflect and respect heterogeneous conditions. At issue in a moral outcome, by contrast, is which reason set, d or e, is rationally dominant. A successful conclusion of moral deliberation would be $d > e$ or $e > d$, with the consequent establishment of an ordering priority between a or b.

Why? Because of what we mean by morality. If the defining components of morality are to be maintained, a moral outcome is the product of shared reasons among moral equals. Many standard political forms are successful without such demanding requirements. Bargaining, for example, may be consummated without shared reasons. (Each party to the transaction may have a different reason for assenting to the bargain.) Or power may be characterized by coercive resolutions of disagreement over both reasons and actions. Efforts at moral resolution, however, must produce collective outcomes through rational persuasion if an accord on reasons is to be ensured. The need to establish a reasoned priority among alternatives marks off moral outcomes as fusing efforts, where, unlike compound directives, the conditions for orderings are themselves the material for orderings.

The ranking formulae for reasons, however, are unlike the arithmetical combinations of Arrow's theorem. A collective outcome in Arrow's theorem is produced from counting the ordinal arrangements of alternatives set by individuals. The absence of cardinal scales prohibits adding numerical weights for the alternatives. But a collective outcome is still an arithmetical function of a preponderance of rank orders. If, for example, $a > b > c$ and $b > c > a$ are "summed," the $b—R \rightarrow c, a—I \rightarrow c$ outcomes are simple combinations of the individual ordinal rankings. Reasons, however, cannot be counted or summed. The reasoned determination of abortion versus no abortion is not a matter of combining ordered units, but of exploring the considerations supporting one course of action versus another. The nonadditive logic of reasons is clearly expressed in judicial decisions. Imagine the absurdity of a legal outcome produced simply from counting the number of earlier decisions on an issue. A moral outcome, like a legal outcome, is negotiated through rules, arguments, and evidence, not through numerically collecting rank orders.

The nonadditive logic of reasoned outcomes supports intuitive feelings that morality is not a matter of mere numbers. That a preponderance of individuals endorses a point of view seems never enough, in itself, to establish the morality of the point of view. The hostility of morality to additive formulae is explained by the supervenience of moral outcomes on reasons. But, also, a distinction is suggested between preferences and choices, or even picking and choosing. Arrow's individuals order alternatives, nothing more. No reasons are advanced to justify the primitive preferences expressed in the ordinal rankings. Moral agents, by contrast, choose on the basis of reasoned considerations. The rational basis of moral choice is revealed through supporting reasons. The introduction of moral considerations to the theorem thus provides a rational feature to the initial orderings, based on reasoning, that is not present in the unsupported preferences of Arrow's individuals.

7

That reason-giving rationality requires nonadditive composition rules is demonstrated in yet another way. Richard Wollheim (1962) elaborates a paradox of participation that is developed on the condition that individuals are moral agents. Think of a voter morally committed to a substantive policy, *a,* which policy is contrary to an alternative policy, *c* (only *a* or *c* can be realized, or some other policy, but not *a* and *c*). He votes for *a*. But the outcome of the election is *c*. The citizen is also morally committed to democratic decision rules, *b,* and so he is obligated to support *c* as the legitimate product of the democratic machinery. He is thus faced with two contrary moral commitments, *a* and *b,* when he can logically only endorse *a* or *b*.

Critics have suggested that this paradox of democracy is really a more general contradiction between the outcome of any decision rule and any preference when the preference doesn't correspond to the results obtained from the utilization of the decision rule (Weiss 1973). I may prefer heads over tails, but find that the flip of a coin produces tails over heads. Attach a moral commitment to heads and to coin-flipping as a method for resolving disputes, and the paradox occurs. Wollheim's paradox seems to be a self-contradiction occurring as a result of simultaneous moral endorsements of a substantive outcome and a decision rule, the endorsements in each case being rational yet producing a contradiction when joined.

Many resolutions have been proposed for Wollheim's paradox (partial survey in Weiss, 1973). Two of the more powerful efforts at managing the paradox are developed along utilitarian lines. One allows that commitments to *a* and *b* represent simultaneous moral claims. But they still may be compatible if the *b* commitment is grounded in the belief that justice requires subordinating individual judgments in order to promote a just social order. The solution, in spite of the fame of its author with another line of argument, is "rule utilitarian": it elevates social rules (when just) over individual judgments. The commitments to *a* and *b* are both moral, but the commitment to *b* is overriding because it is derived from the commitment to a just decision rule for the society at large (Rawls 1964).

A second solution, introduced by Donald Weiss (1973), is "act utilitarian." Here, it is maintained that a full exploration of moral commitment reveals a moral principle, *P,* behind every moral evaluation, which principle provides evaluative criteria for moral judgment. The logic of a moral commitment requires that the moral agent act so as to maximize the fulfillment of *P,* which particular moral evaluations express. Now the fulfillment of any principle in social conditions introduces considerations of what others will do. Once these considerations are introduced, however, actions to fulfill *P* may require the selection of alternatives immediately contrary to *P* (a tactic well-known in game theory). If, for example, social groupings are sufficiently divided to produce conflict if the outcome of a generally accepted decision rule is rejected, then it might be morally preferable (in terms of fulfilling P) to accept an outcome contrary to one's moral commitment in order to bring about the realization of P in the long run. Imagine this arrangement: (1) everyone does A; (2) one-third of the people do A, two-thirds do B; (3) everyone does B. One might consistently prefer (1) over (3) while still preferring (3) over (2); and if a majority vote for B means (3) or (2), but not (1), then P might be more successfully fulfilled over time in the governed harmony of (3) than in the divisive implications of (2).

The intriguing factor introduced by Weiss is time. What is a moral conflict in a static model of society becomes consistent strategy in a process model. But it is important to understand why long-range considerations tell in Wollheim's paradox. Future returns do not solve all participation problems. They do not, for example, transform the ineffective vote into an effective vote. The future instead gives reasons to accept (or, if not important enough, reject) immediate outcomes. Wollheim's paradox expresses a conflict between sets of reasons. One bids the voter to accept the outcome of an election on the commitment to a decision rule. The other set advises the rejection of the outcome on the commitment to a contrary outcome. Long-range considerations may adjudicate this conflict.

Both of the contrary commitments, however, depend on the legitimacy of the procedure for reaching collective outcomes. Wollheim likens the practice of majority rule to a machine: preferences are fed in and outcomes are produced from adding these preferences. But the reason for endorsing the "machine" is that it is a morally acceptable device for resolving conflict. If it were a faulty machine, one that arbitrarily favored some individuals (Arrow's problem), then Wollheim's paradox would not occur. If the machine works, then the choice of alternatives presented by the paradox can be rationally ordered by weighing future returns against present returns (or on some other weights, e.g., the oblique-direct constraints suggested by Wollheim in the original article).

William Riker (1981) has argued that the democratic machine is chronically arbitrary, and so cannot receive the moral endorsements that create Wollheim's paradox. The arbitrary character of majority rule is set by these realities: (a) a variety of criteria express majority preference, (b) the different criteria produce different expressions of majority preference, (c) no rule exists that can select a criterion as the true expression of majority preference, and (d) the criteria are manipulable by individuals.

For example, the Condorcet criterion specifies that the majority preference is the alternative with a clear majority over each other alternative, while the Borda criterion requires that the majority alternative rank most frequently ahead of others in the collection of individual preferences. Theorists from C. L. Dodgson to Riker have shown that these two criteria produce different majority preferences. But if different criteria exist for majority rule (and there are others in addition to the Condorcet and Borda tests), and each criterion seems morally acceptable, then Wollheim's democracy does not exist; for there is no single machine to which individuals can give moral allegiance.

The reality of competing criteria suggests that disequilibrium is the characteristic feature of majority rule. Duncan Black (1958), for example, recognized the two dimensions of manipulation that have since been explored in more recent literatures: agenda control by authorities and insincere expressions of preferences by voters. Either of these types of manipulation dissolves the initial assumption of Wollheim's paradox—that the democratic machine expresses majority preference. If authorities can manipulate outcomes through agenda control, or individuals rationally vote insincerely in elections, then the people do not rule in Wollheim's sense. Thus, there is no reason for individuals to be morally obligated to the outcomes of the machine.

The rational problems surveyed here are proofs that any aggregation machine is bound to be faulty. Imagine Wollheim's individual casting a vote for a when one or all of the following occur: (1) the outcome is not simply contrary to a by majority preference, but results in b when everyone prefers a (a Prisoners' Dilemma problem); (2) an individual vote has no effect on the outcome of the machine (efficacy failure); (3) the outcome fails acceptable tests of rationality and/or equity (Arrow's theorem). A machine that fails such rational and moral tests cannot carry the moral authority needed to generate Wollheim's paradox.

But a deeper problem is also exposed by Wollheim's paradox. Wollheim's individual morally endorses a. He must therefore have reasons to support a, and these reasons must establish the importance of a when contrasted with alternatives. If, as Wollheim recognizes, the choice of a is prudential only, then no important conflict occurs if even a sound aggregation machine produces some other alternative contrary to a. But if a is moral, and thus supported by reasons, the individual will demand both less and more of the democratic process as realistically understood. His moral demands on the democratic machine will be minuscule, perhaps nonexistent, when its flaws are illuminated. But he will demand that some collective choice rule address the reasons for alternatives as well as the alternatives themselves.

Reasons have many functions in moral discourse. They provide gross (moral versus prudential) and fine (types of moral action) rankings of alternatives. They give morality its prescriptive quality. And they introduce collective considerations into the beginning logic of individual choice. But their main contribution to collective choice is to furnish a second type of ranking and accord. Think of an individual, 1, who opposes abortion on reasons drawn from fetal rights. Now suppose a second individual, 2, also opposed to abortion but on different convictions: that zero-growth population trends suggest a need for additional births to supply future inductees for the military. Individual 1 will likely be pleased at the no abortion conclusion of 2, but appalled at the supporting reason. Individuals 1 and 2 are not in full moral agreement—the moral accord is faulty—because of different reasons for their moral conclusions on what to do. Think of one as the moral instructor of the other. The moral lesson will have been incompletely consumed if the pupil does not understand why something is to be done in collaboration with what is to be done.

If Wollheim's individual is selecting a on moral grounds, then his complete preference for a democratic outcome is for a to be adopted for the reasons that make a the moral choice. Some interpreters say that a moral choice must be dictatorial (Little 1952). But this is not quite right. A moral choice extending to others requires that individuals accept the alternative and its reasons freely, not from coercion. The role of agency in morality is not free of controversy. Coercing-to-morality is a complicated issue, made more so by recent elaborations of power. The simple model of direct force easily defines out moral predicates: someone beaten into the performance of a good (or bad) deed hardly qualifies as a Good (or bad) Samaritan. But the manipulation of agendas and general conditions is less easily excluded from agency. If, for example, alternatives of choice, $a, b, c,$ are restricted to $a, b,$ then the agent who chooses $a > b$ can still in some sense be said to have been controlled and to have acted intentionally, volitionally, and (though in an even more weakened sense) knowledgeably. But he cannot have accepted the full set of reasons for choice if he is a member of an unorganized or numerical association, since at least some of the reasons would be obscured by the manipulations of agendas. Wollheim's individual is making a moral choice for the society—the alternative is to be the collective choice—only if he also requires that his civic colleagues subscribe to *a* and its reasons in the way in which he prefers *a* for reasons.

We can now see why any set of additive composition rules must fail to accommodate moral agency. If moral agents must have reasons expressed in collective outcomes, then even flawless aggregation machines cannot produce moral outcomes; for moral resolutions are not established by counting heads and allowing some preponderance of individuals to dominate. On a moral issue, a decisive majority is as oppressive as Arrow's decisive singleton. The deeper problem exposed by Wollheim's paradox is a conflict between moral commitment and preference-aggregation democracy. The parallel in collective choice is a conflict between moral language and the tenets of methodological individualism. If individuals are only arithmetical units to be added for a collective outcome, the resulting distribution cannot be described as dictatorial or exploitive. And no moral problem occurs. If dictatorship or exploitation are authentic problems, on the other hand, then moral agency must be assumed. And then aggregation must give way to some reasoned method for reaching collective outcomes.

It does not, of course, follow from the use of deliberation in ranking orderings that deliberative bodies escape combination problems. Criteria of adjudication may be self-contradictory; reasons (as recognized) may be connected to preference orderings in such imaginative ways that the connecting rules themselves may have to be ordered to reach a reasoned outcome; and meta-disputes over what is to count as a reason may have to be addressed as a condition for reaching a reasoned collective outcome. But at least Arrow's breakdowns do not occur, for universal domain is given up when reasons are introduced to collective choice. Reasons, whatever else they do, cannot allow all logically possible orderings of alternatives to be legitimate candidates for choice.

8

A reconstruction of the concept of rationality in Arrow's theorem leads to a form of rationality that stresses reasoning in opposition to ordering rules (connectivity, transitivity). It is one indication of the hold that methodological individualism has on collective choice that the literature has so much to say about rationality, yet so little to say about reasons. Reason-giving rationality, nevertheless, is a well-known alternative to the means-ends rationality at the core of rationality models in collective choice. Individuals can be rational not simply in terms of how consistently or optimally they order alternatives, but in terms of the reasons that can be advanced to justify their preferences. Both coherence and correspondence theories of truth support this form of rationality. Reasons, in the former, are part of an internal structural of concepts meeting tests of coherence. In the latter, reasons correspond to more objective laws and principles. In both coherence and correspondence theories of reasoning, however, individuals use reasons to make their preferences intelligible, to explain or justify their actions.

Arrow's theorem is the apotheosis of unconditional combinations. Two types of conditional outcomes, however, satisfy the requirements of collective rationality. One is the compound outcome that authenticates local orderings by means of meta-rules. This outcome is a rational representation of the social partitioning that is one solution to Prisoners' Dilemma. The other outcome, represented by fused reasons, fulfills the incomplete moral concerns of the theorem. Several conclusions follow from the recognition of these two alternative types of collective outcome.

1. Reason-giving rationality, though not accommodated by aggregation machines, is still closer in spirit and logic to the terms set out by Arrow than are many other alternatives to the theorem. Reasons do not introduce cardinality or Borda scales, or holistic terms that impose settlements from the collective to the individual level (e.g., the state as an organic whole), or many of the social factors that give up in other ways the simple (atomistic) individualism of the theorem (e.g., custom, social rules, statute law, etc.). Reasons are attached to individual orderings that are conceptually distinct from each other and ordinally arranged.

2. Yet, in spite of the affinity of reason-giving rationality for the general framework of the theorem, this form of rationality qualifies the methodological individualism on which the theorem is based. Arrow's individuals are atomistic units, arranging alternatives from isolated values. Social outcomes are the combined products of individual rankings. But if individuals, as individuals, rank on reasons, then the standard aphorism of methodological individualism—"The whole is equal to the sum of its parts"—permits emergent values and is not even always true. Wholes may be unrepresentative sums, failing to reproduce values found in constitutive parts. Or wholes may be outcomes from nonadditive composition rules.

3. The development of collective rationality without arithmetical combinations is accomplished in two quite different ways with the use of reasoned orderings.

First, the compound directive gives up both transitivity as a measure of collective rationality and the composition rules of the theorem. Since the outcome of Arrow's theorem is a single ordering for the entire set of individuals, transitivity is understandably (though erroneously) assigned to this ordering. Compound directives are meta-rules authenticating multiple orderings on different warranting conditions. Each conditional ordering is transitive. But they are not combined. Thus there may be no single transitive ordering representing the collective outcome. The outcome is no less rational in the absence of transitivity, however. Indeed, if pluralism is warranted, then the imposition of a single ordering would itself be irrational.

Second, a reasoned outcome maintains transitivity but gives up the composition rules. Arrow's theorem produces (when transitivity is maintained) a logical rationality not equivalent to an outcome dominant on persuasive reasons. When moral choice is introduced to the theorem, the outcome is like Arrow's outcome in its rational, rather than logical, dominance. Indeed, a truer sense of collective rationality is achieved through reasoned synthesis than through the arithmetical combinations of Arrow's theorem. The outcome can express a transitive ordering and be the product of reasoned deliberation.

4. Both uses of conditional orderings introduce more complex and interesting senses of rationality than found in Arrow's theorem. The compound directive stresses the rationality of heterogeneity in opposition to combinations. Moral outcomes emphasize homogeneous outcomes. But both outcomes, because established by reasoned considerations, promote strong alternatives to Arrow's version of collective choice by calling into question the notion of an "individual." Morality interprets this term beyond its primitive logical status in the theorem, enriching it with human agency. Reasons prescribe for classes of individuals. The discrete and countable unit of methodological individualism must, in reason-giving rationality, choose for that class of individuals affected by the predicate in the chosen alternative.

5. Neither development of conditional orderings is a solution to the "paradox" Arrow offers us. No surprise here, for a really good rational problem should be airtight to begin with. It should offer no escape as long as the defining terms are maintained. The strategy employed here

has been to restrict and put into relief the scope of the theorem, while staying as close as possible to its rational and moral dimensions. The result of such a strategy should, if successful, disclose the location of the theorem in a pattern or tradition or thought. No less has been accomplished there, although it requires more speculative observation.

Arrow's theorem, in its definition and rules, expresses a relationship of the individual to society that has dominated political theory at least since the seventeenth century. Some have identified the basic social form as a market model of possessive individuals (Macpherson 1967). The reliance on simple preferences, unconstrained and without justifying reasons, is certainly a part of any market model. But the more basic form is that of a collection of autonomous individuals constituting a society with no features beyond those provided by combining the individuals as discrete units. We have labeled this form as the numerical model of society. Arrow's theorem represents the logical extremes of the numerical tradition, its distinctive assumptions and rules of social order transformed into a rational and moral dilemma.

A longer tradition puts into narrow relief the singular individualism of this legacy. Aristotle conceives of individuals as inseparable from the polis, and the polis as an extension of common understandings among individuals. The lines of inquiry away from the theorem lead as much to this classical past as to the present. The organic society of Aristotle's political philosophy suggests exactly those alternative relationships of individual and society that void both the rational and moral dilemmas that Arrow's theorem so powerfully demonstrates. That at least one fusion of the individual with society can fulfill moral as well as rational concerns is an important disclosure, especially to those main lines of recent democratic thought that have for centuries relied on the individualistic assumptions of Arrow's theorem.

NOTES

1. As with all generalizations, this one has exceptions. One outstanding exception is the work done by the late James Reynolds (who gave me the idea years ago of introducing reasons to collective choice theory). See, for example, Reynolds and David Paris, "The Concept of Choice and Arrow's Theorem," *Ethics* 89 (1979): 352–71. Also see the (mostly unsuccessful) efforts to develop alternatives to transitivity, e.g., quasi-transitivity and acyclicity. Review in William Riker, *Liberalism Against Populism,* pp. 130–32.

2. William Riker and Peter Ordeshook, *Positive Political Theory,* pp. 48–53. I have dropped the more complicated notational systems used by Riker and Ordeshook, but the point should be clear in reading this part of their text.

3. Philosophers have urged these two considerations on definitions of moral reasoning since Plato (though not without controversy). The second—reasons—is especially prominent in recent Western moral philosophy. See, for example, Steven Toulmin, *Reason in Ethics* (Cambridge: Cambridge University Press, 1950); Alan Gewirth, *Reason and Morality* (Chicago: University of Chicago Press, 1978); R. M. Hare, *The Language of Morals* (Oxford: Clarendon Press, 1952) and *Freedom and Reason* (Oxford: Clarendon Press, 1963), wherein can be found the artistically impressive demarcation of "morally good reasons" and "good moral reasons." Reason-giving rationality is also accepted as an explanatory device in those approaches to social events that stress the "internal" meanings of action in opposition to deductive-nomological explanations, e.g., Peter Winch, *The Idea of a Social Science* (New York: Humanities Press International, 1958). It is found as well in all forms of participant-regarding field work in anthropology and sociology, such as ethnographic interviewing.

4. See the discussion of these points in Thomas Nagel's "What Is It Like To Be A Bat?" *Philosophical Review* 83 (October 1974): 435–50, reprinted with reflections by the editors in Douglas R. Hofstadter and Daniel C. Dennett, eds., *The Mind's I* (New York: Basic Books, 1981). Obviously, even if a human being could experience the world as a bat, the phylogenetic distance between humans and bats makes comparisons between the experiences very doubtful.

5. David Braybrooke and Charles Lindblom, *A Strategy of Decision* (New York: Free Press, 1963). Of course, the actual relationship between inflation and unemployment is not at issue in this illustration, which only represents the logic of conditional orderings.

6. Steven Strasnick, "The Problem of Social Choice: Arrow to Rawls," *Philosophy and Public Affairs* 5 (1976): 241–73.

7. Robert Nozick, *Anarchy, State, and Utopia,* p. 209.

8. John Rawls, *A Theory of Justice,* pp. 82–83.

9. A translation of Gödel's proof can be found in Jean van Heijenoort, ed., *Frege and Gödel* (Cambridge, Mass.: Harvard University Press, 1970). The main components in the proof are Theorem VI, which proves that there is a proposition that can neither be proved nor negated by a formal system that meets certain conditions, and Theorem XI, which proves that, for any recursive consistent class of formulas, the sentential formula stating that the class is consistent is not provable within the class. See the lovely (and themselves recursive) descriptions of such regresses in Douglas Hofstadter, *Gödel, Escher, Bach: An Eternal Golden Braid* (New York: Basic Books, 1979). No one knows how to solve these problems. They simply represent limits on computational languages. For example, the halting problem (identified by Alan Turing in 1937 before the development of computers) has no solution. Suppose (in LISP) HALTS (func ARG) as (func ARG) halts → T, (func ARG) ∞ → NIL. Then (func ARG) halts → (* halts func ARG) ∞ and (func ARG) ∞ → (* halts func ARG) halts. As defined, (DE * halts (func ARG) (COND ((halts func ARG) (* halts func ARG)) (T))). Now suppose the function halts. Then it runs forever (∞). Suppose it runs forever (∞). Then it halts. Nothing in computer programming or theory can avoid such contradictions.

10. Hofstadter, in *Gödel, Escher, Bach,* sees these levels of activity as possibly corresponding to different and incompatible neural substrates, on pp. 584–85, a possibility that fortunately need not be explored for the discussion here.

6

Rational Forms

1

I magine an individual ranking preferences on sets of knowable values, settling on means to get these preferences (means produced by rational, constrained by moral, rules), and acting more or less consistently in terms of these means-ends systems. Such an individual is the simple unit of classical rationality. Now suppose the more complicated case. Say that an individual is rational in terms of preferences, means, and actions—yet the outcomes of these efforts do not measure up to the criteria employed by the individual and, on occasion, contradict these criteria. This latter individual is found in the infinitely more complicated settings of game theory and collective choice. He is faced with this problem: that the rationality of his own actions is in part a function of his social structure, the rules he uses to combine values, and the actions of others (discussion and bibliographic review in McClennen 1983).

Such an individual is represented in chapters two through five, summed up here.

1. An absence of assurance and coordination among individuals can make second-best choices rational to all. The joint outcome of such choices is a rationally inferior product from the point of view of the participating individuals. A failure of efficacy has similar irrational outcomes. If any single individual has negligible effect on a social effort, it is not rational for single individuals to participate. Yet general participation may be exactly what is needed to produce a desirable good.

In both cases, rational action for the individual leads to an irrational or sub-rational collective outcome.

2. Sometimes individuals cannot combine their preference orderings in any way that leads to a rational joint ordering. Collective choice produces either a decisive individual (one whose orderings are automatically the orderings for all), an intransitive joint ordering, or a failure of other ordering or moral rules. Thus, separate individuals find that combination rules do not simultaneously satisfy both moral and rational expectations in collective choice.

3. The concept of rationality contains the polar extremes of numerical individualism and those holistic considerations suggesting exit routes away from the rational problems. Ordering senses of rationality, where alternatives are arranged according to logical tests like transitivity, complement the sense of individuals as countable and discrete. Another version of rationality, reason-giving, introduces holistic models of a political society.

Here is the connecting point between (1), (2), and (3):

4. Rational conflict between individual and whole is a product of both surface and deep conditions. At the surface level are found representations of participation problems, like Prisoners' Dilemma, a general failure of participation in large groups, and the conflict exposed by Arrow's theorem. Solutions to representations are limited to the conditions they address. They represent only marginal changes in the numerical language of the rational problems. Failures of assurance and coordination are manageable by generalized and/or selective coercion. But this strategy is antagonistic to the volitional character of voting. Efficacy failures respond contingently to a reduction in the size of the social unit and, in a more limited way, to the introduction of participation rules that grant decisiveness to each individual. Where defection and efficacy problems merge, as with the "free rider," a combination of some or all of these particular strategies is useful. Social cohesion (more information, contact, etc.) is a condition that avoids both assurance, coordination, and efficacy failures. But neither the more restricted (coercion) nor the more general (cohesion) measures in this set of management strategies directly addresses the combination problems represented by Arrow's theorem. Conditional orderings, as we have seen, offer a way out of Arrow's paradox (even though such orderings themselves can lead on occasion to impossibility outcomes). Conditionals, however, are undeveloped in the literature as a solution to the problems of assurance, coordination, and efficacy.

More general solutions are promised, however, by the common ground on which the participation problems occur. One limiting assumption in all four problems is the numerical model of society. This model (expressing methodological individualism) (1) identifies individuals as numerical units, and (2) operates with arithmetical combination rules. Changes in these two assumptions promise a social form that avoids the rational breakdowns represented by the problems. A grouping of management strategies (directed at the representations of the problems) suggests the tensions within the numerical model as holistic features are introduced to, or recognized in, collective choice theory.

strategy	representation in which effective
generalized coercion generalized incentives	simple Prisoners' dilemma
	N-person iterated Prisoners' Dilemma
social cohesion ("signalling," conditional strategies, etc.; size-reduction as a means)	simple Prisoners' Dilemma
	N-person iterated Prisoners' Dilemma
	efficacy
social partitioning social structuring	simple Prisoners' Dilemma
	N-person iterated Prisoners' Dilemma
	efficacy
long-range returns low discount rates	N-person iterated Prisoners' Dilemma
	Wollheim's paradox
exchange	none
D-terms	none
other-regarding calculations	none

decisive individuals (either through participation rules or as a consequence of strategic advantage)	simple and N-person iterated Prisoners' Dilemma efficacy
selective incentives	efficacy (in organized groups)
size-reduction	efficacy
conditional rationality/ ranking on reasons (rather than through aggregation)	Arrow's theorem Prisoners' Dilemma (all types) efficacy

Both generalized coercion and decisive individuals have impressive scope as management strategies. But they are unsatisfactory on equity grounds. A reasoned ranking of alternatives is more successful, but only by jettisoning arithmetical summation rules. In several cases, however, the strategies attempt to close the distance among individuals (common responses to coercion, cohesion, a merger of present and temporary selves, size-reduction, reasoned outcomes) as a way of solving the problems. Where divisons are maintained, as in partitioning and the use of selective incentives, a closer connection is established among subgroups. The atomism of the numerical model is, in a variety of ways, modified. In particular, the idea of individuals joined on reasoned rather than numerical grounds points to a general solution of the rational problems.

2

The traditions of the social contract and utilitarianism both complement the interpretations of "individual" found in collective choice theory. Contract theory begins with discrete individuals who then, on a variety of conditions and purposes, transfer some assemblage of rights and authority to an artificial person (thus encoding into the theory the possibility of an adversarial relationship between individual and political society). Utilitarianism sums individual utilities to reach a collective outcome, which outcomes can then legislate (unless modified) against the interests of those who are not in the greater, or preponderant, part.

The breakdowns in collective choice represented by Prisoners' Dilemma and Arrow's theorem are developed on these conditions, for the language of exploitation and dictatorship that guides these breakdowns requires that the individual and the collective be not only separate but capable of adversarial relationships. The formal games and theorems of collective choice extend the traditions of the social contract and utilitarianism to the more general consideration that there can be no ruling *part* of a society on the interpretation of individuals as discrete and countable units.

The more general consideration, however, simply accelerates inquiry toward reinterpretations of "individual" that permit rule without the divisiveness suggested by the exploitive Prisoners' Dilemma cell or Arrow's dictator. The possible reinterpretations are multiple. Individuals are divisible even as countable units. For example, conditions can partition individuals into several selves, each of which can be in conflict with the others. Plato asked how a man can be in two volitional states at once (both wanting and not wanting something). Imagine an individual in two sets of conditions, say (1) agreeing to enter a health resort only on condition that the doctors not release him until he loses ten pounds ("no matter what I say"), and then (2) demanding release after a two-pound weight loss ("no matter what I said"). The two conditions produce partitions between self (1) and self (2), and nothing may be available to say which is the authentic or authoritative self.[1] Or individuals can be extended through identification with others or by means of reasons to establish membership in rational classes of individuals.

Which reinterpretation is more productive—greater fractionalization or greater unity—is best settled through a restatement of some expectations in collective choice. Individuals in all of the various games and theorems are viewed as moral agents, meaning (among other things) that they are conceived in terms of self-defining or self-legislating powers. Stated simply, the rational problems are problems of other minds. In Prisoners' Dilemma, the sensibility of split choices, equally rational, mandates defection. If the other were a mirror image player, an identical mind, coordination and assurance dilemmas would not occur. Nor would efficacy be an issue (a vote of one would be a vote of all, as in Rawls' original position). Different orderings and different reasons give moral qualities to the combination-rule failures of Arrow and Wollheim. Wollheim's paradox makes the point effectively. The acceptance of majority rule is based on the assumption that other minds are feeding preferences into the machine. If the machine alone generated the contrary outcome, or other machines were the source of the majority vote, then the moral agent would face no problem: he rejects the democratic outcome. The problem occurs on the assumption that human beings—moral agents—are ranking alternatives for reasons; and majority rule is a moral and rational rule to accommodate these beings when they disagree.

The broad guidelines suggested by these conceptions lead us toward a reinterpretation of individuals that maintains the qualities of mind that inform collective choice. The same constraints extend to the forms of association that meet rationality and equity tests. It is by now self-evident that organized collectives are better suited to reconcile the full sets of assumptions in collective choice than are unorganized or random collectives (juries, for example, meeting tests of reason and equity that electorates chronically fail). What is yet unclear, however, is what types of organization not only meet the tests, but fulfill the self-legislating powers ascribable to individuals.

3

The equity assumptions in collective choice prohibit control by others, and then reinforce and extend the self-reflective dilemmas created by self-legislating individuals. The problems of rational discontinuity, seen in this more complete way, are inconsistencies between equity and reasoned (reflective) rationality that are created by the use of arithmetical composition rules (that combine individuals without extending them to collective dimensions). The recognition of individuals as reason-giving agents requires institutions that avoid reflexive dilemmas without controls that offend the self-legislating powers of moral agents.

The dilemmas of collective choice occur is substantial part because of the resistance in the various theories to *any* control of individual preferences. Arrow's conditions of nondictatorship and universal domain express this resistance in particularly effective terms: no individual can be decisive over any other, no restriction on preferences is allowed. So great is the commitment to autonomy in collective choice theory that any control is liable to be viewed as equivalent to a form of dictatorship. Thus Riker, in recognizing that Arrow's problem does not arise if there are only two alternatives (on May's theorem, 1952), nevertheless rejects any institutional narrowing of possible alternatives as an unjustifiable constraint.

It is not simply an empirical matter—as Dahl, for example, argued—that the American (or any other) system does not work in the neat way the Wilsonians wanted. More important is the fact that what they wanted was itself morally wrong from a liberal democratic view, because to get binary choice one must enforce some method of reducing options.[2]

So we are faced with a dilemma. Simple majority decision between two alternatives, while narrowly fair, is unattractive because it requires unfair institutions to operate it.[3]

Are such uncompromising celebrations of autonomy justifiable? There are powerful arguments to support autonomy even against *moral* authority. Wolff assumes that a state is defined by the possession and moral exercise of authority, and that authority is the putative moral right to command and the right to be obeyed by another person(s) (1970). If moral autonomy is self-legislation, represented by an individual who gives laws to himself, then moral autonomy and authority are in direct conflict. No state is ever justifiable. Only unanimous direct democracy, in which self-legislating individuals find themselves in a pleasing state of spontaneous coordination, does not contradict authority. Coordinated individuals, however, do not constitute a system of authority. Legitimate authority is a contradiction in all of its forms—exactly what Arrow's theorem documents in formal terms.[4]

The rejection of all control of individuals in collective choice theory is a variation on this core conflict between autonomy and authority. Wolff uses the same model of rational and autonomous moral agents that is found at the background level in Arrow's theorem. As Arrow proves that no individual can be decisive over any other without violating one or more of the features of this model (as extended by the axioms and conditions of the impossibility theorem), so Wolff discovers that all authority, or the exercise of direction through commands, is inconsistent with moral autonomy. In both cases, what I have called the liberal model does not tolerate any restriction of individual autonomy. Once individuals are accepted (as they are in the liberal model) as self-legislating, all direction must seem pernicious, even that which wears the cloak of morality. A closer inspection of autonomy and authority, however, suggests institutions in which the conflict does not occur. These institutions, in turn, offer a way out of the impasse of collective choice (developed in literatures so various as to include both Wolff and Arrow).

Consider first Jeffrey Reiman's (1972) rebuttal to Wolff. Authority and morality are first segregated on the grounds that "moral authority" is a contradiction. Moral action, by definition, is autonomous action. A moral duty is to do *what* is moral, and not to obey a command because of *who* issues it (authority). The moral test of state legitimacy, according to Reiman, is a moral evaluation of the consequences of political authority. If the consequences of political authority are morally better than the consequences of no authority, then there is a prima facie duty to obey the law. (The same test can be applied to all types of political systems—democratic, authoritarian, etc.) Thus, political authority and moral autonomy are reconcilable on the autonomous judgment of individuals that they are justified in obeying laws that do not have (cannot have) the status of morally binding commands.

Additional amendments in the concept of authority enlighten other reconciliations between autonomy and authority. One can, first, expand the notion of a political system to cover exchange. Here, autonomous agents accept collective decisions because the decisions are produced by the autonomous actions of each and every individual. Authority, in exchange, is a token for self-interest, an idiosyncratic use of the concept, to be sure. But unlike straight power events (compelling compliance through the use or threat of force), exchange outcomes have legitimate binding power. They bind individuals in direct ratio to their success as expressions of interests. In this sense, they are also unlike persuasive arguments in that they avoid validity or soundness tests. The narrow view of authority as residing in persons, who are obeyed because of who they are rather than what they say, will not fit exchange. But certainly the laws of a political system can be obeyed because they originate in exchange transactions. Autonomy and governance can in this way be accommodated to each other.

A second expansion of authority is both more congenial to the core meaning of the concept and more helpful in understanding connections between autonomy and authority. Richard Friedman (1973) famously bifurcates authority into two categories: *in* authority and *an* authority. The first is a procedural authority, created when individuals cannot agree on what is to be done but do agree on who is to decide what is to be done. Figures who are in authority are essentially equal to those whom they command. The second is epistemic authority. Here, individuals accept an authority figure out of deference to the authority's superior knowledge or ability. The authority figure is superior, not equal, to those over whom he has authority. In both types of authority, the core concept of "a surrender of private judgment" is realized, but in different ways on different justifications.

The distinction between *in* and *an* authority suggests a reconciliation between individual autonomy and authority on shared reasons. *An* authority is the more promising possibility. The surrender of private judgment on epistemic gounds shifts the locus of authority from the authority figure to the body of knowledge and shared rules establishing epistemic authority. Obligation to *an* authority is not strictly to the authority figure, but to the knowledge that the figure represents. Individuals defer to *an* authority because such an individual is the expression of an superior knowledge that is authoritative for both authority figure and respondent. If *A* is an authority, than one has good reason to believe that what *A* says is true (Flathman 1980). And the good reasons are grounded in the common recognition of a body of knowledge and the authority figure's connections to that knowledge. The rational agent is not in conflict with authority, for deference originates in reasoned judgment made freely.

Notice, however, that this reconciliation of autonomy and authority is possible only if the individual is rational on reasoned (conditional) grounds. A model of rationality that allows only the unconditional expression of preferences cannot accommodate epistemic authority. The deference to a figure *in* authority is possible on traditional models of rationality. Surrendering private judgment to a procedural authority requires some pragmatic judgment that a system of authority (as such, this kind) is better than no authority or some alternative form of authority. These judgments are expressible as preference orderings. Contract theorists speak assuringly of a vote to establish both authority as such and types of authority. But deference to procedural authorities does not reconcile individual autonomy and authority; for the surrender of private judgment to procedural authority gives up precisely the individual's autonomy to decide rationally on the merits of decisions. This type of surrender is inconsistent with moral autonomy. Epistemic authority, by contrast, preserves and even enhances merit insofar as the epistemic authority is more knowledgeable than the lay person. The surrender to epistemic authority, moreover, allows the individual merit review, for such authority is not discretionary but subordinate to the body of knowledge that is its source and establishment. The individual deferring to epistemic authority must do so on reasoned conditions, and these conditions perfect rather than restrict moral agency.

Compatibility between the rational agent (using models of conditional rationality) and epistemic authority is drawn up on collective grounds. Both respondent and authority defer to the knowledge that establishes lines of authority. The authority figure possesses the knowledge (unequal amounts of it), the respondent has reason to believe in the knowledge and believe that the authority figure possesses it. The reasons for making law or policy (advanced by the authority) are not always the same as the reasons for accepting law or policy (advanced by the respondent). But both authority figure and respondent share (although unequally) in a common resource of knowledge. Drawn up in idealized form by Plato, knowledge dominates both ruler and ruled. The rationality of individuals is settled by participation in the content, rules, and practices of this body of knowledge. Rationality is not possible prior to being part of a system of knowing. It is easy to see why the idea of a social contract among individuals or between individuals and a sovereign is not consistent with epistemic authority. Individuals and epistemic authorities must be members of the same collective order at the outset; and authority is established by a natural inequality of this order rather than by formal agreement. Mainly, however, individuals are rational by virtue of membership in this order, rather than as discrete creatures who coalesce on separate rational calculations.

The communal arrangement established by reasons offers a political society that is unlike either anarchism or many standard conceptions of the state. Reasoned associations obviously are not compatible with the use or threat of coercion, a feature often used to define the modern state. Collective outcomes formed on shared reasons are more congenial on the surface with anarchism, a form of association requiring that individuals always make decisions based on arguments and evidence that they themselves have personally formed and evaluated. The anarchist fusion of individual and community is also a form of reasoned association. Ritter (1980) describes the traditional anarchist community as one of independent thinkers who know each other's thoughts. This reciprocal awareness is especially important in the sense of community developed by Proudhon and Kropotkin. But the sharing of independent thought is also found in Godwin, whose model community is analogous to a conversation among sincere and rational persons.

Reasoned communities, however, depend on rules that may be hostile to the anarchist emphasis on situational logic. Anarchism opposes all systems of law. Law, for the anarchist, is always coercive by virtue of its remoteness, generality, and permanence. Law is, in a word, external. It is insensitive to the particular circumstances of decisions. A rational deliberation on anarchist conditions cannot be controlled by prior standards, whether utilitarian, deontic, or the authority of others. A rational decision for the anarchist is bound only by the particular situation in which the decision is made, not by rules that prescribe for types of situations (Ritter 1980).

The problem is that reasons are general and prescriptive by their own logic. If individuals use reasons, they are already members of a general system of evidence and argument that prescribes for classes of events and individuals. The anarchist reliance on social censure seems to recognize the generality of reasons. Censure secures noncoercive obedience by giving reasons to individuals to comply with social directives. But reasons cannot secure rational compliance unless they are generalizable; and if generalizable, then the individuals convinced by reasons must be members of a common epistemic system of rules. Anarchists seem to ignore this communal logic of reasons in limiting rational decisions to particular situations.

Imagine a special (and idealized) type of forum. In this forum, each individual endorses orderings of alternatives on the basis of supporting reasons. Sometimes these individuals are able to reach agreement with each other by exploring the reasons (justifications, implications, consequences, etc.) on which the orderings rest. When they cannot agree, they are able to present their points of view to a court empowered to adjudicate differences (which authority is acknowledged by the participants). Each case receives an individual hearing. Court decisions are reached on the basis of public criteria of justice, and the reasons for the decisions are announced in the forum. Inequalities of counsel are cancelled at the start (through any of a variety of devices, including court-appointed attorneys). Appeals are allowed until a final decision is made. Sometimes the court decides on local criteria. Sometimes the decision requires global criteria. But each decision is made on a case-by-case basis; and the pattern of decisions is regulated by collective principles (monitoring the overall pattern of outcomes).

The juridical democracy suggested by this idealized forum escapes the main objections of anarchism to legal systems. A legal government is a system of control applied by a small number of officials who issue general, standing rules to all members of society and who enforce these rules with fixed penalties for each type of offense.[5] An ideal forum charged with ranking and fusing reasons is not a legal government as defined. Each individual in the forum is given a hearing. The generality of decisions is internal, found in the practice of making reasoned decisions. If the forum is seen as metaphor for society, the anarchist rejection of a citizen-person distinction can be overcome. But what cannot be consistent with the forum is the anarchist insistence on particular decisions isolated from each other. The connecting tissue of reasons may force anarchism away from its reliance on reasoned deliberation if decisions are to be isolated. But if anarchism persists in using reasons to define individual autonomy, a form of epistemic authority must be part of the anarchist community, where all subscribe to the rational dominance of a system of knowledge.

4

The metaphor of a forum, like all metaphors, is not the reality of politics, but an idealization against which to measure and compare alternative attempts to reconcile authority and autonomy. Riker (1982) has persuasively developed a conception of politics that accommodates the proofs and theorems of collective choice, in effect a conception that introduces a form of authority that respects the rational and equity criteria of Arrow's theorem. Politics is defined by chronic disequilibria (such as cyclical majorities) in which losers (a) generate new alternatives that may be able to beat current winners, and/or (b) invent new dimensions of politics in which old equilibria are upset. The art of politics is the ability to find some alternative or dimension that can win when set against the proposal that (provisionally) holds power.

"Winning" does not mean representing, or effectively cultivating, a consensus among eligible voters. All versions of populism, roughly defined as the expectation that the people should rule in a democracy, are abandoned with this definition of politics. A Madisonian view of democracy is endorsed in place of populism. Here (again, roughly defined) authorities rule for periods of time, and then are subject to an electoral process that can remove them from office if a winning alternative or dimension is introduced. Riker likens the process of politics to natural selection. New issues are like genetic recombinations, constantly and (more or less) randomly produced; and some (issues, genes) survive and flourish while others do not. The definitive characteristic of such a process is its indeterminacy. The direction of the process can be charted retrospectively, but it cannot be predicted; for it has no a priori direction.[6] To take a phrase from a different (and, given the metaphysics of this view of politics, surprising) literature in philosophy of science, we would say that explanation and prediction in political inquiry are not symmetrical (Scriven 1959B).

To this rejection of covering law explanations must also be added the less welcome observation that politics, on this account, is an essentially irrational process. The randomness of politics is clear from the descriptions. Riker's basic claim is that a variety of aggregation rules (Condorcet, utilitarian, Borda, Kemeny, etc.) are available to produce collective outcomes; that nothing ranks the rules on rational or moral grounds; that each rule yields cycles and is manipulable; and that it is not even clear when and if manipulation occurs in the use of any of the rules. Thus, voting, as such, lacks a causal relationship between preference-expression and collective outcomes, and the same rule does not necessarily produce the same outcome when applied in circumstances that appear identical. In addition, the outcomes from each of the rules are affected by any of a number of seemingly arbitrary arrangements, such as the order in which the alternatives are presented. These features of aggregation rules are practically a fulfillment of a lexical definition of randomness.

The irrationality of the process is a consequence of its randomness. Since outcomes are random, participation in politics is less transparent than buying a ticket in a lottery (where at least the odds are known). One cannot know the meaning of the collective outcome from the procedures (whether it is the expression of majority preferences), nor provide any reasons for one produced outcome against any other that might have been produced. The process, then, is arbitrary as well as random, meaning that there are no reasons to support one realized outcome over another. Popular will may have a meaning not expressed in collective choice. But this notion is difficult to support, requiring as it would a conception of popular will independent of the procedures to express it (equivalent to seeking a shape for water in the absence of a container). If the aggregation rules and outcomes are arbitrary, then there is nothing to prevent popular will from taking on a variety of shapes equally arbitrary. Such a process offers no incentives for participation that are related to any expression of popular will in collective outcomes. The irrationality is this: the practice of democracy is constituted by a set of procedures that connect (in some way) individual preferences and collective outcomes; and to the degree that such procedures fail to do this, participation in a democracy has no relationship to the acknowledged goals of the practice. The active citizenry in an aggregationist democracy is like a broker trying to buy and sell stocks by whispering numbers in the wind at a vacant lot—a curious figure who is irrationally pursuing goals that cannot be realized by the procedures he uses.

Does Madisonian theory rescue democracy from this irrational state? If there is no rational relationship between preferences and outcomes, then even Madisonian democracy is irrational. Riker's Madisonian democracy tolerates rule by authorities who may not prepresent popular will so long as the people have the opportunity to reject them in regularly scheduled elections. This checking function of elections is then to demarcate democracies from authoritarian systems of rule, where no elections occur. The problem with even this less ambitious set of expectations, however, is that the action of "rejecting" or "controlling" authorities is senseless in the absence of a causal relationship between preferences and outcomes. How can elections be seen as an expression of disapproval if all aggregation rules fail as devices to express preferences in collective outcomes? The critiques of populism bear as heavily on Madisonian democracy: they suggest that any "rejection" might be false or invalid because of possible manipulation by factions in the body politic. The only distinction between democratic and authoritarian systems on this account of politics is the greater instability of democratic rule, an instability created by the chronic disequilibria of electoral systems rather than by any capacity of the people to check or reject authorities. This is an important distinction, since it recognizes the value of periodic elections in preventing stable consolidations of power. But no theory of democracy is content to interpret democratic norms in terms simply of unstable rule, least of all Madisonian theory. A more complete picture of the irrationality of aggregation-rule politics is also suggested. Even basic concepts—rule, authority, consent, representation—have no meaning within democratic theory when rational connections between preferences and outcomes have been dismissed.

If the first problem with this account of politics is that it accomplishes more than it intends by rendering even Madisonian democracy unworkable, the second problem is that it underestimates the compatibility of individual autonomy and liberty with authority. Epistemic authority (as we have seen) is rule by a system of knowledge in which the autonomy of individuals is preserved as they are rational. (The only restriction on liberty is drawn from that system of rules in terms of which an individual reasons.) Given the compatibility of autonomy/liberty with epistemic authority, it is reasonable to ask if there is a conception of politics that preserves the rational and equity expectations of democratic rule.

The answer to this question is suggested by the ways in which disequilibrium is avoided with a suspension of Arrow's condition of universal domain. There is first the obvious avoidance of the impossibility theorem with a restriction of alternatives to two. There are also theorems demonstrating the possibility of nonrandom productions of collective outcomes from preferences if constraints on alternatives exist. Kramer's (1977) model, for example, establishes (on the conditions that parties seek to maximize votes) a trajectory between winning platforms leading to a set of alternatives closest to majority winners, which set defines equilibrium. The standard critiques of Kramer's model (discussed by Riker, 1982;190–92) are: (a) that parties do not always try to maximize votes (and thus the condition for the model may be false); and (b) that the dimensions of issues also can change as platforms change. (This second critique is made on the grounds that, e.g., structural linguistics demonstrates that an infinity of statements can be generated by inserting intermediate phrases in sentences, thus permitting issue language to change even more readily than platforms change.) The critiques can be set aside for the sake of this observation—that the model attempts to recognize equilibria on a restriction of the number of both parties and alternatives. This species of solution appeals precisely as it negotiates the dismissal of universal domain with the restricting activities of institutions.

The appeal of the solution is, in part, a function of its realism. It is difficult to conceive of any society that has met the condition of universal domain. Alternatives are routinely buried by institutions, never reaching the stage of decision making. Such burials can be pernicious, as the critics of modern democratic theory have pointed out (Bachrach 1967; Lukes 1974), or benign, as in the avoidance of morally undesirable issues. (That candidates in democratic societies cannot seriously run for office on a Nazi program can hardly be considered an inequitable restriction on individual autonomy.) Or the restriction of alternatives may simply reflect the filtering out of bizarre or unfeasible alternatives (the latter is an initial interpretation, by Arrow, of the effects of the independence condition). Certainly Madisonian democracy violates universal domain. The role Madison assigned to institutions—as constraints on popular will—unavoidably restricts alternatives (and thus it is contradictory to endorse Madisonian democracy *and* universal domain). If so compelling an alternative to populist democracy also violates universal domain, perhaps it is the condition that must be abandoned in the search for resolutions of aggregation problems.

5

One helpful way to begin a critical examination of universal domain is by introducing some of the richer models of rationality currently used in social theory. Three models of the rational individual dominate recent traditions in the social sciences. The first is a classical model of rationality. Here, rational individuals maximize goals within feasibility sets. Rationality is developed in terms of consistency tests (e.g., transitivity) and on assumptions of perfect and costless information and a fixed environment. The second is the "satisficing" model advanced as a more empirically sound alternative to classical rationality. Rational individuals in this second model set minimum requirements and then select alternatives that satisfy these requirements. The conditions include imperfect information, information costs, and a static environment. (This second model has been famously expanded and amended to various forms of disjointed incrementalism.) The third model is game-theoretic. Here, conditions oscillate between models one and two—perfect information (as in Olson's free rider), imperfect information (as in Prisoners' Dilemma), maximum goals, minimum goals, and so on—with one exception: the game-theoretic model assumes a changing environment as the actions of other individuals affect the rationality of choices and preferences. Rationality is strategic rather than parametric.[7]

These three models are different complements of one another. Classical rationality is restricted to theoretical or laboratory settings. The "satisficing" model applies to nonexperimental phenomena, including especially large organizations. Game-theoretic models are used in fluid conditions of choice. The models are identical, however, in their individualistic premises. Each sets out the conditions on which individuals secure their goals through the selection of appropriate means. Two of the three models contain language that refers to other individuals. The extension of the "satisficing" model to incrementalist logic requires that the decisions of others, typically in other organizational niches, be counted on to restore rational imbalances. Strategic calculations in gaming situations, by definition, incorporate the actions of others into rational decisions. But in both cases the individual remains a separate unit even when using this referential language.

One of the intriguing issues in refining these three models is the effect of decision costs on rational calculations. Bayesian decision rules, for example, can be used in all three models. But the rationality of Bayesian rules is an issue in the second model because of the costs of securing information. Three alternatives are suggested. One is a reliance on rules that, on more general calculations, maximize utility. This more procedurally oriented rationality frees the individual from Bayesian calculations in particular cases by allowing him to rely on rules established in general utility-maximizing procedures. A second alternative is the use of heuristics—intuitions, hunches, stereotypes, constructs, etc.—that yield grosser calculations approximating correct solutions without the finer and more costly calculations that require greater amounts of information. A third, and especially elegant, alternative to Bayesian calculations is Simon's (1982) "satisficing" model, which requires only that alternatives be divided into two subsets, approved and disapproved, and then any alternative in the approved subset is a rational selection. All three alternatives can be considered as utility maximizing strategies from a meta-perspective that weighs information costs. But each modifies or rejects the more demanding statistical combinations that particular Bayesian decisions require.

The dominant consideration in the rationality of decision rules, however, is the social practice in which decisions are to be made. Imagine, for example, calculating the trajectory of an artillery shell aimed to hit a static target. One can use variants of Newtonian mechanics or, given certain assumptions about information costs, simply raise or lower the barrel of the artillery unit until a hit is achieved. The latter, heuristic, method of calculation can be appropriate depending on the end to be achieved. Now imagine calculating the trajectory of a space capsule designed to land human beings on the moon. Hit-and-miss methods are no longer appropriate. Only the finest calculations will do, and, if the information is too costly, then the effort is not attempted. We would say that the information costs are parameters for the attempt, rather than grounds for seeking substitute forms of rationality.

Or think of buying bread versus buying a house. Or seeking care for a parakeet versus medical care for a parent. Or consider the experiments described in Tversky and Kahneman (1982) that suggest the rationality (and widespread use) of heuristics in identifying professions from minimal but suggestive information. Contrast such a use of heuristics with hunch poker players, who inevitably (logically, statistically) fail when opposing players who use strict probability calculations. The general considerations in determining the advisability of various decision rules seem to be: (1) the value involved (especially whether vital or trivial), (2) the relevance and importance of probability in the social practice (identifying professions versus playing poker), and (3) whether the decision is repetitive (and thus whether corrective measures of a pragmatic sort—raising and lowering the barrels of artillery—are possible).

Each of these three models of a rational choice is contrasted with Arrow's rationality by the explicit use of considerations beyond ordering tests, primarily information from the environment. The strongest and most helpful contrast is between Simon's "satisficing" model and Arrow's version of a rational choice. Simon's justification for a satisficing strategy is based on two propositions: (1) cognitive limitations and (2) information costs. Because the human intellect cannot process limitless amounts of information and because the acquisition of information is itself costly, the argument goes, it is rational for individuals to group alternatives into the two unranked sets.

It is also rational in Simon's model to accept organizational influence on alternatives.[8] Organizations can set priorities among goals, factor and interpret alternatives, and in general set agendas that limit the alternatives that individuals consider. Although the justification for organizational influence is wide and varied, the acceptance of cognitive limits is especially important in "satisficing" traditions. Given that individuals cannot handle large amounts of data, it is rational to depend on organizations to process information.

The spareness of Arrow's rationality makes it difficult to determine how information is to be handled by individuals ranking alternatives on the conditions of the theorem. It is tempting to think that universal domain requires classical approaches to information. The condition does require that the agenda of choice be within the control of individuals. Arrow begins by assuming a set of alternatives, X. Universal domain specifies that the domain of social choice, v, is unrestricted in the sense that every logically possible combination of orderings of alternatives in X must be a possible choice.[9] Individuals, in short, must have liberty to order alternatives in the choice set in the way they wish without restrictions. This agenda of choice (all finite nonempty subsets of X) cannot be restricted by organizations.

The information appropriate to rank the alternatives in v favors classical rationality. If the initial set of alternatives is large, then an unbounded model of rationality would seem to be required with universal domain, assuming that the liberty to order alternatives in any combination has no cogency unless individuals can survey and select from a very large set of items. (And X need not be too large for classical rationality to be required. If X contains only 10 alternatives, the agenda would include 3,628,800 possible combinations without counting indifference orderings.) If the initial set of alternatives is small, then classical rationality may still be used on the restricted set, in the sense that complete information could be obtained on the limited number of combinations in the domain of choice.

A reading of the theorem that stops with these observations would conclude that "satisficing" or incrementalist strategies are ruled out by universal domain insofar as they rely on organizational decision making, and that unbounded rationality (with respect to the domain of choice) is the proper rational strategy to pursue. But this reading misses an important point about Arrow's theorem. It is a curious (and largely unmentioned) feature of the theorem that the axioms and conditions are all silent on the scope of X. Universal domain establishes the range of the social choice function from the alternatives in X. A state could severely limit the alternatives in X without violating any of the equity or rationality conditions in the theorem.[10] Or, put in terms of the strategies that individuals can employ in ranking alternatives, incrementalist and gaming methods are not ruled out in expanding or limiting that initial set of alternatives.

It is with the distinction between the set of alternatives, X, and the domain of choice, v, that the important differences between Simon and Arrow on rationality can be seen. Arrow's theorem is indifferent about the way in which the set of alternatives is determined. Rational choice, for purposes of the theorem, simply requires that individuals order alternatives in accordance with connectivity and transitivity, and that the domain of possible orderings includes all possible logical combinations of alternatives in the nonempty set, X. Simon's version of rationality is concerned with the strategies that individuals employ in managing information about alternatives and in ranking alternatives. The different approaches to rationality then intersect in two helpful ways. One is a point of criticism. A large number of combinations in v revives the traditional (and decisive) arguments that unbounded rationality depends on unrealistic expectations of cognitive abilities. A second is more congenial. Simon's strategy can be used without contradiction in managing (factoring, interpreting, limiting) the alternatives in X, and as a device to enrich the ordering rationality that addresses the choice domain, *v*. The introduction of rational strategies to the choice set, however, does require abandoning universal domain.

But the abandonment is not cause for distress. One of the self-evident truths about Arrow's theorem is that the impossibility results can be avoided by changing the conditions or axioms. Give up some of the conditions or axioms and the proof goes through without a contradiction. Whether the game of change and maintenance is played well, however, depends on how close the proposed change is to the premises and ends of the theorem. Arrow's proof demonstrates conflicts between liberal moral values, especially those of autonomy, and aggregation rules. The ordering rationality of Arrow's theorem is an instrument congenial with liberal autonomy, given that it can only order alternatives and not address whether some alternatives should be in the choice set in the first place. But moral choice, so clearly needed if individuals are the moral agents the theorem assumes them to be (in accepting nondictatorship, among other equity conditions), requires a reasoned examination and justification of alternatives. Reason-giving rationality, far from contradicting Arrow's premises, seems to fulfull liberal values in representing the rational choices of moral agents.

The judgment that all restrictions of alternatives are unfair relies on an ordering rationality that is flawed even in terms of the premises of Arrow's theorem. A reasoned version of rationality recognizes communal arrangements among individuals, for what counts as a reason and what marks off good from bad reasons are the conventional rules and criteria accepted in social practices. Institutions, as the conditions for reason-giving rationality, can interpret and limit alternatives without offending moral and rational tests. Authority drawn up on epistemic grounds recognizes the typical ways in which moral reasoning acts on alternatives *before* choices are made. The methodological individualist will object that authority breaks the isolation of individuals from each other in the theorem. But that is precisely the point when moral values are introduced. Reason-giving rationality recognizes individuals as members of a moral community, which can restrict alternatives on the accepted conventions of moral reasoning.

6

Does a restriction of alternatives violate requirements in democratic practices? Strictly speaking, no. A reasoned restriction of alternatives affects Arrow's theorem in two ways. First, if the number of alternatives in the initial set of alternatives, X, is reduced to just two, then majority rule leads to no contradiction on Arrow's conditions (May 1952). Second, though, a restriction of the alternatives in the choice set, v, does violate universal domain. If epistemic institutions are the instruments of restriction, however, then democratic expectations can be maintained in the shared conventions that control both authorities and respondents. Like the promisor who is bound by his commitment, rational constraints on choice can be established and maintained by consent. But the rational instrument that authorizes a restriction of alternatives, reasoned rationality, is antagonistic to one component of democratic arrangements. Conditional rationality expands the contradictions of the theorem and requires the dismissal of the unrestricted preference-aggregation democracy on which the proof is developed.

In one important sense this conflict between reason-giving rationality and aggregation rules is not surprising. Liberalism maintains that the individual is to be shielded from collective regulation on a wide range of issues. If reason-giving rationality more fully expresses the liberal moral values of Arrow's theorem than the ordering rationality used in the proof, we would expect the contradictions demonstrated in the proof between liberal values and aggregation to be more rather than less pronounced as rationality is restructured along reasoned lines. But it is also important to examine whether all or just some democratic arrangements are abandoned with the use of reason-giving rationality.

Dahl (1982) outlines a set of beliefs, and procedures following from these beliefs, for making binding decisions in a procedural democracy. Specifically, the beliefs are these: (1) a specific collection of people has a need for binding decisions (involving both setting the agenda and at the decisive stage); (2) binding decisions ought to be made only by persons who are subject to the decisions; (3) equally valid claims justify equal shares; (4) the preferences of a significant number of members as to the decision are equally valid and no member's preferences are of overriding validity (and equal qualification exists); and (5) the good of each member is entitled to equal consideration and each member is assumed to be the best judge of his or her own interests in the absence of a compelling showing to the contrary. If all these conditions are accepted, then procedures for making binding decisions must satisfy the following criteria: political equality, effective participation, enlightened understanding, final control of the agenda, and inclusiveness. To the extent that procedures satisfy the criteria, then, on Dahl's view, the political system satisfies procedural democracy.

It does not stretch our conception of democracy to separate both the beliefs and the criteria of such procedural democracies from unconstrained preference aggregation. The normative features of the beliefs require a reasoned inquiry into preferences that aggregation cannot satisfy or even support (especially the determination of equally valid claims and the settlement of an entitlement to equal consideration). The key belief allowing aggregation rules is (4) above, which is a necessary condition in forming outcomes on a preponderance of individual preferences. But not only is the determination of such a condition possible only through rational inquiry, there is no reason to think that the condition will always, or even usually, obtain; and if condition (4) above does not occur, then the aggregation of unconstrained preferences may not meet even rudimentary tests of fairness (including treating unequal individuals unequally—for example, those with greater interests in, or intensity for, an outcome). Some rational method for ordering claims, not simply adding them, would be required.

The liberal acceptance of individuals as self-legislating requires that the conditions for reasoning be introduced to the conditions for democracy. The compatibilities are extensive. The use of reasons occurs within systems of full communication (Habermas 1970), impartiality (Rawls 1971; Ackerman 1980), and adjudication rules that can rank and fuse claims. Also, self-legislating individuals are entitled to equal regard in systems of reasoning. The main incompatibility between reasoning and democratic systems is that reasons cannot be counted. Systems of reasoning can tolerate the aggregation of preferences constrained by rules, but cannot always tolerate the conditions of universal domain and nondictatorship as formally specified in Arrow's theorem. Rational discourse can always restrict alternatives and justify the dominance (not the dictatorship) of some alternatives over others on reasons. If individuals prefer alternatives for reasons, and these reasons must be introduced to democratic procedures, then effective participation must include features of an (idealized) forum to reach collective outcomes. Aggregation cannot be the decisive method to satisfy the criterion of effective participation.

The compatibilities between open rational inquiry and democratic institutions are well-known (Smith 1957; Thorson 1962). Epistemic authority encourages such compatibilities, subordinating as it does both authority figure and respondent to the rules and substantive content of fields of knowledge. One consequence of such generalized subordination is that authority is substitutable (DeGeorge 1970), meaning that positions of authority must be accessible to whoever acquires the relevant knowledge. Also, epistemic authority can only be exercised in the context of a critical dialogue whose purpose is to recognize valid claims and authenticate the credentials of those who advance claims. When such a dialogue is elaborated in terms of Popper's (1968) falsificationist thesis, the exercised authority is provisional indeed. The system of authority (a) guarantees general access to authority on publicly recognized criteria of intellectual merit, (b) subordinates all individuals to rules, and (c) subjects claims to repeated tests that can falsify and question authority. This is authority congenial with many (though not all) of the expectations of democratic institutions. Epistemic authority is not democratic when developed in terms of the intuitive truths of Plato's political philosophy. But when elaborated by the norms of critical inquiry, there are broad areas of compatibility.

Or, put in terms of the exercise here, epistemic authority can avoid Arrow's problem while maintaining *both* the liberal respect for individual autonomy found in the theorem with the main features of democratic rule that the theorem celebrates. The compatibility between liberalism and democracy, however, can only be negotiated by introducing reason-giving rationality to collective choice in place of the ordering rationality found in Arrow's theorem. The concept of rationality, on this examination, is the most productive item on Arrow's list of axioms and conditions for understanding the contradictions his proof exposes and for identifying exit routes away from his conclusions.

7

The breakdowns documented in collective choice prevent a causal relationship between preferences and outcomes. Both populist and Madisonian democracy fail on the absence of such relationships, since the language of "rejection" is as unintelligible as the language of "popular will" in aggregation rules. It is then reasonable to ask if there are political forms that do not depend on causal relationships between preferences and outcomes. The guiding question in collective choice is how to produce collective outcomes by aggregating the preferences of discrete and countable individuals. A recognition of individuals as self-legislating agents raises a different question that may identify such forms: What conditions must a political society meet to ensure that rational discourse is the source of collective outcomes?

The first condition is that aggregation machines be restricted to their zones of validity. These zones are defined as elections when no more than two alternatives are at issue. This restriction of aggregation will unavoidably violate Arrow's condition of universal domain; for, given the logical and empirical possibilities of multiple alternatives on any issue, only an imposition (by institutions or individuals) can reduce alternatives to two. The second condition is that reasoned methods for reaching collective outcomes (analogously represented by the ideal forum) be used as both alternatives to aggregation, and as the standard against which to evaluate the rationality and equity of reducing alternatives to two.

These two conditions assign considerable weight to the rules that can authoritatively govern on the rational and equity criteria of collective choice, in opposition to the more direct reliance on the aggregations of preferences unconstrained by rules. The problem of establishing a rational and equitable political society is redirected away from preference aggregation to an alternative satisfaction of the condition on which preference aggregation is itself justified.

The justification for restricting aggregation and expanding the more juridical practices of society begins with an antagonism between additive rules and reasons that is part of a standard argument in modern philosophy. As abstracted and compressed from Wittgenstein, it yields a distinction between head counting and appeal to a rule. Wittgenstein asks:

> If someone asks me: "What colour is this book?" and I reply "It's green"—might I as well have given the answer "The generality of English-speaking people call that 'green'"?[11]

Wittgenstein goes on to answer no, on the grounds that the acquisition of language requires learning correct and incorrect uses of terms. The correct use of a term is governed by a rule used to correct deviations from proper usage. Unlike a scientific hypothesis or law, deviations from the rule do not count against the linguistic rule (although—and this must be added to Wittgenstein's argument—continued and patterned deviation can finally cause a modification of the rule). Mistakes of language are expectations in the use of linguistic rules. An attitudinal survey (a head count) of what people say is a correct use of a term is not equivalent to what the rule is because (a) the rule is an antecedent prescription for the expression of such attitudes, and (b) the rule is itself used to correct deviant expressions in language use.

A reason, like rules in general, is not equivalent to what people say. Reasons are supported by considerations drawn up in accord with conventional rules of inference and evidence. Adding preferences will not establish rational outcomes any more than head counting is equivalent to rules. Reasons, like the logic of rules, are (a) antecedent prescriptions for preference aggregation and (b) devices to judge and correct preference patterns that deviate from rational norms.

The institutional form that is able to accommodate reasons, a forum, is an instrument capable of measuring the internal dimensions of social life. Another set of distinctions, parallel to those between head counting and rule appeal, suggests the changes that result from the use of background concepts in collective choice. Students of society have traditionally divided over the proper methods to be used in social inquiry. One school of thought holds that the methods of social science are continuous with those of natural science. Another tradition maintains that social phenomena are distinct, having qualities (intentionality, meaning, value) unlike natural phenomena and, on the basis of these qualities, require distinct (nonnatural) methods, especially those methods stressing the rational qualities of social action in opposition to the computational methods that establish frequencies of association among events. All who argue a discontinuity thesis stress the reconstruction of subjective reality at the expense of empirical regularities. Even what is to count as an empirical regularity is said to be hostage to conceptions of sameness that are themselves within the social conventions that are the subjects of study (Winch 1958).

Individuals who are rational on reasoning, or self-legislating, grounds express the full dimensions of their preferences on conditional orderings where the conditions are reasons. Such reasoned discourse favors a distinction between social and natural phenomena. The additive rules of collective choice represent continuity claims in social science. Majority rule, for example, is a device easily extended to natural phenomena, for it is an extension of arithmetics that establish a preponderance of unit values. Reasons, however, are items distinctive of human affairs. They are not found in the natural world. That addition fails to accommodate reasons is understandable to those who separate the social and the natural. It is also understandable that the institutions sensitive to reasons are also wholly inappropriate as consolidators of items in the natural world. Additive rules view individuals as natural units. Only their "external" features are to be considered. But this view fails to provide moral and rational outcomes. Rational success is obtained by considering "internal" features—reasons for action. Reason thus represents the endorsement of *verstehen* over natural science methods of joining individuals, specifically those of addition.

Note also that the use of reasons does not rely on causal relationships between preferences and outcomes. A procedure that attempts to order or fuse reasons as a way of reaching a rational outcome is faulty if influenced by a preponderance of preferences, or by any causal effect from one or more of the individual claimants. The only effects can be reasoned, e.g., evidence and argument, which are not causal but philosophical, in the sense that they are more like the appearance of understandings than the production of lawlike outcomes from antecedent conditions. Certainly the deductive form of a causal relationship (Hempel 1966) does not cover reasoned deliberations of the sort found in juridical forums, for juridical procedures may be creative and outcomes may be emergents from rules and evidence. The dismissal of at least that form of causal relationship sought in the use of aggregation rules frees collective choice from those crippling failures that deny both populist and Madisonian forms of democracy (though without restoring either form).

The introductory theme is repeated: only as moral agents are assumed to exist do the rational problems occur, and only as concepts and rules reflect the needs of moral agents—the internal dimension set out by reasons—are the problems solvable. The acceptance of other minds, however, complicates the use of forums. Juridical deliberations are notorious targets for antirealist critiques. There are, in law, many interpretations of rules and events. None, to the antirealist, is privileged. And, as a consequence, juridical decisions are said to be vulnerable to the same pressures from groups and individuals that influence other decision rules. Jurisprudence becomes as much sociological as rational.

Here the requirements for rational continuity are both demanding and interesting. One well-known answer to sociological jurisprudence is a resurrection of classical themes: fixed principles can be discovered by human reason. But a more recent effort (complementing classical political philosophy) also appeals. Listen to R. G. Collingwood on minds:

> Similarly, your thought of the table is what you know of the table, the table as known to you; and if we both have real knowledge of the table, it seems to follow that our thoughts are the same not merely similar; and further, if the mind is its thoughts, we seem to have, for the moment at least, actually one mind; we share between us the unity of consciousness which we said to be the mark of the individual.[12]

Set aside, for the limited purposes of the discussion here, the problems of this view (e.g., are thoughts of different duration the same thoughts, etc.). The thesis expressed is that all thought is in principle public, not private, and that minds can be as one in thinking the same objects. The view of mind as public, with no privileged dimensions, is congruent with philosophies far removed from Collingwood's (Wittgenstein's, in particular). The possibilities of mental unity are encouraging thoughts for the success of a forum in reaching collective outcomes on shared reasons (reasons as devices to establish one mind).

But the main contribution of this line of analysis is to deny the distinctions between direct and reflective activity that leave the forum unfulfilled as an instrument for reasoned outcomes. On Collingwood's view, no meta-thought stratifies the life of the mind. Thought of thought is still thought of the objects of thought, and thus reflection on the minds of others is a thinking of the same objects and the establishment of one mind. The forum rejects the external perspectives of natural science in favor of the agent's point of view. The unity of minds envisaged by Collingwood (a unity that may endorse pluralism as easily as uniformity) may neutralize the heirarchy of claimant-judge that characterizes juridical institutions.

It is at this juncture that MacIntyre's (1981) important contribution bears. MacIntyre distinguishes between the emotivist self and the self found in traditional societies. The emotivist self has no social content nor social identity, for it denies the validity of all governing criteria. It is either a speck of nothingness (Sartre) or inseparable from roles (Goffman). The self of traditional societies, by contrast, identifies with social groups, and this identification sets boundaries to the self by providing a conception of a whole human life within social practices. Now, it is one important feature of a social practice that the authority of standards be accepted, since such authority in part defines a practice. The point advanced here is supported with this part of MacIntyre's elaboration. Hostility between individual autonomy and authority is produced only on an emotivist view of the self, where all values are viewed as noncognitive and individuals are conceived as existing independent of social practices. When individuals, or selves, are defined within practices, no such hostility occurs; for individuals whose identities are formed by social life will be embedded within patterns of authority. These authority patterns provide the standards which both govern and form individuals. The distinction between types of selves also dissolves the mystery of Collingwood's public mind. It can be no more and no less than the mental representation of those shared values that permit governance without dictatorship; and the trick of such governance is made possible by defining individuals as traditional (or practice) rather than emotivist selves.

A redefinition of the individual in terms of social categories also recasts the puzzles of *time.* The logic of Prisoners' Dilemma provides an incentive to regard the future highly; for an indifference to future returns can contribute to coordination problems, and thus exploitation outcomes, in the present. The isolated and autonomous self can be isolated from his future if he uses a high enough discount rate. Such an individual is one form of McIntyre's emotivist self; no rational history exists in its transitions from one moral commitment to another. If, however, the individual is conceived as a member of a system of rules to which he submits on rational grounds, then he is not free from those obligations that bind him to future occasions. Rules do not truncate present and future by the discrete intervals assumed in the use of discount rates. Social practices, as slopes across individual spans of existence, can connect individuals to future selves by the same rational methods that extend individuals to one another in the present.[13]

Conflicts between selves in different conditions and at different times can be adjudicated by the same methods that resolve conflicts among separate individuals. An individual set in a social context is not located solely in the present, nor isolated from others. He is rather part of a context that extends beyond the immediate concerns of the self. Seen in this way, the issue in governing is not, as it is often presented in collective choice, Which individual is to be authoritative? It is rather, Which system of rules is to govern? This question, though not without its own set of problems, moves inquiry to a holistic level at which the conflicts among selves, or between present and future, do not occur in the way that they are presented in collective choice theory. No *part* governs when rules are authoritative. Social practices govern.

8

Theories of democracy routinely demarcate state authority from private practices, permitting an increase in the scope of liberty with a decrease in the scope of the state. Even a Hobbesian state can, in this way, tolerate considerable liberty (on "the silence of the laws"). But the presentation here is more ambitious, requiring that liberty be developed within a rational system that constrains freedom by virtue of its rules. Does the individual who is absolutely unconstrained by any obligation (rational or moral) have authentic freedom? That such an individual is in a chronic state of conflict and even contradiction with collective outcomes, and even with his own past and future selves, suggests that liberty itself may require the constraints that reason-giving rationality provides.

The entire discussion here has demonstrated the importance of social structures in defining and resolving the problems of rational continuity among individuals—from Prisoners' Dilemma through Arrow's problem, failed efficacy, and Wollheim's paradox. If there is one lesson to draw from collective choice, it is that the rationality of individuals is a function of the structures in which they act. An acceptance of reason-giving rationality provides the resource to recognize those structures that avoid rational breakdowns—the rules on which reasons are formed, advanced, and defended. The location of such structures in the background concepts of collective choice should itself suggest that moral autonomy is not abandoned with epistemic authority.

The task of political inquiry, once individuals are accepted explicitly as reasoning agents, is to recognize the juridical forms that are compatible with individual minds. The mistake encoded in collective choice theory is to view authority as the hostile antithesis of moral autonomy. This view is expressed in the acceptance of such conditions as universal domain and nondictatorship. But individuals who are rational on reasons must rely on rules that govern; and the unity of individual minds can be located in the rules by means of which self-legislation occurs. Only a simplistic noncognitivism could view such epistemic authority as a form of dictatorship or a restriction of rationality. Authority, when assigned to rules, can fulfill rather than restrict autonomy by providing the connection among individuals that rational thought requires. If aggregation fails to fill the space between preferences and collective outcomes, democratic procedures may be closer to realization with the introduction of epistemic authority.

NOTES

1. The example from Thomas Schelling, Abrams Lectures at Syracuse University, spring 1983. Is the self who tries to control the genuine self (rather than the one who tries to escape control)? To say this requires principles to justify authority as the source of authenticity. See Jon Elster's discussion in *Ulysses and the Sirens* (Cambridge: Cambridge University Press, 1979). Also, can Arrow's decisive singleton occur within the set of multi-

ple selves? And can there be an impossibility result with three or more selves and alternatives?

2. William Riker, *Liberalism Against Populism,* p. 63.

3. Riker, *Liberalism Against Populism,* p. 65.

4. Alan Ritter, *Anarchism: A Theoretical Analysis* (Cambridge: Cambridge University Press, 1980), has pointed out that unanimous direct democracy also fails anarchist tests in other ways: that force can be used to ensure later compliance with the unanimous decision; that public deliberation produces a fallacious uniformity of opinion; and that the vote as such discourages dissent and (as proved in numerous studies of voting) can rationally favor insincere expressions of opinion.

5. H. L. A. Hart, *The Concept of Law* (Oxford: Clarendon Press, 1961) and quoted approvingly by Ritter (1980) as describing what it is about the law that anarchists oppose.

6. Riker, *Liberalism Against Populism,* pp. 209–11.

7. J.R. Hicks, *A Revision of Demand Theory* (Oxford: Oxford University Press, 1956), for the classical model; Herbert Simon, "A Behavioral Model of Rational Choice," *Quarterly Journal of Economics,* 69 (1955):99–118, for "satisficing"; and R. D. Luce and H. Raiffa, *Games and Decisions,* for developing and clarifying theories of game rationality. These are the standard references. Many extensions and variations have enriched the fields. See, for a truly heroic discussion of these areas, Jon Elster, *Ulysses and the Sirens,* and *Logic and Society* (New York: John Wiley & Sons, 1978). I have appropriated the term "parametric" rationality from Elster.

8. Herbert Simon, *Models of Bounded Rationality* (Cambridge, Mass.: MIT Press, 1982).

9. Recall that universal domain means that the domain of f consists of all logically possible profiles, u, and that at every u, the domain of $Cu = f(u)$ includes all finite nonempty subsets of X.

10. All variations on Arrow's theorem begin with the assumption that X represents a nonempty set of at least three alternatives, but no version of the theorem provides any further requirements for X. See Jerry Kelly, *Arrow Impossibility Theorems.*

11. *Remarks on the Foundations of Mathematics* (Oxford: Basil Blackwell, 1967), p. 90.

12. *Religion and Philosophy* (London: McMillan, 1916), p. 101. See also the study of Collingwood and Karl Popper by Peter Skagestad, *Making Sense of History* (Oslo: Universitetscarlaget, 1975).

13. Thus meeting Robert Nozick's identity condition that the future be part of the individual self. See *Philosophy and Explanation* (Cambridge, Mass.: Harvard University Press, 1981), section I, "The Identity of the Self," especially pp. 84–86.

7

Primitive Terms

1

Connections between individuals and wholes are plagued by any number of fallacies. Students of logic concede two at the beginning of their studies: the ecological fallacy (inferring characteristics of individuals from group characteristics, like average, mean, median, etc.); and the fallacy of division ("The university is not academically sound, therefore no member of the university is academically sound," and "Not everyone at the university is a scholar, therefore no one at the university is a scholar"). Both are well-known logical errors. One issue in such fallacies is whether to accept them at face value or view them as anomalies avoidable with a different interpretation of the concepts critical to the fallacy.

The rational problems surveyed here are demonstrations that a particular theory of individualism—that which maintains individuals as discrete and countable—cannot successfully produce collective outcomes while maintaining rational and equity conditions congenial to that theory. One can leave it at that. Or one can turn to background concepts as the source for reinterpreting the problems and identifying solutions that stay as close as possible to the theories of collective choice in which the problems occur. The main line of argument here is that two competing models of a political society are fixed at the background level of collective choice, and solving the rational problems requires the replacement of one model (numerical) with another (holistic).

The presence of two competing models is seen clearly in an inspection of the background assumptions of collective choice, especially as they express liberal values. The assumptions are conveniently (though not without overlap and strained classifications) assignable to three categories. One is metaphysical: (1) causality: individuals are in a cause-and-effect relationship with collective outcomes; (2) non-emergence: nothing is to appear in aggregated outcomes that is not found in individual values (stated precisely by Arrow's independence condition, loosely expressed as a requirement that combination rules not be creative); and (3) the atomistic (discrete, countable) status of individuals. A second set of assumptions consists of moral requirements. They are (1) autonomy, (2) equal effects, and (3) equal claims (also used to designate fair starting conditions in markets). The third set contains methodological propositions or premises. They are (1) reasonless (or unconditional) orderings, and (2) additive composition rules.

That these three sets of assumptions are advanced as a coherent package cannot be doubted. The rational problems discussed here are proofs that the package cannot be maintained as a single unit. The middle set of moral assumptions represents a holistic model, in the sense that liberty and equality are concepts that can be developed only within reasoned discourse. The first and third sets are features of numerical association, unable to sustain moral conditions.

The tight (and contradictory) union of the three sets of assumptions, however, can be best seen by marking the effects that occur as changes are made in one term: "individual." Start with the first set of assumptions and allow individuals to self-legislate on reasons. Reasons can be used only on the acceptance of a system of rules. The third metaphysical assumption has changed. An individual who reasons is a member of a class of individuals, occupying a category within a conceptual system. Individuals are now more accurately seen as located on a grid of rational communities, no longer isolated from each other (even though the communities, or systems of claims, can be antagonistic). The two other metaphysical assumptions are immediately affected. Individuals are no longer in a causal relationship with their societies. And emergence is an expected feature of collective choice.

Begin with causality. There is no sense to viewing individuals as antecedent units when they are members of reasoning systems. Such individuals are embedded in a system of concepts no part of which is consistently prior temporally to any other. (Even the notion of temporal priority is senseless when applied to rational discourse.) Simple causal relations do not always require antecedence. Think of two interlocked gears where one is turned by a drive shaft, causing the other to move also. The causal variable in this case is not antecedent; it occurs simultaneously with the dependent variable. But causal relationships do at least isolate relationships that are asymmetric in effect. To say that a causes b is to say that a and b are in a relationship such that the effects of a on b are not matched by the effects of b on a (the powered gear turning the passive gear, and not vice versa). Whether causal relations are lawlike, allowing for the deduction of dependent events from causal events and covering laws, is less settled (Hempel and Oppenheim 1948; Scriven 1959A; Hanson 1958; Popper 1961; Winch 1958).

Even the settled version of causality, however, does not accommodate the operations of reasoned discourses. Imagine a small claims court, where two individuals are advancing arguments before a judge who is expected to decide in favor of one or the other. Viewing the relationships between the two individuals as asymmetric is bound to distort the rich context of such verbal exchanges and deliberations. We would say that each of the participants is in a holistic system and brings to this system various competing rational communities with the arguments introduced. A set of simultaneous equations would more accurately depict these relationships, for each individual is in a complex set of symmetrical relations in a system of mutual dependencies. General equilibrium theory in economics is a suitable parallel, where changes in any one variable alter the system state. Or the solar system. Or the simple equation, $v = t/p$ (the volume of gas equals a ratio of its temperature and pressure). In each case, a system of mutual effects is a richer conceptualization of relationships than causal primacies. No events can be selected as causal and no relationships can be singled out as asymmetric. The fragmented asymmetries of causality give way to functional relationships in a system of events. The reasoning individual is in this way not in a causal relationship with collective outcomes, but is part of the system of reasoning required in conditional rationality. Decisive individuals are indispensable rather than causally preeminent.

Emergence is part of this system of reasoning. Technically, an emergent is an outcome that cannot be predicted from statements about the features of events and a theory otherwise explaining their relationships (Nagel 1953, 1961). Among the types of emergents are (1) mutations, which are not predictable but yet do not count against the validity or completeness of explanatory laws, and (2) anomalies, also not predictable but which do set limits on the scope or validity of explanatory laws. The emergents in Arrow's theorem (a decisive set, an intransitive collective ordering) are anomalies, not mutations. But they are anomalies only because concepts in collective choice are compromised by such outcomes. Shift now to the small claims court as temporary exemplar of reasoning systems. The judge can arrive at novel conclusions from available rules and evidence. His methods of reasoning can include counterfactual logic as he introduces hypothetical worlds to legal discourse.[1] The judge who chronically speculates on contrary-to-fact conditionals in small claims court may offend conventional limits. But any jurist's form of reasoning produces emergents more analogous to mutations rather than anomalies, for rational deliberation is open rather than closed in being able to arrive at novel and counterintuitive outcomes.

Once the metaphysical assumptions are changed, the methodological assumptions follow suit. Reasonless orderings are abandoned by definition. Arithmetical compositon rules give way to rational fusion and ordering. The problem at this stage with aggregation is that addition produces outcomes by concentrating only on features of the individual units to be combined, with no reference to the characteristics of a system or to the features of individuals as members of a system. Yet, as we have seen, structures are decisive in forming the Prisoner's Dilemma and influence the logic of Arrow's theorem as background concepts. It is also not even clear that "individual" means anything as a countable term, separate from membership in human groups. The nonadditive logic of reasoning, by contrast, is developed within the context of group or systemic features, producing outcomes within the contraints of a system of rules. The structure of society, as relations among parts, is a decisive influence on outcomes.

The differences in types of associations now become prominent. The numerical associations of collective choice, random collections of individuals (like the passengers on an airline flight, or the pedestrians on a particular street), have been abandoned. Organized associations, governed by rules, are required with the use of conditional rationality. Here, the equations of chapter two are more fully understandable. The constitutive rules of organized associations are interactive terms within which "individual" is a residual category (its meaning a function of membership in organizations). Reasons, when decisive in reaching outcomes, form unitary associations in defining individuals as members of rational classes. A holistic model is in this way the natural consequence of changing the term "individual" from a preference-expressing to a reasoning (self-legislating) agent. The middle (second) set of assumptions, representing holistic (moral) language, now is compatible with the other two sets because all vestiges of the numerical model have been dismissed.

2

The conflicts between numerical and holistic models of society are found within what is perhaps the protean form of individual-whole discontinuities—the generalization argument. Offered as a response to the individual who does not participate in a collective effort the plea is, "What if everyone did that?" A return to valid and invalid forms of the generalization argument tells us why numerical collectives do not accommodate such a commonplace appeal, while collectives with rules or values connecting individuals do.

Consider the following sequence of examples.

1. If everyone lied on their tax returns, the consequences would be undesirable. Therefore, no one ought to lie on their tax returns.

2. If everyone took Professor Winters' seminar, the consequences would be undesirable. Therefore, no one ought to take Professor Winters' seminar.

3. If everyone practiced birth control, the consequences would be undesirable. Therefore, no one ought to practice birth control.

4. If everyone were president, the consequences would be undesirable. Therefore, no one ought to be president.

5. If everyone voted Republican, the consequences would be undesirable. Therefore, no one ought to vote Republican.

6. If everyone on the scientific team worked on the nuclear warhead, the consequences for the world would be undesirable. Therefore, no one on the team ought to work on the warhead.

7. If no one voted, the consequences would be undesirable. Therefore, everyone ought to vote.

Example (1) represents a valid expression of the generalization argument in hypothetical form. Singer (1963) recognizes two principles in the derivation of the generalization argument. One is a principle of consequences *(PC):* "If the consequences of everyone's doing x would be undesirable, then not everyone ought to do x." The other is a generalization principle (GP): "If not everyone ought to act or be treated in a certain way, then no one ought to act or be treated in that way without a reason." Thus, "If not everyone ought to do x, then no one ought to do it." Taken together, PC and GP generate the generalization argument: "If the consequences of everyone's doing x would be undesirable, then no one ought to do x."[2] The tax case fits the argument in providing a reason why no individual should lie on his tax return—because of what would happen if everyone did so. This simple case is a hypothetical generalization, in that the reason for not lying is valid for an individual no matter how many others do or do not lie on their tax returns.

Examples (2) and (3) are expressions of the generalization argument where numerical considerations must be considered, and considered as part of the social practice the examples describe. If all in a sufficiently large undergraduate student body take any seminar, this excess of students will make teaching impossible. But from this reality it does not follow that no one ought to take the seminar, only that the class should not exceed the critical number beyond which teaching possiblities decline. Singer's "invertibility" may seem to bear here, for an action with undesirable consequences if everyone and no one acts is ruled out of consideration by the generalization argument. But the persistence of threshold events is clear in (3). Let (3) refer to a society with a birth rate considerably below replacement levels. Then, while everyone practicing birth control is undesirable and no one practicing birth control may be desirable, a fraction of the population practicing birth control may still be best. Or, the undesirable consequences of everyone doing x seem in (2) and (3) to lead only to the conclusion that some number of individuals below some threshold ought not to do x.

The desirable number of individuals acting is often specified by the social practice. In example (4), the particular features of the office of the presidency tell us that everyone as president is undesirable, but that some individual as president is desirable. We may say more generally that the use of numerical considerations in the generalization argument (what everyone else is doing) will turn on the social practice to which it is assigned; for not only do practices specify desirable numbers of individuals acting, but the meaning of "everyone" depends on the relevant class of individuals identified by a social practice.

Both senses of the generalization argument offer reasons for individuals to act based on what would happen if everyone did something. Consequences are built into collective action, not individual action. Examples (5) and (6), however, connect collective and individual action on the consequences of individual action. Start with (6). Suppose this example (French 1975). In a joint scientific project, (a) each scientist is necessary but not sufficient for the successful development of a warhead, so that (b) the withdrawal of any one scientist would cause the project to collapse. In this case, each individual member of the team bears a special responsibility for the production of the warhead by virtue of being necessary for the project. The collective outcome assigns responsibility to the individual (each and every one). Compare with (5), where no one voter is necessary for the election outcome. If, however, (5) were restructured to present a threshold case, where some one Democratic voter is the difference between victory or defeat for the Republicans, then the responsibility for a Republican victory is decisive for that voter, and the undesirable consequences of a Republican victory do present reasons to vote. And if everyone votes at once, so that no one can say who the threshold voter is, then, as with (6), responsibility is distributed to each and every party voter.

Example (7) demonstrates how efficacy failure affects generalization arguments. If no one votes, the consequences are undersirable. But if everyone votes, no one vote counts for very much. The prescription, "everyone ought to vote," carries its own reason not to vote when it is successfully carried out, for then the individual vote is not efficacious. The generalization argument, however, provides a shift in reference. Any individual ought to vote on the thought that only if all (or a substantial number) vote, can elections take place. On this type of collective consideration voting seems rational. But notice that voting is then no longer an effort to affect outcomes. It is an obligation to maintain a social practice—elections. This will not do. The social practice of voting is a method for determining collective preferences. The overriding reason to vote—to have an effect on the election outcome—has been lost. It appears that so long as the *one* in "No one" is a numerical term, a singleton, efficacy failure prevents a generalization between everyone and one.

The generalization argument establishes rational connections between collective and individual with a simple appeal. Individual action is to be guided by consideration of the consequences that follow "no one" or "everyone" doing the action. But the sequence of examples (1) through (7) suggests how this simple appeal is qualified and expanded.

(1) No general entailments hold between numerical senses of one and everyone (or all).[3] If an action is undesirable because performed by some numerical magnitude, as in examples (2), (3), (4), it does not follow that no single person should perform the action. Nor do the consequences of singleton acts prescribe for aggregates, as seen in example (7). Such actions contain thresholds. The relationship between one and all is nonmonotonic: The sequence of acts is not one of consistently in-

creasing or decreasing value, but of value inversion at a threshold number. (One student in the seminar is acceptable, 3,000 students are not acceptable; one president is fine, 100 are not, etc.). The value of the action is inverted because of the number of actors carrying out the action.

(2) Prescriptions for *one* do follow from the values assigned to collective action if decisiveness is distributed to each individual. Example (6) makes the point. A social practice in which the success of the joint effort depends upon each and every member participating provides a rational continuity between *one* and *all* of the strongest sort; each and every individual is necessary for the aggregate outcome A more general point also instructs: the features of social practices constrain inferences from *all* to *one* voting or being president or practicing birth control: the number of participants that defines a desirable outcome varies with the practice. So, too, does the possibility of prescribing for individuals on the basis of the outcomes. That all vote, occupy the office of the president, or practice birth control, specifies nothing for a single individual's actions. That all are needed to build a warhead does bear on each single individual's actions.

(3) A fairness principle provides reasons for individuals to act. If all are cooperating in a jointly beneficial project, then one has a reason to cooperate as well. But the use of the principle is complicated by the possibility of thresholds and the calculation of effects. If one is cooperating only because others are doing so, then it seems reasonable to measure how and the extent to which one's own contribution counts. The free rider seems to appeal as a rational option whenever we allow our own actions to be governed by how many others are acting in a similar way. Also, even if equivalence is established between individual and collective by more complete descriptions (that extend to thresholds), efficacy problems remain. Lyons' (1965) thesis requires that thresholds be considered as the consequences of individual acts when they are relevant. If an individual action is isolated, thresholds are not considerations. If the individual acts as part of a social practice in which thresholds occur, then thresholds are to be included in the complete description of individual actions. But since the possibility of having a threshold effect must be distributed proportionately to individuals, the failure of efficacy in large groups is not addressed by the numerical sense of the generalization argument.

(4) A hypothetical use of the generalization argument connects individual and collective action by ignoring numerical considerations. Example (1) suggests the controlling language. The popular translation of the generalization argument, "What if everyone did that?" must be interpreted as "What if members of a certain class were warranted in

doing that?" The "everyone" in the tax example then becomes a class of rational actors all warranted in lying on their tax returns. The class is hypothetical, not actual. How many people do in fact lie is irrelevant. The generalization argument requires individuals to rank collective outcomes and then act as a member of that hypothetical collective that produces the best outcome, regardless of whether the relevant class of individuals acts that way or not. The numerical size of this class is thus not a relevant consideration. Unlike examples (2) through (6), the hypothetical use of the generalization argument in (1) defines individuals as members of hypothetical classes, conceived as collectives, rather than as countable units in sets.[4]

These three types of connections between individuals and collectives—decisiveness, fairness, the hypothetical generalization argument—introduce collective considerations to individual choice. The first distributes responsibility to individuals by assigning each a negative power to end a cooperative venture. The collective outcome then must be considered exactly as the outcome of individual action in deliberations on whether to cooperate in the joint exercise. The second bids individuals to consider the actions of others and the benefits of collective action in deciding on defection or cooperation. The third urges individuals to rank collective outcomes hypothetically and then act on the principle that would bring the best outcome if everyone acted on it, whether others in fact act on it or not. Here the individual considers collective outcomes without reference to how others act.

The first and third appeals are continuous, the second is not. In both decisiveness and the generalization argument individuals are acting like collectives. The negatively decisive individual can act to prevent a collective outcome exactly as he can act to prevent an outcome from his actions as an isolated individual. He is the collective writ small. The individual deciding on the basis of a hypothetical generalization argument is joining the collective state that he ranks as highest. He acts as if he were everyone. But the fairness appeal is simply a reason to cooperate; and it is a reason that can be defeated by any number of rational considerations, including a low regard for future returns.

Two conditions, then, provide rational continuity between individuals and wholes: (1) a distribution of decisiveness to each and every single individual, or (2) a conception of individuals as collective, members of that hypothetical class of *everyone* that produces the best outcome.

Turn back to the problem of thresholds. We can see now more clearly that redescribing individual acts to include thresholds can be carried out in quite different ways. In numerical senses of the generalization argument an individual calculates the likelihood of his act being a threshold act. But, again, in large and disjointed collectives efficacy failure interrupts the obligations to participate that fairness principles might establish (Fishkin 1982). Nozick (1981) recognizes differences between a whole and a unity (a different terminology than that used here). A whole—for example, a heap of sand—is not equal to the sum of its parts. (The individual grains of sand are not necessary for any heap of sand; and certainly grains of sand need not be in any relationship to each other for a heap of sand to be.) A unity, for example a sentence, requires for its identity that the parts remain in a certain relationship to each other, and each part may be vital to the continued existence of the unity. Large numerical associations are roughly analogous to heaps of sand. No matter how accurately each individual member calculates thresholds, the individual effect is so negligible that it does not matter if any individual continues as a member of the association or not. The calculation of thresholds remains discrete because of its numerical form.

Two other forms of association provide different calculations of threshold effects. One is an association that contains features of a unity, where at least the decisiveness of individuals—their indispensability—grants to each the capacity to cause a threshold. Here, the description of individual acts includes collective consequences without any discontinuity. Since each individual member matters, the unit and the whole (unitarily conceived) are rational complements. The holistic association presumed in a hypothetical interpretation of the generalization argument offers yet another calculation of thresholds. Here, the individual act is described as if it were the act of everyone, without considering numbers or actual events at all. The linguistic shift is found in the two senses normally ascribed to "no one": "no *one*," where *one* is a singleton; and "*no one*," where the phrase means "not anyone." In the latter case, "no one voting" refers to a hypothetical class of voters, not a single (countable) voter. If the individual identifies in this way as a member of a collective without considering the actual action of others, then efficacy is no longer a rational issue. Whether others are voting, and how many are voting, is not relevant to the rationality of voting. The individual voter is a collective, hypothetically conceived. Those distinctions between one and all on which efficacy failures occur no longer exist. The calculation of thresholds is entirely holistic, for the numerical features of an association do not bear on the calculation.

The collapse of discrete individuals to hypothetical collectives faces the realist objection that the individual still has little effect on outcomes, even when acting as "everyone." But the objection depends on maintaining the reality of discrete, countable individuals. Another reality is as persuasive—that the isolation of individuals can be broken by describing them as embedded in social wholes, inseparable from the outcomes they are thought to cause. Such holism, of course, is totally inconsistent with voting as currently conceived, which, whatever else it requires, does rely on single individuals expressing unconditional preferences for alternatives.

Finally, note that, while fairness principles are not sufficient conditions for participation, they are necessary. A society without redeeming moral features will fail to provide participation incentives even when individuals are indispensable or conceived as collective. An association achieving rational continuity between individual and collective seems to require some combination of rational organization and those principles of fair or just association that participation requires. A reason-giving form of rationality is the substance on which such an association is formed. Reasons, as we know by now, (a) are formed on a network of rules that can organize communities authoritatively, (b) define individuals holistically as members of rational classes, and (c) provide evaluative criteria to address those issues of fairness in the absence of which cooperation has no meaning.

3

The development of a consistent arrangement among the background assumptions through the introduction of reason-giving rationality reconciles the moral needs of collective choice with methods for reaching collective outcomes. Equity is maintained in particular forms of holism (those associations based on an authority founded on shared reasons). The logic of such conceptual change and maintenance is clarified by examining current disputes between realists and relativists.

Realism is the doctrine that science is an inquiry into objective reality. The primitive realist claim is that scientific statements are true or false as they accord with the real world. Sophisticated realism says that terms in the language are governed in their usage by evidence for the existence of the things to which the terms refer. Scientific change is, in general, a successive approximation to truth.[5]

Relativists, by contrast, view science as a practice governed primarily by background considerations, not objective reality. Two objections to realism outline the relativist case. The first is that theory is underdetermined from data. Suppose a set of observation statements derived from a particular theory (necessary if the theory is to be falsified). The observation statements are not falsifiable from experience (or data sets). The theory is, accordingly, maintained. But, it has been shown, an open set of additional theoretical statements is also consistent with those same observation statements.[6] The proof of this consistency does not in itself establish the particular variables explaining why scientists choose one theory over others. But the selective mechanism must be relativistic; for the proof of underdetermination rules out the truth or falsity of theories as the means of selection.

A second objection to realism is drawn from the absence of referential continuity in science. Both realists and relativists agree that natural-kind words like "water" and "gold" have a stable sense and reference in the face of substantial changes in conventions. But science has also relied on other, less fixed, referential language. The problem is illustrated by terms like "phlogiston." At one time the term referred to a substance found in all combustible materials. Now "phlogiston" has been dropped from scientific discourse. It no longer refers to a real substance. The difficulty for realism is that such referential discontinuity is, according to the critics, more typical of science than the stability represented by natural-kind words (Kuhn 1962). One reason (among several) for referential discontinuity is that scientific inquiry employs nonobservables. Nonobservables, to the realist, must be governed by objects in the same way that terms referring to objects are governed. But since terms like "phlogiston" and "quark" are both governed by evidence for their existence, there is no reliable criterion for demarcating the nonexistent from the real.[7]

Relativists solve these two problems by redefining scientific inquiry. Science, for the relativist, is dominated by background considerations (rules and conventions) in retaining or falsifying theories; these background considerations are decisive. Exactly how such considerations influence the choice of theories and adjustment of statements is unsettled. Among the cluster of background items are cognitive values, authority, and—the current favorite—interests.[8] But whichever item is selected to explain scientific practice, the explanation is radically different from realist science. Relativism aims to account for science by causal rather than validity criteria. Scientific belief is said to be determined by factors antecedent to science rather than by truth.

Conceptual change, for the realist, is historically continuous. Conceptual change, for the relativist, is on occasion discontinuous. The primitive term "individual" shifted its sense radically in the seventeenth century. The modern use of "individual" refers to discrete, countable units. The classical sense of an "individual" refers to units embedded in holistic associations. A resolution of the problems surveyed here requires that "individual" be redefined holistically. Are these changes in the concept of an individual continuous or discontinuous?

One understanding of "politics" that cuts across both realism and relativism distinguishes between core and peripheral terms. Imagine that the terms of political language are arranged on inner and outer rings, with the core of a set of such concentric circles consisting of those terms impossible to dismiss without rearranging all, or most, other terms. The core consists of the term "aggregate" (the neutral collection of individual parts) and "directiveness." No referential power is found in the core. The referential terms of politics—those drawn from theories of power, authority, exchange—are on the outer circles. The peripheral terms are influenced by the interpretations given to core terms. But these interpretations are not logically coerced by any feature of the concept of politics. The core terms can be interpreted in a number of ways without breaking any rules found in a definition of "politics."[9]

The closest program in philosophy of science to this understanding of "politics" is I. Lakatos' view of change and maintenance (1970). Lakatos advances a theory of "sophisticated falsification" according to which scientific theories undergo a succession of "problem shifts" which may be deemed regressive or degenerative. Theories qualify as progressive problem shifts if they have three features: (a) excess empirical content (accounting for facts not covered by rival theories), (b) explanations for the unrefuted content of rival theories, and (c) a corroboration of some of their own excess content. In all progressive problem shifts, theories maintain a hard core of unchallenged assumptions. Scientific change occurs in the "protective belt" of auxiliary propositions surrounding the hard core. On Lakatos' view, rival scientific programs are always somewhat commensurable; and not all empirical statements in a theory are equally falsifiable (some may not be falsifiable at all). Scientific change is rational and continuous.

The core terms of politics are like the hard core of research programs. They are unchallenged terms that are maintained throughout theoretical change. No rules, however, are found in the core of politics.

The core is simply a nonidentifying structure that is constant in all theories of politics. It offers a skeletal form that provides the premises for conceptual disputes in political theory, however acrimonious and distant are the disputants. The metaphor is a stable set of points around which are clustered a changing array of political theories. No relativist could tolerate the fixed status of core terms. Realism, on the other hand, is hardly helped by the denial of referential continuity. Lakatos' use of a hard core and protective belt of statements roughly parallels the structural terms in "politics" that exhibit features of both realism and relativism.

A change in core terms, in this case in the primitive term "individual," and, as a consequence of the change, in the composition rules specifying how individuals combine, is a problem shift arising from the need to resolve the anomalies of political thought defined by the rational problems. The core terms are continuous lines in the study of politics, although fresh interpretations of these terms can lead to radically different conceptions of a political society. Shifting the sense of "individual" from discrete to holistic through reasons requires that a political association be corporate in some weak sense, or in the strong sense (as described in chapter two) that parts and wholes are unitary.

A corporate political society, though hardly discontinuous with classical political philosophy, does force substantial revisions in modern political thought. Neither of two recent traditions can be entirely maintained. One is utilitarianism, where collective outcomes are arithmetical combinations of discrete units. The rational problems mark this tradition. Another is the social contract. Here, collective states are formed on a transfer of some individual characteristic, usually authority, to an artificial person created by the transfer. An adversarial relationship between natural individuals and the newly formed corporate person is built into the starting premises; for even as umpire, the artificial state is created to mediate or manage conflicts among natural individuals. Even so, the formation of an agent representing the interests of all is closer to the rational solutions developed here than are utilitarian methods.

The deeper source of rational problem, however, is in the starting premise of both utilitarian and contract traditions: the separation of individuals into discrete units. So long as individuals are distinct figures, rational calculations cannot be consistently continuous with collective rationality. Associations formed on shared understandings, or mutual reasons, avoid these rational problems. The main line of argument developed here establishes several points: (1) the rational problems of collective choice are moral as well as rational; (2) exhibiting the suppressed moral premises provides a solution to the problems; (3) moral concepts, however, require a redefinition of the primitive term "individual"; and (4) redefining "individual" as a class or organic term forces a shift to rational, rather than countable, composition rules. Juridical forums are thus charged with exploring and establishing the fusion needed for rational association. Such forums break with the modern traditions of political thought, even though the core of politics is continuous.

4

The use of core terms brackets the question of whether individuals are more real than groups. A long tradition of classical political philosophy has maintained that the group is the primary human unit and that individuals do not exist except in terms of groups. For Aristotle, individuals are to be derived from political societies, which are antecedent (temporally, conceptually) to individuals. Plato defined human activity by functions, or the exercise of skills by individuals who are members of the political society and are required by virtue of their roles to act in terms of the good of others. It is only those most recent traditions (beginning with the social contract theorists of the seventeenth century) that frame the question in the way it occurs in collective choice, How to derive society from individuals who exist prior to the formation of collective states?

Core terms permit a tiered procedure that accommodates both views. Individuals are the primitive terms to be interpreted by theoretical languages. Some theories attempt to derive social concepts from a combination of physicalist and social languages assumed at the core level. This is the method of collective choice when aggregation is the form of derivation, and the problems created by this effort have filled the discussion here. Other theories turn inquiry in the opposite direction, assigning (not deriving) a social dimension to individuals from the perspective of moral and political philosophy. This latter method recognizes irreconcilable differences between physicalist and social languages, and responds to these difference by viewing individuals in terms of moral agency (as a condition for human association). The first method, by contrast, is never able to separate and then recombine the dual languages of arithmetic and morality that form the starting premises for the derivation. But in both cases a theoretical language is mixed with primitive terms. Only the conceptual clarity and consistency of the mix, not its reality, lead us to favor one method over another.

The method of assigning, rather than deriving, social concepts requires a sense of the political society before collective choice begins. Derivation methods produce social conditions from premises, and in some cases the society is in a constant state of flux or temporary equilibrium (exchange theory), or does not exist (as in certain forms of libertarian thought). No concept of the political need be formed before the derivation, for the method is to produce a state of a political society or ignore such states altogether. If social concepts are to be assigned to individuals as a condition for recognizing and reaching collective states, however, a conception of the political must inform theory at the outset. This conception, moreover, must contain rational and moral languages, since these are the languages of human communities.[10]

The use of rational and moral languages (combined in reason-giving rationality) shifts the sense of any number of political terms. "Covenant," for example, is a more appropriate designation for moral accord than is "contract." "Indispensability" substitutes for "causality." In all cases, the language of participants replaces spectator language. But also the political society itself must be an organism (rather than a machine or a collection of parts) that has the capability to dispense justice. This requirement—that justice be a part of the political society—is not an imposition on collective choice. It is drawn from the background considerations that are unsuccessfully welded together in derivation methods. The conceptual superiority of assignment methods is supported by the failure of derivative approaches to hold conflicting assumptions together in a consistent way. The consistency demanded and not satisfied in current collective choice theory requires a political society held together by reasoning.

A reasoned association is holistic rather than individualistic (in numerical terms). The distribution of authority through rules or practices demarcates the political society from the individuals constituting it. Think of distinctions between terms like "war" and "fight," where the former applies only to societies while the latter describes individual actions. Practice terms (like "war") describe demarcated wholes. The demarcation between political societies and individuals does not exhaust holistic language. A society may also be described by mass nouns. Such nouns do not individuate without the use of extrinsic measures (establishing quantities), and no single extrinsic measure is privileged. Water, for example, is a congeries of molecules in a certain chemical arrangement. But there are no sets of waters, only quantities (weight, mass, etc.). Nor do the constituent elements of water have the complete characteristics of the mass, as a molecule of water will fail to wet anything. Public goods are examples of mass social concepts in applying uniformly to individuals who may not be describable in terms of the features of a public good. It is one of the encourging features of reasoning, however, that a collective outcome formed on reasons may also collapse individuals into a description of the political society. Unanimity on both preferences and supporting reasons presents the political society as a homogeneous mass happily extending to the individual parts. In both demarcated and mass wholes, however, the assignment method begins with holistic features, as opposed to deriving outcomes by aggregating preexisting parts. Even unanimous outcomes are producible from the workings of rational systems.

Political societies seem to range over a spectrum only one segment of which can satisfy the requirements of rational continuity. The equations from chapter two set out a partial range of variations on methods for reaching collective outcomes, and also introduce the nomenclature in use here. Numerical wholes sum discrete units. Practice wholes contain interactive terms that do not extend to all units in the political society. Systemic wholes are those in which (1) interactive relations are distributed throughout the set of all relationships of units, and/or (2) the total outcome is itself an interactive term (though not one that is universally distributed). Unitary wholes are those where (1) the outcome is totally distributed, or (2) the political society is a collective state that is nonindividuating. Epistemic authority seems to be a system of relations in which (a) the criteria for reasoning are universally shared and thus expressible as an interactive term universally distributed, and (b) the outcomes of collective action are non-additive and thus not expressible by the equations. A cautious approach distinguishes between the political society and its outcomes. But caution still affirms the close relationship between the two items that the distinction recognizes. To define a political society in the form of epistemic authority is to introduce an interactive term that requires the dismissal of additive relationships. One distinguishing mark of numerical wholes is that nothing is ascribable a priori to the political society except the rule of addition. Epistemic authority defines a political society in terms of values that can dominate individuals (ruling out alternatives, for example). Defining these values is part of the exercise of defining a political society within which rational (nonadditive) methods produce collective outcomes. One may or may not want to say that a change in the criteria of reasoning changes the political society. But one must say that epistemic authority defines that segment of variation within which political societies can satisfy rationality.

A political society governed by reasoned discourse is an association of claims, where individuals act on each other in terms of the arguments they can advance. Such an association is different from two prominent and rival forms of the just society. Robert Nozick's (1974) market model of justice sketches a hyper-plane of moral space around each individual. The state can guarantee the security of each individual against border crossings by others, but cannot itself regulate individuals against their consent except by providing compensation to them. This morally restricted state is incapable even of coercive taxation, for the moral individual (as in Mill) can only be regulated if he invades the moral space of another. But, on the discussion here, regulation is morally limited only by rational claims, not by the isolation of individuals. Though individuals may endorse rival systems of morality (generating different and conflicting sets of reasons), it is also possible to have a system shared by all individuals. Shared moral systems can easily warrant regulation. If, for example, rationality establishes the priority of need as a basis for allocating resources, then individuals can be distributed along a schedule of needs without violating moral rules. The thought that individuals have inviolable moral rights not to be regulated can only be supported on the assumption that the social order consists of isolated individuals each holding to an isolated morality. But this assumption expresses again the conceptual error leading to the participation problems: confusing the countable individual with moral agency. Moral individuals are easily, by the logic of reasons, brought into hierarchical associations formed on reasoned grounds.

John Rawls (1971) develops a patterned theory of justice. On an account of rational choice in the original position, distributive principles are chosen for the governance of society. One of the principles, the difference principle, justifies inequalities only if they benefit the worst off representative person. The distribution of burdens and benefits is just if the pattern is fair. How the pattern comes about empirically, or which particular persons occupy what positions, is not legislatable by Rawls' theory of justice. Indifference to the empirical origins of patterns suggests an indifference to liberty of exchange;[11] indifference to the locations of particular persons suggests the possibility of tyrannous exchanges of positions.[12] Reasoned outcomes, by contrast, allow for the consideration of particular claims to just returns; and liberty is found not in voluntary exchanges but in the freedom to press particular cases before a rational forum. Thus, unlike all patterned accounts of justice, social outcomes resulting from reasoned synthesis are adjudications of special or general claims. Like market outcomes, reasoned conclusions collect case-by-case patterns. Unlike markets, however, reasons justify the particular settlement of conflicting claims and adjust collective patterns to rational norms.

The liabilities of the forum type of institution described here are not those of the market, or of patterned versions of justice, or rationality generally. The problems are elsewhere. Primarily, (a) effective political units may have to be large,[13] and (b) the costs of reasoned settlements are high, both to competing values like privacy and in the administration of institutions.[14] The connected possibilities of local settlements guided by general meta-rules (roughly represented by school boards, to the degree that local boards follow reasons instead of prejudices) and fusion on moral issues (like United States Supreme Court decisions on constitutional rights, which are invariant across regional differences) provide for types of reasoned outcomes that may evaluate effectiveness and impose costs on different measures. The idea of reasoned settlement may, of course, not satisfy on any calculation of effectiveness and cost. Carlyle said that we have to count heads in order to avoid breaking them. But if the rational discontinuities explored here are deficiencies of a basic "countable" method of producing joint outcomes, then alternative forms of rational synthesis may be needed to avoid breaking the bonds of rationality between individuals and whole.[15]

The general conclusions of this exercise follow.

1. Unit aggregation is not an adequate method for producing rational associations. Collective rationality requires reasons as well as preferences. Numerical collections do not satisfy rational and moral requirements. Reasoned associations can.

2. Reasoned collectives require an ordering or fusion of reasons. The collective outcome can be homogeneous (one ordering for the entire society) or heterogeneous (social partitioning as orderings with local validity). But reasons must justify the collective outcome.

3. The idealized institutional form that fuses or ranks reasons is a democratic forum, where collective outcomes are produced through a procedure that considers the reasons that individuals have for orderings while adjusting collective patterns on rational grounds.

4. The type of institution that establishes collective rationality is also a formal expression of the moral political society. If moral agency requires that reasons cannot be overriden without justification, then

numerical collections fail to meet moral requirements. Even unanimity on arithmetical combinations does not necessarily express a moral outcome. Reasoned collections, however, do respect moral agency. The rational and moral political society are identical.

The four conclusions are justified by levels of rationality. The denial of reductionism and the acceptance of a form of emergence endorse the hierarchical arrangement of juridical over unit-aggregation methods. The rational problems, viewed from this, the last perspective, are failures of lower level methods (in particular, additive rules) to account for those higher level events anticipated by the background assumptions of collective choice. Precisely the human qualities of reasoning—especially a moral sense of equality—create in unit-aggregation methods the conflicts that produce rational problems. Reasons are the higher level methods that explain and order human events successfully. No superiority attaches to such a hierarchy. But different organizing principles clearly emerge as the participation problems are solved.

The importance of juridical forums relocates discussions over democratic rule. The issues now become economies of scale, privacy rights in case evaluation, the nature of authority in small/cohesive social units—in general, the assets and liabilities of those social forms fulfilling rational and moral criteria. A complete discussion of rational and moral social forms should also cover the empirical preconditions for a rational association, an item that may be congenial even to the most hardheaded of empirical scientists.

These conclusions need not be disturbing to supporters of democratic rule. Democracy has many meanings, and at least some of these meanings (Rousseau's) are more credible as working arrangements precisely because of the solutions to the rational problems discussed here. It is true that democracy in the modern sense is established to reach collective decisions in the absence of shared reasons or justifications. Also, various devices, like lot or exchange, can supplement democratic decision rules when rational problems occur. But the problems treated here are too basic to be avoided by supplements. Since aggregation is itself a casualty, the supplements would have to become the rule. Also, the supplements do not always work. Exchange, as we have seen, does not solve the rational problems. Lotteries are blind to reasons. They assign equi-probability when rankings or inequalities may be justified. (This is why reasons are almost always used to establish classes of persons subject to lotteries, as in, e.g., a military draft.) The forum in any case is not antidemocratic. It may be immensely impractical as a form of collective choice. But at an ideal level it simply demonstrates that, whatever its liabilities, juridical democracy is superior to unit-aggregation democracy in avoiding some of the rational problems of collective choice. And the superiority is established by means of the background concepts in collective choice: juridical institutions more fully realize a liberal community of moral agents than do institutions relying on arithmetical composition rules.

Finally, the line between methodology and normative theory has never been an easy one for political theorists to follow. One such line does exist between a primitive term "individual" and forms of democracy. From approximately the seventeenth century, political theorists have worked with a model of discrete, rational, and autonomous individuals to derive the state (Hobbes, Locke, Rousseau, Rawls), to use as a maximizing platform (Bentham, Mill), to seek as an ideal goal (Marx), to provide rules of aggregation (Arrow, Wollheim), or to realize in market economies (Smith, Nozick). An exploration of what we mean by rational individuals suggests conflicts among concepts that can be resolved only with different connections between parts and wholes than some of these traditions tolerate. No less than the full set of composition rules producing collective outcomes may be traceable from what we make of the concept of an individual. A more promising link between basic theoretical particles and normative outcomes is almost unimaginable.

NOTES

1. Conditional statements can be either backtracking or non backtracking. On the basic $x \rightarrow a > b$ form, an individual states that if x were true, he would prefer a to b. The truth conditions of the conditional can be elaborated by either (a) stating how the past would have had to be different for the antecedent to be true, or (b) introducing the antecedent as a hypothetical and then determining (by slicing the world as closely as possible to the conceptual area of the antecedent) which counterfactuals have to be true if the antecedent is true. For example, "If Assad had accepted the United States' plan for withdrawing foreign troops from Lebanon, he would have preferred an independent over a dependent and partitioned Lebanon," is a backtracking conditional (the consequent is earlier in time than the antecedent); while, "If Israel stopped its West Bank settlements, Hussein would prefer negotiations to a protracted conflict between the P.L.O. and Israel," is a non backtracking conditional. I submit this elementary distinction to suggest that conditionals promise a richness of possible analyses, including that of time, that simple preference expressions cannot even approach.

2. Marcus Singer, *Generalization in Ethics* (London: Eyre and Spottiswoode, 1963), pp. 65–66.

3. See my "Individuals and Aggregates: The Generalization Argument Reconsidered," *Social Theory and Practice*[3] (spring 1975): 343–66. A more recent statement on the problems in inferring that someone ought to do non-*a* if the consequences of doing *a* would be undesirable is advanced by E. Ulmann-Margalit in "The Generalization Argument," *Journal of Philosophy* 73 (1976): 511–122. The point generally accepted by now is that if not everyone ought to do *a,* then not everyone ought to do *a*—but that the premise of the generalization argument (not everyone ought to do *a*) does not permit a deduction that some one (countable) individual ought not to do *a.* Or, again, numerical senses of either *everyone* or *one* lead when joined only to a fallacy of composition, not to the valid logical inferences sought in the generalization argument. See also the helpful discussion in Jon Elster, *Logic and Society,* Ch.5.

4. This point is generally acknowledged in discussions of the generalization argument. For example, Marcus Singer, *Generalization in Ethics,* "Their (universal terms like 'everyone' and 'no one') scope is restricted to each and every member of a certain *class* of persons." p. 68 (italics in original). This class, in the generalization argument, is invariably established or recognized by reasons, for "the reason given must be capable of applying beyond the particular person in the particular situation to a *class* of persons in a certain type of situation." p.24 (italics added).

5. Richard Boyd, "Scientific Realism and Naturalistic Epistemology," *Philosophy of Science* (1980) for one especially interesting version of realism.

6. The Duhem-Quine thesis here is treated extensively in Pierre Duhem, *The Aim and Structure of Physical Theory,* trans. P.P. Wiener (Princeton, N.J.: Princeton University Press, 1954), and W.V.O. Quine, "Two Dogmas of Empiricism," in *From A Logical Point of View* (Cambridge, Mass.: Harvard University Press, 1953), with more general treatments in *Word and Object* (Cambridge, Mass.: MIT Press, 1960), Ch. 1, 2. See also Craig's theorem, a formal proof demonstrating that any observation statement of a theory is also an observation statement of another formal system having no theoretical terms in William Craig, "On Axiomability within a System," *Journal of Symbolic Logic,* 18 (1953): 30–32, and "Replacement of Auxiliary Expressions, " *Philosophical Review,* 65 (1956): 38–55.

7. See especially the work done in what is called the "strong program" in sociology of knowledge, represented by Barry Barnes, *Scientific Knowledge and Sociological Theory* (London: Routledge & Kegan Paul, 1974): Barnes, *Interests and the Growth of Knowledge* (London: Routledge & Kegan Paul, 1978); and David Bloor, *Knowledge and Social Imagery* (London: Routledge & Kegan Paul, 1976). See also the network model developed by Mary Hesse, *The Structure of Scientific Inference* (London: Macmillan, 1974); and the more general appraisals in M.J. Mulkay, *Science and the Sociology of Knowledge* (London: George Allen & Unwin, 1979); and Larry Laudan, *Progress and Its Problems: Towards a Theory of Scientific Growth* (London: Routledge & Kegan Paul, 1977).

8. Bloor, especially, relies on interests as the main causal factor.

9. See my "The Structure of 'Politics,'" *American Political Science Review* 72 (September 1978): 859–70.

10. This part of the program complements Eugene F. Miller's efforts to define the political, and indeed offers a different justification for the effort—because derivation methods fail in the ways documented here. See Miller's "On the Meaning of 'Political,' " *The Review of Politics* 42 (January 1980): 56–72.

11. Nozick, *Anarchy, State and Utopia,* pp. 153–66, 198–213.

12. James Fishkin, *Tyranny and Legitimacy* (Baltimore, Md.: Johns Hopkins University Press, 1979), pp. 82–90.

13. Robert Dahl and Edward Tufte for some conflicts between size and access/effectiveness, in *Size and Democracy* (Stanford: Stanford University Press, 1974). Generally, economies of scale in the production of public goods may mandate large social units. Some goods, like system defense, almost logically require comprehensive efforts.

14. A helpful overview of the costs and benefits of institutional expressions of markets versus political systems can be found in Guido Calabresi and Philip Bobbitt, *Tragic Choices* (New York: W.W. Norton & Co., 1978). Included in the discussions are some thoughts on competing costs in different types of reason-giving institutions.

15. See, for example, the use of the "dialogue" by Bruce A. Ackerman in *Social Justice in a Liberal State* (New Haven, Conn.: Yale University Press, 1980). Ackerman argues for a neutral dialogue among persons to resolve social issues, an admittedly liberal social order. I argue for forums, institutions that can establish warranted rankings among issues. Such institutions may not fulfill all of the expectations of liberalism. But they do at least represent the background ideals of a liberal community.

Select Bibliography

Ackerman, Bruce A. 1980. *Social Justice in the Liberal State.* New Haven, Conn.: Yale University Press.

Arrow, Kenneth. 1977. "Extended Sympathy and the Possibility of Social Choice." *American Economic Review* 67: 219–125.

Bachrach, Peter. 1967. *The Theory of Democratic Elitism.* Boston: Little, Brown & Co.

Baier, Kurt. 1977. "Rationality and Morality." *Erkenntnis* 11: 197–223.

Barry, Brian. 1980. "Is It Better to be Powerful or Lucky?" *Political Studies* 28: 183–94, 338–52.

———. 1973. *The Liberal Theory of Justice.* Oxford: Clarendon Press.

———.1967. "The Public Interest." In Anthony Quinton, ed. *Political Philosophy.* Oxford: Oxford University Press.

Barry, Brian, and Russell Hardin, eds. 1982. *Rational Man and Irrational Society?* Beverly Hills, Calif.: Sage Publications.

Black, Duncan. 1958. *The Theory of Committees and Elections.* Cambridge: Cambridge University Press.

Buchanan, James, and Gordon Tullock. 1962. *The Calculus of Consent.* Ann Arbor: University of Michigan Press.

Dagger, Richard. 1981. "Understanding The General Will." *Western Political Quarterly* 34: 359–71.

Dahl, Robert. 1982. "Procedural Democracy." In Peter Laslett and James Fishkin, eds. *Philosophy, Politics and Society.* New Haven, Conn.: Yale University Press.

Dahl, Roberts, and Edward Tufte. 1973. *Size and Democracy.* Stanford: Stanford University Press.

DeGeorge, Richard T. 1970. "The Function and Limits of Epistemic Authority." *Southern Journal of Philosophy* 8: 199–204.

Dworkin, Ronald. 1978A. "Liberalism." In Stuart Hampshire, ed. *Public and Private Morality.* Cambridge: Cambridge University Press.

_____1978. *Taking Rights Seriously.* Cambridge, Mass.: Harvard University Press.

_____.1981. "What Is Equality?", Parts 1 and 2, *Philosophy and Public Affairs* 10: 185–246; 283–345.

Fishkin, James. 1982. *Size and Obligation.* New Haven, Conn.: Yale Unversity Press.

Flathman, Richard. 1980. *The Practice of Political Authority and the Authoritative.* Chicago: University of Chicago Press.

French, Peter. 1975. "Types of Collectives and Blame." *Personalist* 56: 160–69.

Friedman, Richard B. 1973. "On the Concept of Authority in Political Philosophy." In Richard Flathman, ed. *Concepts in Social and Political Philosophy.* New York: Macmillan Publishing Co.

Gauthier, David. 1978. "Social Choice and Distributive Justice". *Philosophia* 7:239–52.

Habermas, Jurgen. 1982. *Reason and the Relationalization of Society* (1982). Boston: Beacon Press.

_____1970. "Towards a Theory of Communicative Competence." *Inquiry* 13:360–75.

Hanson, Norwood. 1958. *Patterns of Discovery.* Cambridge: Cambridge University Press.

Hardin, Garrett. 1968. "The Tragedy of the Commons." *Science* 162:1243–48.

Hardin, Russell. 1971. "Collective Action as an Agreeable n- Prisoners' Dilemma." *Behavioral Science* 16:472–79.

_____1982. *Collective Action.* Baltimore: Johns Hopkins University Press.

Hare, R.M. 1965. *Freedom and Reason.* Oxford: Oxford University Press.

_____1952. *The Language of Morals.* Oxford: Oxford University Press.

_____1981. *Moral Thinking: Its Method, Levels, and Scope.* Oxford: Oxford University Press.

Harsanyi, John. 1975. "Can the Maximin Principle Serve as a Basis for Morality?" *American Political Science Review* 69:595–606.

Hart, H.L.A. 1955. "Are There Any Natural Rights?" *Philosophical Review* 64:175–91.

Hempel, Carl 1966. *Philosophy of Natural Science.* Englewood Cliffs, N.J.: Prentice-Hall.

Hempel, Carl and Paul Oppenheim 1948. "The Covering Law Analysis of Scientific Explanation." *Philosophy of Science* 15:135–74.

Hicks, J.R. 1956. *A Revision of Demand Theory.* Oxford: Oxford University Press.

Kelly, Jerry 1978. *Arrow Impossibility Theorems.* New York: Academic Press.

Kohlberg, Lawrence 1980. *Essays on Moral Development.* San Francisco: Harper & Row Pubs.

Kramer, Gerald H. 1977. "A Dynamical Model of Political Equilibrium." *Journal of Political Economy* 16:310–34.

Kuhn, Thomas 1962. *The Structure of Scientific Revolutions.* Chicago: University of Chicago Press.

Lakatos, I. 1970. "Falsification and the Methodology of Scientific Research Programmes." In Lakatos and A. Musgrave, eds. *Criticism and the Growth of Knowledge.* Cambridge: Cambridge University Press.

Little, I.M.D. 1952. " Social Choice and Individual Values." *Journal of Political Economy* 60:422–32.

Luce, R.D., and H. Raiffa. 1958. *Games and Decisions.* New York: John Wiley & Sons.

Lukes, Steven. 1968. "Methodological Individualism Reconsidered." *British Journal of Sociology* 19:119–29.

_____1974. *Power: A Radical View.* New York: Macmillan Publishing Co.

Lyons, David. 1965. *Forms and Limits of Utilitarianism.* Ithaca, N.Y.: Cornell University Press.

MacIntryre, Alasdair. 1981. *After Virtue.* Notre Dame, Ind.: University of Notre Dame Press.

MacKay, Alfred F. 1980. *Arrow's Theorem: The Paradox of Social Choice.* New Haven, Conn.: Yale University Press.

Macpherson, C.B. 1967. *The Political Theory of Possessive Individualism.* Oxford: Oxford University Press.

May, Kenneth O. 1952. "A Set of Independent Necessary and Sufficient Conditions for Simple Majority Decision." *Econometrica* 20:680–84.

Mill, John Stuart. 1971. *Utilitarianism.* Samuel Gorovitz, ed. New York: Bobbs-Merrill.

McClennen, Edward F. 1983. "Rational Choice and Public Policy: A Critical Study." *Social Theory and Practic* 9:335–79.

Moe, Terry M. 1980. "A Calculus of Group Membership." *American Journal of Political Science.* 24:593–632.

Nagel, Ernest. 1961. *The Structure of Science,* ch. 11. New York: Harcourt, Brace & World.

_____. 1953. "The Meaning of Reduction in the Natural Sciences." In Philip P. Weiner, ed. *Readings in Philosophy of Science.* New York: Charles Scribner's Sons.

Nozick, Robert. 1974. *Anarchy, State and Utopia.* New York: Basic Books.

_____. 1981. *Philosophical Explanations.* Cambridge, Mass.: Harvard University Press.

Olson, Mancur. 1965. 1971. *The Logic of Collective Action.* Cambridge, Mass.: Harvard University Press.

Popper, Karl. 1968. *The Logic of Scientific Discovery.* London: Hutchinson Publishing Group.

_____.1972. *Objective Knowledge* Oxford: Clarendon Press.

_____.1961. *The Poverty of Historicism.* New York: Harper & Row Pubs.

Putnam, Hilary. 1969. "Is Logic Empirical." In R. Cohen and M. Wartofsky, eds. Proceedings of the Boston Colloquium for the Philosophy of Science, *Boston Studies in the Philosophy of Science,* vol.5. Dordrecht: Reidel.

Rawls, John. 1964. "Legal Obligation and the Duty of Fair Play." In Sidney Hook, ed. *Law and Philosophy: A Symposium*. New York: New York University Press.

———.1971. *A Theory of Justice*. Cambridge, Mass.: Harvard University Press.

Reiman, Jeffrey. 1972. *In Defense of Political Philosophy*. New York: Harper & Row Pubs.

Riker, William. 1982. *Liberalism Against Populism*. San Francisco: W.H. Freeman & Co.

———.1981. "Why Wollheim's Paradox is not a Paradox of Democracy." In Gordon Tullock, ed. *Toward A Science of Politics*. Blacksburgh, Va.: Public Choice Center, Virginia Polytechnic Institute and State University.

Ritter, Alan. 1980. *Anarchism: A Theoretical Analysis*. Cambridge: Cambridge University Press.

Scriven, Michael. 1959A. "The Covering Law Position: A Critique and an Alternative Analysis." In Leonard I. Krimerman, ed. *The Nature and Scope of Social Science: A Critical Anthology*. New York: Appleton-Century-Crofts.

———.1959B. "Explanation and Prediction as Non-Symmetrical." *Science* 130:477–82.

Sen, Amartya. 1974. "Choice, Orderings and Morality." In Robert Korner, ed. *Practical Reason*. New Haven, Conn.: Yale University Press.

———. 1970. "The Paradox of the Paretian Liberal." *Journal of Political Economy* 78:152–57.

Simon, Herbert. 1982. *Models of Bounded Rationality*. Cambridge, Mass.: MIT Press.

Singer, Marcus. 1963. *Generalization in Ethics*. London: Byre & Spottiswoode.

Smith, James Ward. 1957. *Theme for Reason*. Princeton: Princeton University Press.

Strasnick, Steven. 1977. "Ordinality and the Spirit of the Justified Dictator." *Social Research* 44:668–90.

———. 1976. "Social Choice and the Derivation of Rawls's Difference Principle." *The Journal of Philosophy* 73:85–99.

Suppes, Patrick. 1966. "Some Formal Models of Grading Principles." *Synthese,* 6:284–306.

Taylor, Michael. 1976. *Anarchy and Cooperation*. New York: John Wiley & Sons.

Thom, Rene. 1975. *Structural Stability and Morphogenesis: An Outline of a General Theory of Models*. Reading, Mass.: Benjamin Cummings Publishing Co., 1975.

Thorson, Thomas Landon. 1962. *The Logic of Democracy*. New York: Holt, Rinehart & Winston.

Tullock, Gordon. 1968. *Toward a Mathematics of Politics*. Ann Arbor: University of Michigan Press.

Tversky, Amos, and Daniel Kahneman. 1982. *Judgment Under Uncertainty: Heuristics and Biases*. Cambridge: Cambridge University Press.

Weiss, Donald. 1973. "Wollheim's Paradox: Survey and Solution." *Political Theory* 1:323–28.

Winch, Peter. 1958. *The Idea of a Social Science.* New York: Humanities Press.

Wolff, Robert Paul. 1970. *In Defense of Anarchism.* New York: Harper & Row Pubs.

———. 1977. *Understanding Rawls.* Princeton: Princeton University Press.

Wollheim, Richard. 1962. "A Paradox in the Theory of Democracy." In Peter Laslett and William Runciman, eds. *Philosophy, Politics and Society* (Second Series). Oxford: Basil Blackwell.

Index

RATIONAL ASSOCIATION

was composed in Itek 10-point Times Roman on a Digitek and leaded 2 points
with display type set in Avant Garde Demi Bold
by Ampersand Publisher Services, Inc.;
printed by sheet-fed offset on 50-pound, acid-free Glatfelter Antique Cream,
Smyth-sewn and bound over binder's boards in Joanna Arrestox B,
by Maple-Vail Book Manufacturing Group, Inc.;
with dust jackets printed in 2 colors
by Philips Offset Co., Inc.;
and published by

SYRACUSE UNIVERSITY PRESS
SYRACUSE, NEW YORK 13244-5160